⌐ BEYOND FEELINGS ⌐

BEYOND FEELINGS
A GUIDE TO CRITICAL THINKING
FOURTH EDITION

VINCENT RYAN RUGGIERO

Professor Emeritus of Humanities

State University of New York, Delhi

Mayfield Publishing Company

Mountain View, California

London • Toronto

Library of Congress Cataloging-in-Publication Data
Ruggiero, Vincent Ryan.
Beyond feelings: a guide to critical thinking / Vincent Ryan
    Ruggiero.—4th ed.
        p.   cm.
    Includes bibliographical references.
    ISBN 1-55934-357-5
    1. Critical thinking. I. Title
    BF441.R85 1994   94-8839
    153.4′2—dc20   CIP

Manufactured in the United States of America
10 9 8 7 6 5 4 3 2

Mayfield Publishing Company
1280 Villa Street
Mountain View, California 94041

Sponsoring editor, James Bull; production editor, Larisa North; manuscript editor, Carol Dondrea; cover designer and production artist, Jean Mailander. The text was set in 10/13 Palatino and printed on 50# Ecolocote by Malloy Lithographing.

Cover illustration: *Relativity* by M. C. Escher, © 1994 M. C. Escher/Cordon Art—Baarn—Holland. All rights reserved.

 This book is printed on recycled paper.

CONTENTS

I THE CONTEXT

⧈

II THE PROBLEMS

III A STRATEGY

IV SOME CONTEMPORARY ISSUES

To the Instructor

When the first edition of this book appeared in 1975, the dominant intellectual focus was still subjectivity, *feelings*. That focus, the legacy of the 1960s, was originally a necessary reaction to the rationalism and behaviorism that preceded it. It declared, in effect, "People are not robots. They are more than the sum total of their physiology. They have hopes, dreams, emotions. No two humans are alike—each has a special perspective, a unique way of perceiving the world. And any view of humanity that ignores this subjective side is a distortion."

Yet, despite its value, the focus on feelings went too far. Like many other movements, what began as a reaction against an extreme view became an extreme view itself. The result of that extremism was the neglect of thinking. This book was designed to answer that neglect. The introduction to the first edition explained its rationale as follows:

> The emphasis on subjectivity served to correct a dangerous oversimplification. But it is the kind of reaction that cannot be sustained for long without causing an even worse situation—the neglect of thinking. Worse for two reasons. First, because we live in an age of manipulation. Armies of hucksters and demagogues stand ready with the rich resources of psychology to play upon our emotions and subconscious needs to persuade us that superficial is profound, harmful is beneficial, evil is virtuous. And feelings are especially vulnerable to such manipulation.

Secondly, because in virtually every important area of modern life—law, medicine, government, education, science, business, and community affairs—we are beset with serious problems and complex issues that demand careful gathering and weighing of facts and informed opinions, thoughtful consideration of various conclusions or actions, and judicious selection of the best conclusion or most appropriate action....

[Today's college student] has been conditioned not to undervalue subjectivity, but to overvalue it. And so he does not need to have his feelings indulged. Rather, he needs to be taught how to sort out his feelings, decide to what extent they have been shaped by external influences, and evaluate them carefully when they conflict among themselves or with the feelings of others. In short, he needs to be taught to think critically.

There is an unfortunate tendency among many to view feeling and thought as mutually exclusive, to force a choice between them. If we focus on one, then in their view we must reject the other. But this is mistaken. Feeling and thought are perfectly complementary. Feeling, being more spontaneous, is an excellent beginning to the development of conclusions. And thought, being more deliberate, provides a way to identify the best and most appropriate feeling. Both are natural.

Thinking, however, is less automatic than feeling. To do it well demands a systematic approach and guided practice....

The general attitude toward thinking has changed considerably since the mid-1970s. The view that critical thinking is an important skill to which education should give prominence is no longer a minority view. Hundreds of voices have joined the chorus calling for the addition of critical thinking objectives to existing courses and even the creation of special courses. There is little disagreement that the challenges of the 1990s demand minds that can move beyond feelings to clear, impartial, *critical* problem solving and decision making.

This edition of *Beyond feelings* retains the successful four-part design of the first three editions. The first five chapters help students understand the *context* in which critical thinking takes place and overcome attitudes and ideas that undermine the development of their critical thinking skills. The next ten chapters help students recognize and solve *problems* that arise in thinking. This section includes the most common logical fallacies.

The final five chapters provide a strategy for dealing with issues. Concluding the text are contemporary issues for analysis.

This edition gives additional emphasis to the role of critical thinking in constructing sound arguments and evaluating other people's arguments. Also, Chapter 14, "Logical Fallacies," has been revised. It now includes additional fallacies and provides a classification system so that students can anticipate when errors are most likely to occur. New applications have been added throughout the text.

I wish to express my appreciation to all those who contributed to the preparation of this edition. My special thanks to Natalie Dandekar of the University of Rhode Island, Karan Hancock Gier of the University of Alaska, Anchorage, Edna Maye Loveless of La Sierra University, Donna Miller of Cerritos College, Lynn Hankinson Nelson of Rowan College of New Jersey, Jon A. Schlenker of the University of Maine at Augusta, and Jon Stratton of Walla Walla Community College, and to Jim Bull and Larisa North of Mayfield for their skillful direction of the project.

To the memory of Howard Trumble,
whose quiet practice of the skills
detailed in this book was an inspiration
to me, to his family, and to all who knew him

INTRODUCTION

Beyond Feelings is designed to introduce you to the subject of critical thinking. The subject is undoubtedly new to you because it is not taught in most elementary and secondary schools. In fact, until fairly recently it was not taught in most colleges. During the 1960s and much of the 1970s, the emphasis was more on subjectivity than on objectivity, more on feeling than on thought.

Over the past fifteen years, however, a number of studies of America's schools have criticized the neglect of critical thinking, and a growing number of educators and leaders in business, industry, and the professions have urged the development of new courses and teaching materials to overcome that neglect.

It is no exaggeration to say that critical thinking is one of the most important subjects you will study in college regardless of your academic major. The quality of your schoolwork, your efforts in your career, your contributions to community life, and your conduct of personal affairs will all depend on your ability to solve problems and make decisions.

The book has four main sections. The first, "The Context," will help you to understand such important concepts as *individuality, thinking, truth, knowledge,* and *opinion* and to overcome attitudes and ideas that

1

obstruct critical thinking. The second section, "The Problems," will teach you to recognize and avoid nine common errors that often occur, singly or in combination, during the thinking process. The third section, "A Strategy," will help you acquire the various skills used in addressing problems and issues. This section includes tips on identifying and overcoming your personal intellectual weaknesses, as well as techniques for becoming more observant, clarifying issues, conducting inquiry, evaluating evidence, analyzing other people's views, and making sound judgments.

At the end of each chapter you will find a number of applications to challenge your critical thinking and provide exercise for your skills. These applications cover problems and issues both timely and timeless. The fourth section of the book, "Some Contemporary Issues," presents additional important issues that continue to occupy the attention of the best thinkers of our time.

In brief, *Beyond Feelings* is designed to help you acquire the intellectual skills necessary to solve the exciting problems of today and tomorrow.

I

THE CONTEXT

CHAPTER ONE

WHO ARE YOU?

Suppose someone asked, "Who are you?" It would be simple enough to respond with your name. But if the person wanted to know the entire story about who you are, the question would be more difficult to answer. You'd obviously have to give the details of your height and age and weight. You'd also have to include all your sentiments and preferences, even the secret ones you'd never shared with anyone—your affection for your parents; your desire to please the crowd you associate with; your dislike of your older sister's husband; your allegiance to your favorite beverage, football team, brand of jeans, and music.

Your attitudes couldn't be overlooked either—the impatience you have when an issue gets complex, your aversion to English courses, your rejection of communism, your fear of high places and dogs and speaking in public. The list would go on. To be complete, it would have to include all your characteristics—not only the physical but the emotional and intellectual as well.

To provide all that information would be quite a chore. But suppose the questioner was still curious, and now asked, "How did you get the way you are?" If your patience were not yet exhausted, chances are you'd answer something like this: "I'm that way because I choose to be, because I've considered other sentiments and preferences and attitudes

5

and made my selection. The ones I chose fit my style and personality best." That answer is a natural enough one, and in part it's true. But in a larger sense it's not true. The impact of the world on all of us is much greater than we usually realize.

◇ INFLUENCES ON IDENTITY

You are not only a member of a particular species, *Homo sapiens,* but you exist at a particular moment in the history of the species. Being a young adult today is quite different from being a young adult thirty years ago, and very different from being a young adult in A.D. 1500 or 10,000 B.C. The world's state of progress differs, and likewise its knowledge and beliefs and values. The opportunities for learning and working and relaxing are not the same. So people's daily thoughts and actions vary.

Variations in place and circumstance also can make a difference. If you're from a large city, the odds are you look at many things differently from someone in the country. A person raised for eighteen years in New York City or Los Angeles who goes to college in a town of 3000 will find the experience difficult. So will a person raised on an isolated farm. But probably for opposite reasons!

If you are an American sports enthusiast, you're probably interested in football, baseball, or basketball. But if you were Chinese, you'd be much more familiar with and excited about Ping-Pong, and if you were European, soccer. If one of your parents is an automobile mechanic, you undoubtedly know more about cars than the average person. If the other is a teacher, you'll tend to have a somewhat different perspective on school and teachers than do other students.

In much the same way, all the details about your family very likely have some bearing on who you are. Their religion, race, national origin, political affiliation, economic level, and attitudes toward one another, all have made some contribution to your identity.

Of course, people may reject what they are taught at home. People between the ages of eighteen and twenty-one often have sharp and apparently permanent differences with their parents in terms of beliefs and values on many issues. Still, whether you accept or reject what you are taught, your present position grows out of those teachings. It is a response to your upbringing. Given different parents with a different culture and different values—growing up, say, in Istanbul rather than Dubuque—your response would necessarily be different. You would, in that sense, not be the same person.

◇ THE ROLE OF MASS CULTURE

In centuries past, the influence of family and teachers was the dominant, and sometimes the only, influence on children. Today, however, the influence exerted by mass culture (the broadcast media, newspapers, magazines, and popular music) is often greater.

By age eighteen the average teenager has spent 11,000 hours in the classroom and 22,000 hours in front of the television set. He or she has done perhaps 13,000 school lessons, yet has watched more than 750,000 commercials.

What effects does mass culture have on young people (and many adults, as well)? To answer, we need only consider the formats and devices commonly used. Modern advertising typically bombards the public with slogans and testimonials by celebrities. This approach is designed to appeal to emotions and create artificial needs for products and services. As a result, many people develop the habit of responding emotionally, impulsively, and gullibly to such appeals.

Television programmers use frequent scene shifts and sensory appeals such as car crashes, violence, and sexual encounters to keep audience interest from diminishing. Then they add frequent commercial interruptions. This author has studied the attention shifts that television viewers are subjected to. In a dramatic program, for example, attention shifts might include camera angle changes;* shifts in story line from one set of characters (or subplot) to another, or from a present scene to a past one (flashback) or to fantasy; and shifts to "newsbreaks," to commercial breaks, from one commercial to another, and back to the program. Also included are any shifts of attention that occur *within* commercials. I found as many as 78 shifts per hour, excluding the shifts within commercials. The number of shifts within commercials ranged from 6 to 54 and averaged approximately 17 per fifteen-second commercial. The total number of shifts came out to over 800 attention shifts per hour, or over 14 per minute.**

A century ago even uneducated Americans were accustomed to listen attentively to political debates lasting five or six hours. And the speakers used bigger words and longer sentences than are common today. What many people today perceive to be dullness in teachers, text-

---

*This is typically accomplished by using two or more cameras and switching from one camera to another.
**There are about eleven minutes of commercials per hour, the exact time varying by network. Thus, at a rate of four per minute, the total number of commercials per hour is 44. This calculates, therefore, to 78 shifts outside commercials plus 748 shifts within commercials (17 shifts per commercial times 44 commercials per hour) for a total of 826.

book authors, and work assignments, may actually be their own deficiency. Television viewing (and other modern entertainments) may have prevented them from developing a mature attention span and accepting the normal rhythms of life.

Finally, mass culture promotes values that oppose those held by most parents. Play is presented as more fulfilling than work, self-gratification more desirable than self-control, and materialism more meaningful than idealism. People who adopt these values without questioning them may end up sacrificing worthy goals to their pursuit of "a good time" and lots of money.

◇ EFFECTS ON BELIEFS

The social and psychological theories of our time also have an impact on our beliefs. Before the last few decades, children were urged to be self-disciplined, self-critical, and self-effacing. They were urged to practice self-denial, to aspire to self-knowledge, to behave in a manner that ensured they maintain self-respect. Self-centeredness was considered a vice. "Hard work," they were told, "leads to achievement, and that in turn produces satisfaction and self-confidence." By and large, our grandparents internalized those teachings. When they honored them in their behavior, they felt proud; when they dishonored them, they felt ashamed.

Today the theories have been changed—indeed, almost exactly reversed. Self-esteem, which nineteenth-century satirist Ambrose Bierce defined as "an erroneous appraisement," is now considered an imperative. Self-centeredness has been transformed from vice into virtue, and people who devote their lives to helping others, once considered heroes and saints, are now said to be ill. (The popular term for their affliction is "a disease to please.") The formula for success and happiness begins with feeling good about ourselves. Students who do poorly in school, workers who don't measure up to the challenges of their jobs, substance abusers and lawbreakers—all are typically diagnosed as deficient in self-esteem.

In addition, just as our grandparents internalized the social and psychological theories of their time, so most contemporary Americans have internalized the message of self-esteem. We hear people speak of it over coffee, we hear it endlessly invoked on talk shows. Challenges to its precepts are usually met with disapproval.

But isn't the theory of self-esteem self-evident? No. A negative perception of our abilities will, of course, handicap our performance. Dr. Maxwell Maltz explains the amazing results one educator had in improving the grades of schoolchildren by changing their self-images. The educator had observed that when the children saw themselves as stupid in a particular subject (or stupid in general), they unconsciously acted to confirm their self-images. They believed they were stupid, so they acted that way. Reasoning that it was their defeatist attitude rather than any lack of ability that was defeating them, the educator set out to change their self-images. He found that when he accomplished that, *they no longer behaved stupidly!* Maltz concludes from this and other examples that our experiences can work a kind of self-hypnotism on us, suggesting a conclusion about ourselves and then urging us to make it come true.[1]

Maltz's research documents that lack of confidence impedes performance, a valuable insight. But such research doesn't explain why the more global concept of self-esteem has become so dominant. The answer to that question lies in the popularization of the work of such humanistic psychologists as Abraham Maslow. Maslow described what he called the hierarchy of human needs in the form of a pyramid, with physiological needs (food and drink) at the foundation. Above them, in ascending order, are safety needs, belongingness and love, the need for esteem and approval, and aesthetic and cognitive needs (knowledge, understanding, etc.). At the pinnacle is the need for self-actualization, fulfillment of our potential. In Maslow's view, the lower needs must be fulfilled before the higher ones. It's easy to see how the idea that self-esteem must precede achievement was derived from Maslow's theory.

However, other, different theories might have been adopted. One notable one is Austrian psychiatrist Viktor Frankl's, which was advanced at roughly the same time as Maslow's, and was based on both Frankl's professional practice and his experiences in Hitler's concentration camps. Frankl argues that there is a higher human need than self-actualization—*self-transcendence,* the need to rise above narrow absorption with self. According to Frankl, "the primordial anthropological fact [is] that being human is being always directed, and pointing to something or someone other than oneself: to a meaning to fulfill or another human being to encounter, a cause to serve or a person to love." A person becomes fully human "by forgetting himself and giving himself, overlooking himself and focusing outward."

Making self-actualization (or happiness) the direct object of our pursuit, in Frankl's view, is ultimately self-defeating; such fulfillment can occur only as "the unintended effect of self-transcendence."[2] The proper perspective on life, Frankl believes, is not what it can give us but what it expects *from* us; life is daily—even hourly—questioning us, challenging us to accept "the responsibility to find the right answer to its problems and to fulfill the tasks which it constantly sets for [each of us]."[3]

Finding meaning, according to Frankl's theory, involves "perceiving a possibility embedded in reality" and searching for challenging tasks "whose completion might add meaning to [one's] existence." But such perceiving and searching is frustrated by the focus on self: "As long as modern literature confines itself to, and contents itself with, self-expression—not to say self-exhibition—it reflects its authors' sense of futility and absurdity. What is more important, it also creates absurdity. This is understandable in light of the fact that meaning must be discovered, it cannot be invented. Sense cannot be created, but what may well be created is nonsense."[4]

How very different contemporary America would undoubtedly be if the emphasis of the past several decades had been on Frankl's theory rather than on Maslow's and the other humanistic psychologists' theories. All of us would certainly have been affected—we can only imagine how profoundly—in our attitudes, values, and beliefs.

◇ Becoming an Individual

What does individuality mean and to what extent can a person be an individual? In the current popular imagination, individuality means "doing your own thing," responding to life's situations in whatever way seems most natural. The problem with that notion is that it ignores all the shaping forces we have been discussing. It denies the fact that each of us has been channeled and conditioned to a great degree. It pretends there is some inner self untouched by all that we have experienced, all that has happened to us.

The fact is that if you define individuality in the popular way and act on that definition, you'll be acting like Pavlov's famous dog. Pavlov rang a bell whenever he placed food in front of the dog. After a while, he conditioned the dog to drool when it heard the bell, even though no food was presented. The dog was doing what came naturally to it. But what came naturally was influenced by its experience. The dog was controlled by a force outside itself.

Obviously, individuality must be something more than that. It must be the habit of developing your own personal responses to people, issues, and situations, rather than mindlessly endorsing the responses you have been conditioned to make. These guidelines will help you achieve individuality:

1. Treat your first reaction to any person, issue, or situation as tentative. No matter how appealing it may be, refuse to embrace it until after you have examined it.

2. Decide why you reacted as you did. Consider whether you borrowed the reaction from someone else—a parent or friend, perhaps, or a celebrity or fictional character on television. If possible, determine what specific experiences conditioned you to react this way.

3. Think of other reactions you might have had to the person, issue, or situation.

4. Ask yourself whether one of the other reactions is more appropriate than your first reaction. And when you answer, resist the influence of your conditioning.

To ensure that you will really be an individual, and not merely claim to be one, apply these guidelines throughout your work in this book, as well as in your everyday life.

◫ APPLICATIONS

Note: One of the best ways to develop your thinking (and writing) skills is to record your observations, questions, and ideas in a journal and then, as time permits, to reflect on what you have recorded—considering the meaning and application of the observations, answering the questions, elaborating on the ideas (and, where appropriate, challenging them), and recording your insights. An inexpensive bound notebook or spiral notebook will serve the purpose. A good approach is to record your initial observations, questions, and ideas on the left side of the page, leaving the right side blank for our later analysis and commentary. The value of this reflective process is so great that you should consider keeping such a journal even if your instructor does not make it a formal part of the course.

1. Do a brief study of attention shifts such as the one described in the chapter. Videotape a half-hour show on a VCR. Then play the tape back twice, the first time counting the number of shifts within the program excluding commercials, and the second time counting only those within commercials. Complete the necessary arithmetic and be prepared to share your results in class.

2. Reflect on your findings in application 1. Write several paragraphs discussing the implications of those findings for education, business, and family life.

3. Imagine how different America might be if Frankl's emphasis on self-transcendence (and personal responsibility), rather than Maslow's emphasis on self-actualization and popular culture's emphasis on self-esteem, had been dominant for the last thirty years. List as many ways as you can in which our society might be different today and comment on whether each would be beneficial or harmful. Be prepared to explain your views in class discussion.

4.   Watch MTV for at least an hour. Analyze how men and women are depicted in the songs. Note significant details. For example, observe whether men are depicted in power roles more than women, whether women are portrayed as objects of male desire. Decide what attitudes and values are conveyed. (You may wish to videotape the show as you are watching so that you can review what you have seen, freeze significant frames for closer analysis, and have a record of your observations for later reference or class viewing and discussion.)

5.   Suppose you asked a friend, "How did you acquire your particular identity—your sentiments and preferences and attitudes?" Then suppose the friend responded, "I'm an individual. No one else influences me. I do my own thing, select the sentiments and preferences and attitudes that suit me." How would you explain to your friend what you learned in this chapter?

6.   Ask yourself the question "Who am I?" Write down ten answers to this on ten separate slips of paper. Use the first three paragraphs of this chapter to help you choose your answers. Arrange the pieces of paper in order of their importance to you. Which self-descriptions are most important to you? Why?

7.   Identify the various positive and negative influences that have shaped you. Be sure to include the particular as well as the general and the subtle as well as the obvious influences. Which of those influences have had the greatest effect on you? Explain the effects as precisely as you can.

8.   Note your immediate reaction to each of the following questions. Then apply the four guidelines given in this chapter for achieving individuality.

   a.   Should freshman composition be a required course for all students?

   b.   Should athletes be tested for anabolic steroid use?

   c.   Should creationism be taught in high school biology classes?

   d.   Should polygamy be legalized?

   e.   Should the voting age be lowered to sixteen?

9. *Group Discussion Exercise:* Discuss each of the following questions with two or three classmates, applying the four guidelines for developing individuality that are given in this chapter. Be prepared to share your group's ideas with the class.

    a. Should extremist groups like the Ku Klux Klan be allowed to hold rallies on public property?

    b. Should the prison system give greater emphasis to the punishment or to the rehabilitation of inmates?

    c. Should doctors and clinics be required to notify parents of minors when they prescribe birth control devices for the minors?

CHAPTER TWO

WHAT IS CRITICAL THINKING?

When Arthur was in the first grade, the teacher directed the class to "think." "Now, class," she said, "I know this problem is a little harder than the ones we've been doing, but I'm going to give you a few extra minutes to think about it. Now start thinking."

It was not the first time Arthur had heard the word used. He'd heard it many times at home but never quite this way. The teacher seemed to be asking for some special activity, something he should know how to start and stop. Like his father's car. "Vroom-m-m," he muttered half aloud. Because of his confusion, he was unaware he was making the noise. "Arthur, please stop making noises and start thinking."

Embarrassed and not knowing quite what to do, he looked down at his desk. Then out of the corner of his eye he noticed that the little girl next to him was staring at the ceiling. "Maybe that's the way you start thinking," he guessed. He decided the others had probably learned how to do it last year, that time he was home with the measles. So he stared at the ceiling.

As he progressed through grade school and high school, he heard that same direction hundreds of times. "No, that's not the answer, you're not thinking—now *think!*" And occasionally he would hear from a particularly self-pitying teacher given to talking to himself aloud: "What did

I do to deserve this? Don't they teach them anything in the grades anymore? Don't you people care about ideas? Think, dammit, THINK."

So Arthur learned to feel somewhat guilty about the whole matter. Obviously this thinking was an important activity that he'd failed to learn. Maybe he lacked the brain power. But he was resourceful enough. He watched the other students and did what they did. Whenever a teacher started in about thinking, he screwed up his face, furrowed his brow, scratched his head, stroked his chin, stared off into space or up at the ceiling, and repeated silently to himself, "Let's see now, I've got to think about that, think, think (I hope he doesn't call on me), think." Though Arthur didn't know it, that's just what the other students were saying to themselves.

Because Arthur's situation is not all that uncommon, your experience may have been similar. That is, probably many people have told you to think, but no one ever explained what thinking is, how many kinds of thinking there are, and what qualities a good thinker has that a poor thinker lacks.

Thinking is a general term covering numerous activities, from daydreaming to reflection and analysis. Here are just some of the verbs Roget's *Thesaurus* includes for the word *think*:

appreciate	consult	fancy	reason
believe	contemplate	imagine	reflect
cerebrate	deliberate	meditate	ruminate
cogitate	digest	muse	speculate
conceive	discuss	ponder	suppose
consider	dream	realize	weigh

However, all of those are just the *names* that thinking goes under. They really don't explain it. The fact is after thousands of years of humans' experiencing thought and talking and writing about thinking, it remains in many respects one of the great mysteries of human existence. But though much is yet to be learned, a great deal is already known.

◇ ONE BRAIN OR TWO?

Brain function research has revealed the importance of a small bundle of nerves found between the left and right sides of the brain. Until recently that bundle, the corpus callosum, was thought to have no significant function. Now, however, scientists know that the brain is not *one* center of thought and learning but *two*. Each side has control over certain skills. When the corpus callosum is intact, the two sides work in harmony (although one may dominate). But when the corpus is cut or damaged, the left side of the brain is no longer aware of what the right side is doing and vice versa. Experiments performed with patients in this condition reveal that when one eye is covered and the other eye is shown an object, the hand controlled by the "blind" eye cannot later identify the object by touch. It is a familiar object to one part of the brain but totally unfamiliar to the other.[1]

We now know, too, that each half of the brain has its own memories and its own train of thought. The left half deals mainly with words and is associated with analysis and logical thinking. The right half deals mainly with sensory images and is associated with intuition and creative thinking.[2] Despite the separateness of the hemispheres, however, the brain's functions are profoundly integrated.

Some researchers regard the brain as synonymous with the mind. Western philosophy, however, has traditionally held that there is an important difference between the two. According to this view, the brain is a physical reality whereas the mind is metaphysical—that is, nonmaterial.

◇ CRITICAL THINKING DEFINED

Critical thinking is the process of evaluating ideas. More specifically, it is testing the accuracy of statements and the soundness of the reasoning that leads to conclusions. Critical thinking helps us interpret complex ideas, appraise the evidence offered in support of arguments, and distinguish between reasonableness and unreasonableness. Both problem solving and decision making depend on critical thinking, as does the analysis and discussion of controversial issues.*

One of the keys to proficiency in critical thinking is skill in asking relevant questions. Where the uncritical accept their first thoughts and others' statements at face value, critical thinkers challenge all ideas in the following manner:

Thought	*Question*
Professor Vile cheated me in my composition grade.	Did he grade everyone on the same standard? Were

---

*The word *critical* often carries a negative connotation, implying excessive faultfinding. That connotation does not apply to the term *critical thinking*.

He weighted some themes more heavily than others.	the different weightings justified?
Before women entered the work force, there were fewer divorces. That shows that a woman's place is in the home.	How do you know that this factor, and not some other one(s), is responsible for the increase in divorces?
A college education isn't worth what you pay for it. Some people never reach a salary level appreciably higher than the level they would have reached without the degree.	Is money the only measure of the worth of an education? What about increased understanding of self and life and increased ability to cope with challenges?

Critical thinking also involves the use of questions to inquire about issues, probing them more deeply than is customary and looking for new insights. Consider, for example, the subject of values. When it is being discussed, some people say, "Our country has lost its traditional values" and "There would be less crime, especially violent crime, if parents and teachers emphasized moral values." Critical thinking would prompt us to ask:

What is the relationship between values and beliefs? Between values and convictions?

Are all values valuable?

How aware is the average person of his or her values? Is it possible that many people deceive themselves about their real values?

Where do one's values originate? Within the individual or outside? In thought or in feeling?

Does education change a person's values? If so, is this change always for the better?

Should parents and teachers attempt to shape children's values?

◇ CHARACTERISTICS OF CRITICAL THINKERS

A number of misconceptions exist about critical thinking. One is that being able to support beliefs with reasons makes one a critical thinker. Virtually everyone has reasons, however pathetic they may be. The test of critical thinking is whether the reasons are good and sufficient.

Another misconception is that critical thinkers never imitate others in thought or action. If that were the case, then every pigheaded person would be a critical thinker. Critical thinking means making wise decisions, regardless of how common those decisions are.

A third misconception is that critical thinking is synonymous with having a lot of right answers in one's head. There's nothing wrong with having right answers, of course. But critical thinking is the process of finding answers when they are not so readily available.

Yet another misconception is that critical thinking cannot be learned, that one either "has it" or does not. On the contrary, critical thinking is a matter of habit. The most careless, sloppy thinker can become a critical thinker by developing the characteristics of a critical thinker.

We have already noted one characteristic of critical thinkers—skill in asking appropriate questions. Another is control of their mental activities. American philosopher John Dewey once observed that more of our time than most of us care to admit is spent "trifling with mental pictures, random recollections, pleasant but unfounded hopes, flitting, half-developed impressions."[3] Good thinkers are no exception. However, they have learned better than poor thinkers how to stop that casual, semiconscious drift of images when they wish and how to fix their minds on one specific matter, examine it carefully, and form a judgment about it. They have learned, in other words, how to take charge of their thoughts, to use their minds actively as well as passively.

Here are some additional characteristics of critical thinkers, as contrasted with those of uncritical thinkers:

Critical Thinkers . . .	*Uncritical Thinkers . . .*
Are honest with themselves, acknowledging what they don't know, recognizing their limitations, and being watchful of their own errors.	Pretend they know more than they do, ignore their limitations, and assume their views are error-free.
Regard problems and controversial issues as exciting challenges.	Regard problems and controversial issues as nuisances or threats to their ego.
Strive for understanding, keep curiosity alive, remain patient with complexity, and are ready to invest time to overcome confusion.	Are impatient with complexity and thus would rather remain confused than make the effort to understand.
Base judgments on evidence rather than personal preferences, deferring judgment	Base judgments on first impressions and gut reactions. They are unconcerned

whenever evidence is insufficient. They revise judgments when new evidence reveals error.	about the amount or quality of evidence and cling to earlier views steadfastly.
Are interested in other people's ideas, so are willing to read and listen attentively, even when they tend to disagree with the other person.	Are preoccupied with self and their own opinions, and so are unwilling to pay attention to others' views. At the first sign of disagreement, they tend to think, "How can I refute this?"
Recognize that extreme views (whether conservative or liberal) are seldom correct, so they avoid them, practice fairmindedness, and seek a balanced view.	Ignore the need for balance and give preference to views that support their established views.
Practice restraint, controlling their feelings rather than being controlled by them, and thinking before acting.	Tend to follow their feelings and act impulsively.

As the desirable qualities suggest, critical thinking depends on mental discipline. Effective thinkers exert control over their mental life, direct their thoughts rather than being directed by them, and withhold their endorsement of any idea—even their own—until they have tested and confirmed it. John Dewey considered this mental discipline to be identical with freedom. That is, he argued that people who do not have it are not free persons but slaves. Here are his words:

> If a man's actions are not guided by thoughtful conclusions, then they are guided by inconsiderate impulse, unbalanced appetite, caprice, or the circumstances of the moment. To cultivate unhindered, unreflective external activity is to foster enslavement, for it leaves the person at the mercy of appetite, sense, and circumstance.[4]

◇ THE ROLE OF INTUITION

Intuition is instinctive knowing or perception without reference to the rational process. Of all aspects of thinking, it is perhaps the most dramatic and therefore the most fascinating. History records many cases of important discoveries just "occurring" to people. These people may not even be consciously considering the matter. Then all of a sudden the answer comes to them, seemingly out of nowhere.

The German chemist Kekule found the solution to a difficult chemical problem that way. He was very tired when he slipped into a daydream. The image of a snake swallowing his tail came to him—and that provided the clue to the structure of the benzene molecule, which is a ring, rather than a chain, of atoms.[5] The German writer Goethe had been experiencing great difficulty organizing a large mass of material for one of his works when he learned of the tragic suicide of a close friend. At that very instant the plan for organizing his material occurred to him in detail.[6] The English writer Coleridge (you may have read his "Rime of the Ancient Mariner" in high school) awoke from a dream with between two and three hundred lines of a new and complex poem clearly in mind.

Intuition is not restricted to famous men and women. Most of us have had similar though less momentous experiences with it. Two facts are common to all these experiences, great and small alike. The first is that intuition cannot be controlled; the second is that intuition is not completely trustworthy. Even the strongest intuition can prove wrong. For both reasons, though intuition is always a welcome companion to critical thinking, it is never a substitute for it. This, of course, is no cause for concern because many other skills of thinking can be controlled and developed.

◇ CRITICAL THINKING AND ARGUMENT

Critical thinking is especially useful in evaluating arguments. An argument is a line of reasoning offered in support or refutation of a viewpoint.* Not all arguments are sound arguments. A sound argument is one in which the assertions (premises) that are made are accurate and the conclusion follows inescapably from those assertions.** Mistakes occur as often in constructing arguments as they do in arithmetic. Just as we can have accurate numbers, be conscientious, follow proper arithmetic procedure, and yet come up with the wrong answer, so too we can proceed from accurate information to a wrong conclusion. Of course,

---

*Though the term *argument* is sometimes used as a synonym for *quarrel,* there is an important difference between the two: Arguments are thoughtful, quarrels mindless.
**It's possible for a conclusion to be true even if the reasoning process is flawed. Consider this argument: "Fair-skinned people are more susceptible to skin cancer than dark-skinned people. Florida has more fair-skinned people than Michigan. Therefore, the skin cancer rate is higher in Florida than in Michigan." The conclusion happens to be true, *but coincidentally so, not because of the reasoning in this argument.* (The argument is flawed because the second premise lacks a basis in fact.)

when we start with inaccurate or incomplete information or reason recklessly, the chances of error are multiplied. Often the errors in an argument can be traced to inappropriate attitudes toward ideas and the reasoning process.

For example, if you regard your initial thought on an issue as unquestionably valid, you are likely to embrace it uncritically, seek out evidence that supports it and reject evidence that challenges it, and defend it rabidly. Such an approach leaves you vulnerable to self-deception and to manipulation by others. However, if you regard that idea as merely tentative—an interesting possibility but not a conviction—and postpone your acceptance or rejection of it until you have examined it carefully and compared it to other ideas, you are less likely to deceive yourself or be deceived by others.

Let us now consider how arguments are structured. An argument is a kind of verbal equation without mathematical symbols. A numerical equation takes the form $1 + 1 = 2$, or $2 - 1 = 1$; a verbal equation expresses similar relationships without using plus (minus) and equal signs. Here are some examples:

> Fair-skinned people are more in danger of sunburn than darker-skinned people. Ariel is fair-skinned. So Ariel is more in danger of sunburn than darker-skinned people.

> The law prohibits teachers from leading class prayers in public schools. Wynona leads students in prayer in her public school classroom. Therefore, Wynona is breaking the law.

Like numerical equations, arguments may be complex as well as simple. Just as the sum in a numerical equation may represent many numbers ($342 + 186 + 232 + 111 = 871$), so the conclusion of an argument may proceed from many assertions (premises). Just as having an incorrect number in the equation will result in a wrong total, so having an erroneous assertion will lead to the wrong conclusion. In the class prayer argument, if we mistakenly think that the law approves teachers leading students in prayer, our conclusion would be that Wynona is not breaking the law. And that would be erroneous. As these examples illustrate, it is possible for our final answer to be wrong even if we carry out flawlessly the process of addition or logic. We get correct answers (conclusions) only if we have *both* correct data (assertions) and the correct process.

Numerical equations and arguments are not, however, entirely similar. One important difference is that flaws in assertions tend to be more subtle and/or complex than flaws in numbers, and therefore more difficult to detect. Does vitamin C prevent the common cold or lessen its severity? Was Mike Tyson falsely accused of rape? Is television violence a causative factor in real violence? Was JFK killed by a single assassin? In these and many other matters, the evidence is as yet incomplete and/or knowledgeable people disagree.

Consider another important difference between numerical equations and arguments. It is difficult to imagine someone adding up a column of figures and including a figure she is unaware of at that time—the very fact of her being unaware of it would lead to its *exclusion*. Yet arguments often contain hidden premises, clearly implied assertions that we don't recognize when we conceive and express the argument. (Logicians call such arguments *enthymemes*.) If the hidden premise is accurate, no harm is done; but if it is inaccurate, it quietly corrupts the argument without our being aware. Here are some examples of such arguments. Each is first presented as it might occur in informal discussion. Then it is broken down into its component parts, including hidden assertions. The questions critical thinking would address are shown opposite each part.

1. *Argument:* They should never have married—they felt no strong physical attraction to each other during courtship.

Component Parts	Questions to Answer
Stated Premise: They felt no strong physical attraction to each other.	Is this statement completely accurate? That is, did they feel no strong physical attraction to each other?
Hidden Premise: Strong physical attraction is the best, or perhaps the only meaningful basis for marriage.	Is this statement completely accurate? That is, is strong physical attraction the best, or the only, meaningful basis for marriage?
Conclusion: They should never have married.	Do the premises lead inescapably to this conclusion and no other?

2. *Argument:* It's clear why Morton is an underachiever in school. He has very little self-esteem.

Component Parts	Questions to Ask
Stated Premise: Morton has very little self-esteem.	Is this statement completely accurate? That is, does Morton have very little self-esteem?
Hidden Premise: Self-esteem is necessary in order to achieve.	Is this statement completely accurate? That is, is self-esteem necessary in order to achieve?

Conclusion: It's clear why
Morton is an underachiever
in school. (The sense of this
statement is *"This explains
why . . . ."*)

Do the premises lead
inescapably to this conclusion and no other?

3. *Argument:* That book should be banned because it exposes children
to violence.

Component Parts	*Questions to Ask*
Stated Premise: That book exposes children to violence.	Is this statement completely accurate? That is, does the book expose children to violence?
First Hidden Premise: Exposure to violence is harmful.	Is this statement completely accurate? That is, is exposure to violence always harmful? (Note that in the absence of limiting terms, such as "sometimes," the general "always" is implied.)
Second Hidden Premise: Banning is the most appropriate reaction to such material.	Is this statement completely accurate? That is, is banning the most appropriate reaction to such material?
Conclusion: That book should be banned.	Do the premises lead inescapably to this conclusion and no other?

4. *Argument:* Pure water is healthy to drink, and Pristine Mountain
Water brand is pure, so I'm treating my body right by drinking it
rather than tap water.

Component Parts	*Questions to Ask*
Stated Premise: Pure water is healthy to drink.	Is this statement completely accurate? That is, is pure water healthy to drink?
Stated Premise: Pristine Mountain Water brand is pure.	Is this statement completely accurate? That is, is Pristine Mountain Water brand pure?
Hidden Premise: The water from my tap is not pure.	Is this statement completely accurate? That is, is water from this person's tap not pure?

Conclusion: I'm treating my
body right by drinking it
rather than tap water.

Do the premises lead
inescapably to this conclusion
and no other?

It is tempting to think that the longer the passage, the less likely it will contain hidden premises, but this is not the case. It is possible to elaborate an argument with one or more hidden premises into a book-length treatment without detecting and expressing these premises. In fact, the longer the passage, the more difficult it is to identify such premises. Whatever the length of the passage you are evaluating (or composing), be alert for hidden premises.

◇ SUPPORTING ASSERTIONS

Bare assertions are seldom persuasive. Thoughtful listeners or readers want to know the basis on which assertions are made, so they can be sure the statements are accurate. They rightly expect the person advancing the argument to answer the questions a critical thinker would ask about it. Those answers take the form of supporting evidence that is relevant and sufficient to overcome reasonable objections. Evidence may be classified in four broad categories.

ANECDOTAL EVIDENCE

Anecdotes are brief accounts or examples that have a bearing on the issue in question. These may be found in the case literature of related academic field(s), in news stories, or in everyday experience—our own as well as other people's.* To evaluate anecdotal evidence, ask: How typical, or representative, are the anecdotes? Do they represent the exception or the rule?

EXPERIMENTAL EVIDENCE

Experimental evidence is based on controlled studies in the laboratory or field. It is most commonly used in the physical sciences and in some of the social sciences. Experimental evidence may be found by checking the appropriate abstracts, such as those found in *Psychological Abstracts,*

---

*The list of sources for this and the other kinds of evidence is merely illustrative. For an extended list, see Chapter 19.

Sociological Abstracts, and *Dissertation Abstracts International;* and in index-es, such as the *Engineering Index,* the *Applied Science and Technology Index,* and the *General Science Index.* To evaluate experimental evidence, ask: Has the experiment ever been replicated by other researchers? (If other researchers have been unable to replicate the study and verify its con-clusions, the study's validity should be considered questionable.)

STATISTICAL EVIDENCE

Statistical evidence is derived from random sampling of a target group or "population." It may be found by consulting such reference works as *Statistical Abstracts.* To evaluate statistical evidence, consider the reputa-tion of the polling organization; the currency, size, and representative-ness of the sample (Does the sample reflect all sections of the total population as to age, race, gender, and socioeconomic status?); and whether the questions in the poll were free of bias. Ask also whether other statistical studies support these findings.

TESTIMONIAL EVIDENCE

Testimonial evidence is the expressed views of authorities. These are found in a variety of sources, including books, professional journals, magazines, newspapers, and television documentaries. Expert testimony is most helpful when the person goes beyond simple assertion and explains the *why* of his or her position—that is, the relevant historical factors, anecdotal evidence, experimental evidence, and statistical evi-dence underlying the position. To evaluate testimonial evidence, ask whether the person in question has up-to-date, special expertise in the matter. One may be the world's leading authority on one small aspect of his or her discipline, yet be quite out of touch with current research in many other aspects. Ask also whether the person's testimony goes beyond the boundaries of his or her expertise. Remember that people cease to speak as authorities the moment they step outside their fields of expertise. Unfortunately, some individuals have difficulty resisting the temptation to imprudent pronouncement. (A well-known astronomer, for example, regularly speculates in popular magazine articles about ethics and theology.) Ask, too, whether the person paid for his or her testimo-ny. The acceptance of money does not necessarily disqualify one from testifying, but it raises a question about the objectivity of what is said. Finally, ask whether other authorities agree or disagree with the testi-mony given.

One additional question is applicable to all kinds of evidence: Is it relevant to the issue under consideration? Consider the rather substantial body of evidence that has been widely accepted as proving that teaching effectiveness is unrelated to class size; in other words, that classroom teachers can be as effective with fifty students as they are with fifteen. (Many administrators continue to accept such evidence as definitive.) Yet, on careful examination, the evidence is revealed to apply only to classes emphasizing the imparting of information. For classes emphasizing the development of skills—for example, thinking, writing, or speaking skills—that research is irrelevant.

Ideally, argument is a *cooperative* endeavor in which people with different viewpoints seek to find the most accurate perspective on an issue. But given the strength of the human ego, that ideal is seldom achieved, so more often than not argument is *competitive,* each side of the debate striving to "win" by proving the other side wrong. Predictably, in a society as competitive as ours, many people are so fixated on winning that they forget about accuracy and integrity and continue embracing shallow views long after good sense has bid them to discard such views. To maintain a balanced perspective in argument, value knowledge and wisdom more than ego and remember that the measure of any argument—your own or someone else's—is not the depth or sincerity of belief but the quality of the evidence that supports it.

◇ What Constitutes "Sufficient" Evidence?

Because no field is ever completely closed to new discoveries or new inventions, in one sense investigation should never end because evidence is never sufficient. Still, few people have unlimited time at their disposal; practical necessity demands that decisions be made and action taken. The following guidelines reflect this reality:

Evidence is sufficient when it permits a judgment to be made with *certainty*. Wishing, assuming, or pretending that a judgment is correct does not constitute certainty. Certainty exists when there is no good reason for doubt, no basis for dispute. Certainty is rarely attained, especially in controversial issues.

If certainty is unattainable, evidence is sufficient if one view of the issue has been shown to have the force of *probability*. This means that the view in question is demonstrably more reasonable than any competing view. Demonstrating reasonableness is, of course, very different from merely asserting it, and all possible views must be identified and evaluated before any one view can be established as most reasonable.

◇ CRITICAL THINKING AND WRITING

Writing may be used for either of two broad purposes: to discover ideas or to communicate ideas. Most of the writing you have done in school is undoubtedly the latter kind. But the former can be very helpful, not only in sorting out ideas you've already produced, but in stimulating the flow of ideas. For some reason, the very act of writing down one idea has a way of producing additional ideas.

Whenever you write to discover ideas, focus on the issue you are examining and record all your thoughts, questions as well as assertions. Don't worry about organization or correctness. If ideas come slowly, be patient. If they come suddenly, in a rush, don't try to slow the process down and develop any one of them, but jot them all down. (There will be time for elaboration and for correction, later.) Direct your mind's effort, but be sensitive to ideas on the fringes of consciousness. Often they, too, will prove valuable.

If you have done your discovery writing well and have thought critically about the ideas you have produced, the task of writing to communicate will be easier and more enjoyable. You will have many more ideas—tested and proven ideas—to develop and organize.

⌘ APPLICATIONS

1. How closely has your experience with thinking in school matched Arthur's?

2. Do you find it difficult to ponder important matters? Are you able to prevent the casual, semiconscious drift of images from interrupting your thoughts? Do you have less control in some situations than in others? Explain.

3. Rate yourself on each of the seven characteristics of good thinkers that are listed on pp. 18–19. Which are you strongest in? Which weakest? If your behavior varies from situation to situation, try to determine what kinds of issues or circumstances bring out your best and worst mental qualities.

4. Is there any pattern to the way you think about a problem or an issue? Does an image come to mind first? Or perhaps a word? What comes next? And what after that? If you can't answer these questions completely, do this exercise: Flip half a dozen pages ahead in this book, pick a sentence at random, read it, and note how your mind deals with it. (Such thinking about your thinking may be a little awkward at first. If it is, try the exercise two or three times.)

5.   Read each of the following statements carefully. Then decide what question(s), if any, a good critical thinker would find it appropriate to ask.

   a.   Television news is sensational in its treatment of war because it gives us pictures only of injury, death, and destruction.

   b.   My parents were too strict—they wouldn't let me date until I was sixteen.

   c.   It's clear to me that Ralph doesn't care for me—he never spoke when we passed in the hall.

   d.   From a commercial for a news network: "The news is changing every minute of the day, so you constantly need updating to keep you informed."

   e.   The statement of an Alabama public elementary school teacher who had students recite the Lord's Prayer and say grace before meals: "I feel part of my job as a teacher is to instill values children need to have a good life."[7]

6.   Complete the analysis of each of the four arguments in the chapter by answering the questions presented there. Be sure to investigate if necessary.

7.   Evaluate each of the following arguments. First identify the argument's component parts (including hidden premises) and ask relevant questions, as shown in the chapter. Then check the accuracy of each premise, stated or hidden, and decide whether the conclusion is the most reasonable one. Note that checking the accuracy of the premises may require obtaining sufficient evidence to permit a judgment. If you find a premise to be inaccurate or a conclusion to be less than completely reasonable, revise the argument accordingly.

   a.   From a used-car advertisement: "We can guarantee your car loan even if you have a poor credit rating because we sell only quality used cars."

   b.   Children tend to receive more nurturing when only one parent works. Therefore, whenever possible, only one parent should work outside the home.

   c.   The term *family* should be legally applicable to any couple who wishes it, married or unmarried, gay or heterosexual, because love can exist without a marriage license.

d. Serious disease strikes the poor as well as the rich. Yet the poor are often unable to afford health insurance, so when they get ill, they are denied the most effective treatment available. This situation is intolerable in a democratic society. Universal, government-sponsored health care is the only equitable solution to this problem.

8. State your tentative position on each of the following controversial issues, applying what you learned in this chapter. Then select one of your responses, investigate to obtain relevant and sufficient evidence, and decide whether your tentative position is the most reasonable one. Write at least three paragraphs expanding your (original or revised) view into a sound argument. Be sure it contains no hidden premises.

a. The rape laws in some states require that the force used in the act be sufficient to produce a fear in the victim of serious physical injury or death. Some laws also require that the victim earnestly resist the assault. Where those conditions are not present, a rapist will not be prosecuted.

b. In what was believed to be the first national attempt to bring economic pressure to make a television network tone down the sex and violence in its programming, the Coalition for Better Television urged the public to boycott products made by RCA because the network owned by that company, NBC, had "excluded Christian characters, Christian values, and Christian culture from their programming." NBC denounced the move as "an obvious attempt at intimidation."[8]

c. The increase in violent crimes by teenagers and even young children in recent years has prompted many people to urge that the criminal justice system treat juvenile offenders as adults. Some even argue that the most serious offenders should receive the death penalty.

d. The U.S. Supreme Court has considered the cases of two teenagers who committed heinous crimes. In one, a seventeen-year-old raped and then murdered a gas station attendant. In the other, a sixteen-year-old stabbed a liquor store owner eight times, killing her. Many believe the death penalty is appropriate in such cases. Others believe that the death penalty is always inappropriate for minors, regardless of the crime.[9]

e. An unstable man called an Alabama television newsroom and threatened to kill himself. The station notified the police and then dispatched a camera crew to the scene. The crew reportedly stood by, filming, while the man doused himself with lighter fluid and lit two matches in an unsuccessful attempt to ignite himself. They moved in to stop him only after his third, successful attempt. The television station subsequently ran the film footage on the air. One member of the crew explained later, "My job is to record events as they happen." Many people find fault with the television crew's response to the situation.[10]

CHAPTER 3

WHAT IS TRUTH?

For hundreds of years philosophers battled over whether "truth" exists. The argument usually concerned "Truth" with a capital *T*, a kind of complete record of whatever was, is, or will be, error-proof, beyond doubt and dispute, a final test of the rightness or wrongness of people's ideas and theories.

Those who accepted the existence of this *Truth* believed it was a spiritual reality, not a physical one. That is, it was not a celestial ledger or file drawer—yet it was beyond time and space. It was considered an understanding among the gods, or an idea in the mind of God, or simply the sum total of *Reality*. Could human beings ever come to know *Truth*? Some said no, never. Others said yes, but only in the afterlife. Still others said that the wisest and best of humans could catch glimpses of it and that the rest of humanity could learn about it through these special ones.

Those who rejected this notion of an awesome, all-embracing *Truth* argued that it was an empty notion. How could all reality be summed up that way? More important, what possible evidence could be offered in support of its existence? Many who reasoned this way dismissed the idea of *Truth* as wishful thinking, a kind of philosophical security blanket. A few went further and denied even the existence of *truths* (no capital).

Our age has inherited the whole argument. The focus, however, has changed. It seldom concerns Truth anymore. Most people seem to doubt its existence. And even if it does exist, they reason, it's of little help to us in our world and our lives because it is beyond human understanding. Even many people of strong and rather conservative religious views no longer consider the question of Truth important to the understanding or practice of their faith.

Still the problem of truth (no capital) remains, and the position we take toward this question does have an important bearing on how we conduct our thinking and acting. Unfortunately, there is a good deal of murkiness and confusion about the concept. The rest of this chapter will attempt to shed light on it.

What comes through our senses exerts a powerful influence on us. It presents itself as true, and we are inclined to believe it. In addition, what we see is shaped by our individual way of seeing. We focus on what interests us. We filter out of our perception what seems unimportant to us. So we each perceive the world around us, and the events that fill our lives, in a unique way. No two people see the same event precisely alike.

Now if we were to stop our analysis here and consider only the fact of our uniqueness, we might understandably conclude that truth is relative—that is, that it varies from person to person, that one person's truth is another's error, and that there is no higher claim to validity than individual viewpoint.

◇ THE QUALITY OF PERCEPTION

But there is more to consider. *First, we can be mistaken in what we perceive.* The barroom brawler may be so uncertain of his own worth that he sees everything anyone does near him as mocking him. If two students walk by him sharing a joke, completely unaware he is there, he will interpret their laughter as directed at him and start a fight with them. He will have heard them laughing and be absolutely certain they are mocking him. And yet he will be wrong!

College students are often positive that their textbook contains a certain statement. So they answer an exam question with perfect confidence that they are right. Yet when they get the corrected test back and find the question marked wrong, then hurriedly flip open the book, and examine the passage again, they may find it does not say what they thought at all.

Your parents probably watched in awe as Tarzan uttered his famous yell and swung through the treetops to catch the villain. Tell them that Tarzan never made that yell and they'll say, "False, we heard it with our own ears." And yet it's not false. According to one of the men who first played the role of Tarzan, Buster Crabbe, that yell was dubbed into the films in the studio. It was a blend of three voices—a soprano's, a baritone's, and a hog caller's.

At least a dozen times every weekend from September to January, the imperfection of human observation is underlined by that marvel of technology, the instant replay. Is there a fan left in the land who isn't occasionally to be found screaming, "Bad call," only to be proved wrong a moment later? We can be sure enough to bet a week's wages that a pass receiver's feet came down in bounds. And then that unemotional camera shows them plainly three feet out.

The vagaries of perception have long been noted by those who deal with human testimony—notably, trial lawyers, jurists, and psychologists. It is well-established that a number of factors can make us see and hear inaccurately. Darkness, cloudy conditions, or distance from what we are witnessing may obscure our vision. We may be distracted at a crucial moment. If we are tired or in the grip of such powerful emotions as fear or anger, our normal perceptiveness may be significantly diminished. Also, perception may be intermingled with interpretation—the expectation that an event will unfold in a certain way may color our perception of the way the event actually unfolds. Loyalty and affection toward the people or things involved may distort our vision as well. If someone we dislike speaks in a loud voice and is animated, we may regard her as showing off to get attention. But if a friend behaves in the same way, we see her as vivacious and extroverted.

As if all these possibilities weren't enough, the passing of time frequently alters perception in our memories. We forget details and, when later attempting to recall what happened, we resort to imagination to fill in the blanks. Though we may at first be aware that such a process of reconstruction is occurring, this awareness soon fades and we come to believe we are remembering the original perception. As psychologist William James explained:

> The most frequent source of false memory is the accounts we give to others of our experiences. Such acts we almost always make more simple and more interesting than the truth. We quote what we should have said or done rather than what we really said or did; and in the first telling we may be fully aware of the distinction, but [before] long the fiction expels the reality from memory and [replaces it]. We think of

what we wish had happened, of possible [interpretations] of acts, and soon we are unable to distinguish between things that actually happened and our own thoughts about what might have occurred. Our wishes, hopes, and sometimes fears are the controlling factor.[1]

◇ THE QUALITY OF INFORMATION

Second, our information can be inaccurate or incomplete. The quality of a belief depends to a considerable extent on the quality of the information that backs it up. Because it's a big world and reality has many faces, it's easy for us to be misinformed. For example, which way does the water in a sink circle as it goes down the drain? Clockwise or counterclockwise? If you're more of an experimenter than a gambler, you'll find a sink, run some water, and find out the truth. The problem is you can only be half right that way (no matter how much your sink cost). If the sink is north of the equator, the water will circle counterclockwise, and if it's south, clockwise.

Even in more common situations, it's easy to be misinformed. How many drivers take the wrong turn because of faulty directions? How many people get on the wrong bus or train? How many car owners put too much or too little air in their tires on the advice of some service station attendant? Now, if misinformation is common enough in such relatively simple matters, how much more common is it in complex matters like law and medicine and government and religion?

It's possible, of course, to devote a lifetime of study to a particular field. But not even those who make that kind of commitment can know everything about their subject. Things keep happening too fast. They occur whether we're watching or not. There's no way to turn them off when we take a coffee break or go to the bathroom. The college student who hasn't been home in three months may be able to picture the neighbor's elm tree vividly. Yet it may have been cut down two months ago. The soldier may have total recall of his hometown—every sight and sound and smell—and return home to find half of Main Street sacrificed to urban renewal, the old high school hangout closed, a new car in his best friend's driveway.

◇ EVEN THE WISE CAN ERR

So far we've established that people can be mistaken in what they perceive and that the information they receive can be faulty or incomplete. But these matters concern individuals. What of *group* judgment—the carefully analyzed observations of the best thinkers, the wisest men and women of the time? Is that record better? Happily, it is. But it, too, leaves a lot to be desired.

All too often, what is taken as truth today by the most respected minds is proved erroneous tomorrow. You undoubtedly know of some examples. In the early seventeenth century, when Galileo suggested that the sun is the center of our solar system, he was charged with heresy, imprisoned, and pressured to renounce his error. The "truth" of that time, accepted by every scientist worthy of the name, was that the *earth* was the center of the solar system.

A little more than a century ago Darwin scandalized the Western world with his claims that the earth was far older than 5,000 years and that human beings descended from apes. The error of this was obvious to every schoolchild. The truth of the traditional view was based on the Bible itself. How could it possibly be wrong? Here are some other examples you may not have heard where "truth" turned out to be not true:

- For a long time surgeons used talc on the rubber gloves they wear while performing surgery. Then they discovered it could be poisonous. So they switched to starch, only to find that it too can have a toxic effect on surgical patients.[2]
- Film authorities were certain they were familiar with all the films the late Charlie Chaplin ever made. Then in 1982 a previously unknown film was discovered in a British screen archive vault.[3]
- For hundreds of years historians believed that, though the people of Pompeii had been trapped by the eruption of Mount Vesuvius in A.D. 79, the people of neighboring Herculaneum had escaped. Then the discovery of eighty bodies (and the hint of hundreds more) under the volcanic ash revealed that many from Herculaneum had also been trapped.[4]
- Your grandparents probably learned that there are eight planets in our solar system. Since Pluto was discovered in 1930, your parents and you learned there are nine. But if the observations of Joseph L. Brady of the University of California prove correct, your children will learn there are *ten*.[5]
- After morphine was used by doctors for some years as a painkiller, it was found to be addictive. The search began for a nonaddictive substitute. What was found to take its place? *Heroin.*[6]

◇ TRUTH: A DEFINITION

Where does all this leave us? If an individual can be wrong and even the most widely endorsed conviction of an age is not necessarily correct, what definition of truth shall we endorse? Truth can be considered in two ways: (1) as a quality of assertions or statements; or (2) as the aspect of reality the statements are intended to express. The former is more fashionable today, the latter neglected. That is undoubtedly why many people describe their opinions as "my truth" and passionately defend such silly views as "The idea that smoking is harmful may be true for others but not for me." This translates to "Whatever I want to believe is worthy of belief."

The easiest way to avoid such foolishness is to assign the second definition of truth more weight than the first. It really deserves that priority because the reality we are describing is the measure of our assertions about it. Our assertions have value only if they are accurate expressions. The truth about something, then, is what is so about it—the facts in their exact arrangement and proportions. Did time run out before the field goal was kicked? How does gravity work? Who stole your hubcaps? Are there time/space limits to the universe? Who started the argument between you and your mother last weekend? Have you been working up to your potential in this course? To look for the truth in any of these matters is to look for the correct answer, the answer that completely expresses reality in the matter. Whatever difficulty we may find in discerning or stating the truth is beside the point.

That last sentence deserves emphasizing. Much of the confusion about truth arises from complex situations in which the truth is difficult to ascertain or express. Consider a question like "Are there really UFOs that are piloted by extraterrestrial beings?" Although the question is often hotly debated, and people make assertions that purport to express the truth, there is not yet sufficient evidence to say we know the truth about UFOs. That, however, doesn't mean there is no truth about them or that people who affirm their existence and people who deny it are equally correct. It means that whatever the truth is, we do not yet possess it.

Similar difficulty arises from many psychological and philosophical questions like "Why are some people heterosexual and others homosexual?" "Is the cause of criminality genetic or environmental or a combination of the two?" "Are human beings inherently violent?" "Is there an afterlife?" "What constitutes success?" The answers to these questions, and to many of the issues you will encounter in the applications in this book, will often be incomplete or tentative. Yet that fact should not shake your conviction that there are truths to be discovered.

During the Senate hearings on Clarence Thomas's candidacy for the Supreme Court, Anita Hill's charge of sexual harassment was the focus of national debate. Was Thomas guilty, as she claimed, or innocent, as he maintained? Tens of thousands of editorials, letters to editors, articles, and books were written about the case and hundreds of hours of air time were devoted to analysis of the evidence. Many people believed him a villain; many others saw him as a victim of false accusation; still others couldn't make up their minds. But to my knowledge no one advanced the argument that *both stories were true*—that Clarence Thomas was at the same time guilty of the charge and innocent of the charge. If anyone had, he or she would have been attacked by both camps for talking nonsense and trivializing an important issue. However fashionable it may be to speak of "my truth" and "your truth," on significant issues like the Thomas case, people want to know *the* truth, what really happened.

Having the right frame of mind can make your pursuit of the truth less burdensome and give it some of the adventure the greatest thinkers in history experienced. A good way to begin is to keep the following thought in mind: "I know I've got limitations and can easily be mistaken. And surely I'll never find all the answers I'd like to. But I can observe a little more accurately, weigh things a little more thoroughly, and make up my mind a little more carefully. If I do so, I'll be a little closer to the truth."

That's far different from saying, "Everyone makes his or her own truth" or "It all depends on how you look at it." And it is much more reasonable.

❖ APPLICATIONS

1.   Think of a recent situation in which someone referred inappropriately to "my truth." Write two or three paragraphs, in your own words, explaining to that person what you learned in this chapter.

2.   Evaluate the following arguments as you did the arguments in Chapter 2, application 7. First identify the argument's component parts (including hidden premises) and ask relevant questions, as shown in that chapter. Then check the accuracy of each premise, stated or hidden, and decide whether the conclusion is the most reasonable one. Note that checking the accuracy of the premises may require obtaining sufficient evidence to permit a judgment. If you find a premise to be inaccurate or a conclusion to be less than completely reasonable, revise the argument accordingly.

   a.   *Background note: College administrators are debating their campus policy after receiving complaints about professors dating students. They* *endorse the following argument:* There is nothing wrong in two unmarried adults dating, so it is acceptable for professors to date students who are over eighteen years of age.

b. Copying computer software violates the copyright law. Still, I paid full price for my software and my friend not only needs it for his class, but can't afford to purchase it himself. If I give him a copy of mine, he'll be helped and no one will be hurt. (The software company wouldn't have made a sale to him anyway because he's broke.) Therefore I am justified in giving him the software.

c. "All men are created equal," says the Declaration of Independence. Yet lots of Americans are victims of poverty and discrimination and lack of opportunity for education and careers. And the rich and social elites can buy a standard of justice unavailable to the average citizen. Equality is a myth.

3. For years grade school students faced this question on their science tests: "True or False—The famous rings of the planet Saturn are composed of solid material." If the students marked "true," they lost credit, because the "truth" was that Saturn's rings are composed of gas or dust. Then in 1973 radar probes revealed that all those wrong answers were right. Saturn's rings are in fact composed of solid matter.[7] This confusing case seems to suggest that *the truth changed*. Did it really? Explain.

4. The scene is a dormitory head resident's office. Two students are being questioned. A few minutes earlier they were engaged in a fistfight in the hall. The head resident asks them again and again how the fight started. The stories conflict. Because each student seems genuinely convinced that the other one was the aggressor, and there were no witnesses, the resident has no hope of discovering the truth. But is there *a* truth to discover? Or are there two truths, one for each student's story? What light does the chapter shed on these questions?

5. A strange phenomenon that affects a tiny number of the world's inhabitants has interested psychologists for some time. It occurs during what Norwegians call the "murky time," the two months each year during which areas above the Arctic Circle experience almost unrelieved darkness. The effects on people have been discovered to be unfortunate, even dangerous. At worst, people experience severe tenseness, restlessness, fear, and a preoccupation with thoughts of death and even suicide. At best they experience an inability to concentrate, a tiredness, a lack of enthusiasm for anything, suspicion, and jealousy. Part of the cause is seen as lack of sleep. Accustomed to day and night, people become confused by constant darkness.[8] This phenomenon poses an interesting test of truth. Would it be proper to say the phenomenon was true before it was recognized and acknowledged by psychologists? Or did it become true only when they became aware of it? And what of your relation to the phenomenon? Before you became aware of it for the first time, whether reading it here or elsewhere, it was not "true to you." But did that make it any less true? Explain in light of this chapter.

6.   Evaluate the following dialogues in light of what you learned in this chapter. If you lack sufficient knowledge to judge the issue, do some research.

   a.   *Lois:* We should really quit smoking, Francis. The evidence is growing that it's a factor in a number of diseases.

   Francis: Don't get nervous about it, Lois. So far there has been no definitive study—only theories and speculation and "suggested links." Nobody ever died from those. If they come up with a conclusive link between smoking and disease, there will be time enough to quit.

   b.   *Martha:* I don't care what the courts say about abortion—I'm convinced it's murder because the fetus is a human being.

   Marian: If you want to believe that, fine. Just don't impose your beliefs on others and prevent them from exercising their rights.

   Martha: You don't seem to understand. It's not just a fetus in my uterus that's human but the fetus in the uterus of every pregnant woman.

   Marian: Nonsense. You have no right to classify what exists in someone else's uterus. That's her business. You should mind your own business.

   c.   *Barbi:* Television shows about suicide should not be aired.

   Ken: Why?

   Barbi: Because they cause people to commit suicide.

   Ken: That's ridiculous. How can a drama or documentary that shows the tragedy of suicide cause people to commit suicide?

   Barbi: I don't know how it happens. Maybe some people have thoughts of suicide already and the show reinforces them. Or maybe they focus on the act of suicide and lose sight of the tragedy. All I know is that attempted suicides increase after the airing of such shows.

   d.   *Mabel:* I notice when you get a newspaper you immediately turn to the astrology column. Do you really believe that nonsense?

   Alphonse: It's not nonsense. The planets exercise a powerful influence on our lives; their positions in the heavens at the time of our birth can shape our destiny.

Mabel: I can't believe I'm hearing such slop from a science major.

Alphonse: What you fail to understand is that astrology is science, one of the most ancient sciences at that.

e. *Jake:* What did you think of the chapter "What Is Truth?"

Rocky: It's stupid.

Jake: What do you mean?

Rocky: It contradicts Chapter 1.

Jake: I didn't get that impression. Where's the contradiction?

Rocky: In Chapter 1 the author says that we should strive to be individuals and think for ourselves. Now he says that his idea about truth is OK and ours isn't and that we should follow his. That's a contradiction.

7. *Group discussion exercise:* How many times have you been certain something was true, only to find out later that it was not? Discuss those experiences with two or three of your classmates. Be prepared to share the most dramatic and interesting experiences with the rest of the class.

CHAPTER 4

What Does It Mean to Know?

Sally looks up from her composition and asks her roommates, "How do you spell *embarrass*?"

Nancy says, "I'm not sure. I think it has a double *r* and a double *s*. Oh, I really don't know."

Marie smiles her smug smile. "I guess spelling isn't your cup of tea, Nancy. The correct spelling is e-m-b-a-r-a-s-s. Only one *r*."

By this time Sally has already opened her dictionary. "Might as well check to be sure," she says. "Let's see, *embargo, embark* . . . here it is, *embarrass*. Double *r* and double *s*. You were right, Nancy."

Let's consider what happened more closely. Marie *knew* the answer, but she was wrong. Nancy *didn't know*, but she was right. Confusing. What kind of thing can this "knowing" be? When you're doing it, you're not doing it. And when you aren't, you are.

Fortunately, it only appears to be that way. The confusion arises because the feelings that accompany knowing can be present when we don't know. Marie had those feelings. She no longer wondered or experienced any confusion. She was sure of the answer. Yet she was mistaken.

◇ REQUIREMENTS OF KNOWING

Nancy was in a better position than Marie because she answered correctly. Yet she didn't *know* either, for knowing involves more than having the right answer. It also involves *the realization that you have it*.

The answer, of course, may not always be as simple as the spelling of a word. It may require understanding numerous details or complex principles or steps in a process. (It may also involve a skill—knowing *how to do* something. But that is a slightly different use of the word than concerns us here.)

Knowing usually implies something else, too—the ability to express what is known and how we came to know it. This, however, is not *always* so. We may not be able to express our knowledge in words. The best we may be able to say is "I just know, that's all" or "I know because I know." Yet these replies are feeble and hardly satisfy those who wish to verify our knowledge or share it.

◇ ACTIVE AND PASSIVE KNOWING

We can achieve knowledge either actively or passively. We achieve it actively by direct experience, by testing and proving an idea (as in a scientific experiment), or by reasoning. When we do it by reasoning, we analyze a problem, consider all the facts and possible interpretations, and draw the logical conclusion.

We achieve knowledge passively by being told by someone else. Much of our learning comes passively. Most of the learning that happens in the classroom and the kind that happens when we watch TV news reports or read newspapers or magazines is passive. Conditioned as we are to passive learning, it's not surprising that we depend on it in our everyday communication with friends and co-workers.

Unfortunately, passive learning has a serious defect. It makes us tend to accept uncritically what we are told. Of course, much that we are told is little more than hearsay and rumor.

Did you ever play the game Rumor? It begins with one person's writing down a message but not showing it to anyone. Then the person whispers it, word for word, to another person. That person, in turn, whispers it to still another, and so on, through all the people playing the game. The last person writes down the message word for word as he or she hears it. Then the two written statements are compared. What is usually discovered? The original message has changed, often dramatically, by passing from person to person.

That's what happens in daily life. No two words have precisely the same shades of meaning. Therefore, the simple fact that people repeat a story in their own words rather than in exact quotation changes the story. Then, too, most people listen imperfectly. And many enjoy adding their own creative touch to a story, trying to improve on it, stamping it with their own personal style. This tendency may be conscious or unconscious. Yet the effect is the same in either case—those who hear it think they know.

◇ Why Knowing Is Difficult

One reason knowing is difficult is that old unanswered questions continue to resist solution, questions like what causes cancer, what approach to education is best for children, and how can we prevent crime without comprising individual rights.

Another reason is that everyday situations arise for which there are no precedents. When the brain operation known as frontal lobotomy was developed to calm raging violence in people, it raised the question of the morality of a "cure" that robbed the patient of human sensibilities. When the heart transplant and the artificial heart became realities, the issue of which patients should be given priority was created, as well as the question of how donors were to be obtained. When smoking was definitely determined to be a causative factor in numerous fatal diseases, we were forced to examine the wisdom of allowing cigarette commercials to mislead TV viewers and entice them into harming themselves. More recently, when smoking in public places was shown to harm the nonsmoker as well as the smoker, a debate arose concerning the rights of smokers and nonsmokers.

Still another reason why knowing is difficult is that, as generation passes to generation, knowledge is often forgotten or unwisely rejected. Some ancient Greeks knew that whales have lungs instead of gills and are therefore mammals. But later the Romans thought whales were fish, and that false notion persisted in Western minds until the seventeenth century. In that century one man suggested whales are really mammals, and another later established it as fact. The West rediscovered an item of knowledge.[1]

In our time the ideas of "sin" and "guilt" have come to be regarded as useless and even harmful holdovers from Puritan times. The "new morality" has urged people to put aside such old-fashioned notions as obstacles to happiness and fulfillment. Then Karl Menninger, one of America's leading psychiatrists, wrote a book called *Whatever Became of*

Sin?[2] in which he argues that the notions of "sin" and "guilt" are good and necessary in civilized society. He says, in other words, that our age rejected those concepts too quickly and quite unwisely.

Knowledge is often thought of as dead matter stored on dusty shelves in dull libraries. Unfortunately, the hushed atmosphere of a library can suggest a funeral chapel or a cemetery. But the appearance is deceiving. The ideas on those shelves are very much alive—and often fighting furiously with one another. Consider the following cases.

The idea that Columbus was the first person from Europe, Africa, or Asia to land on the shores of North or South America hangs on tenaciously. The opposite idea challenges this again and again. (The evidence against the Columbus theory continues to mount: the discovery of ancient Japanese pottery in Ecuador, traces of visits by seafarers from Sidon in 541 B.C., as well as by the Greeks and Hebrews in A.D. 200 and by the Vikings in A.D. 874.[3] The most recent evidence suggests the Chinese may have discovered America by 2500 B.C.)[4]

The idea that a history of slavery and deprivation have caused black Americans to have less self-esteem than whites was well-established. Then it was challenged by two University of Connecticut sociologists, Jerold Heiss and Susan Owens. Their studies indicate that the self-esteem of middle-class blacks is almost identical to that of middle-class whites and that the self-esteem of lower-class blacks is *higher* than that of lower-class whites.[5] The experience of many educators and social workers, it should be noted, runs counter to this finding.

The notion that when the youngest child leaves home, middle-aged parents, especially mothers, become deeply depressed and feel that life is over for them has many believers. Yet at least one study attacks that notion. It shows that many, perhaps most, parents are not depressed at all; rather, they look forward to a simpler, less demanding life.[6]

Similarly, until recently most scientists were satisfied that senility is a result of the physical deterioration of the brain and is both progressive and irreversible. Then experimenters in an Alabama veterans' hospital found that in many cases the symptoms of senility—confusion, disorientation, and withdrawal from reality—can be halted and even reversed by "a simple program of keeping the aged constantly in touch with the surrounding environment."[7]

Books and articles referring to athletes' "second wind" abound in every library. Yet Nyles Humphrey and Robert Ruhling of the University of Utah have presented evidence that there really is no second wind and that the sensation experienced by many athletes is merely psychological.[8]

◇ A CAUTIONARY TALE

Even authorities who have the most sophisticated measurement tools at their disposal fail to achieve certainty. Consider, for example, the challenge to anthropologists posed by the Tasaday tribe. When discovered in the Philippine island of Mindanao in the late 1960s, the Tasaday were living a Stone Age existence—living in caves in the deep jungle, ignorant of agriculture, subsisting by hunting and gathering. Manuel Elizaldo, an associate of then-dictator Ferdinand Marcos, quickly became their protector, mentor, and go-between with a fascinated world. A number of anthropologists and other experts visited the tribe and studied their artifacts, language, and social structure. Except for a few skeptics, most scholars judged them to be authentic Stone Age people. Prestigious publications like the *National Geographic* wrote about the Tasaday and marveled at the fact that they were such an innocent, gentle people with no words in their language for "weapon," "war," or "hostility."

In 1986, after the Marcos regime collapsed, a Swiss journalist visited the Tasaday and found them living in houses. They reportedly admitted to him that their story was an elaborate hoax perpetrated by Elizaldo. He supposedly told them when to go to the caves and put on the Stone Age act for visiting journalists and scholars. From that time to this, Elizaldo has denied the charge and has had the continuing support of many scientists. Douglas Yen, an ethnobiologist and early Tasaday researcher, originally sought to link the group to neighboring farming tribes, but now believes the Stone Age circumstances were genuine. (He cites a case where little children were shown cultivated rice and displayed amazement.) Carol Molony, a linguist and another early Tasaday scholar, is also a believer. She argues that the tribe, children as well as adults, would have to have been superb actors to eliminate all agricultural metaphors from their speech. A local priest and former skeptic, Fr. Sean McDonagh, also believes the Tasaday to be authentic and says neighboring tribes do, too.

One continuing element of dispute concerns the authenticity of Tasaday tools. Zeus Salazar, a Philippine anthropologist, maintains the loose straps attaching stones to handles suggest a poor attempt to fake Stone Age methods. Yet archaeologist Ian Glover says such looseness has been noted in authentic Stone Age implements. The Tasaday's own statements have not simplified the puzzle. They told NBC and Philippine television that their original story was true, and then told ABC and British television that it was false.

Certainty in this case seems impossible to achieve. The best that can be hoped for may be a high degree of probability, which anthropologist Thomas Headland has arguably achieved. Headland, who exhaustively researched the matter, suggests there was no hoax but there were gross exaggerations and false media reports, as well as some self-fulfilling expectations by anthropologists. It is likely, he believes, that the Tasaday were once part of the neighboring farming tribes who fled several hundred years ago (perhaps to avoid slave traders), and hid in the forest for so many generations that they not only regressed to a Stone Age culture but lost all memory of their more advanced state.[9]

◇ THE PATH TO KNOWLEDGE

Before discussing how knowledge is best sought, let's consider two habits that *impede* knowledge: assuming and guessing. *Assuming* is taking something for granted—that is, arbitrarily accepting as true something that has not been proved, or that there are reasonable grounds for disputing. Because assuming is generally an unconscious activity, we are often unaware of our assumptions and their influence on us.* The main negative effect of unrecognized assumptions is that they stifle the curiosity that leads to knowledge.

Many people, for example, never speculate about the daily life of fish. They may occasionally stop at the pet store in the mall and stare at the tank of tropical fish. But they never display curiosity about the social roles and relationships of fish communities because they assume fish have no such roles and relationships. Yet the fact is, in the words of underwater sociologist C. Lavett Smith, "There are fish equivalents of barbers, policemen, and farmers. Some are always on the move and others are sedentary. Some work at night and some by day."[10]

Most people who are familiar with the Catholic Church's official opposition to abortion assume that this opposition has always existed. The great majority of Catholics share this assumption. Yet at various times in history there have been dramatic shifts in the Church's position. Before the end of the sixteenth century, Catholic ethical practice was to allow abortion during the first eighty days of pregnancy. At the end of that century, one pope (Sixtus V) decided the practice was wrong and declared that abortion was sinful at any stage of pregnancy. Then the next pope (Gregory XIV) decided that abortion was permissible any time

---

*It is, of course, possible to raise assumptions to the conscious level and express them. Most scientific references to assumptions are made in this context.

before the fetus showed signs of movement in the womb. In 1869 still another pope (Pius IX) returned to the view that abortion was always wrong.[11]

Guessing is offering a judgment on a hunch or taking a chance on an answer without any confidence that it is correct. It's a common, everyday activity. For students who don't do their studying for exams, it's a last-ditch survival technique. For an example of guessing, though, let's take a more pleasant subject—drinking beer. Some time ago a professor of behavioral science at a California college conducted a beer taste test among his students. The question was whether they could really tell a good beer from a bad one or their favorite from others. Many students would guess they could. A number of participants in the test guessed that way. However, the test showed that when the labels were removed from the cans, not one student could identify a single brand.[12]

Because assuming stifles curiosity and guessing denies the importance of evidence, neither is likely to lead to knowledge. The most reliable approach is to be cautious in asserting that you know something. Be conservative in your level of assertion—whenever you are less than certain, speak about possibilities and probabilities. Say "I think" or "It seems to me" rather than "I know." Most important, be honest to yourself and others about your ignorance. To admit you don't know something shows good sense, restraint, and intellectual honesty. These are not weaknesses but strengths. The admission of ignorance is the essential first step toward knowledge.

Does this mean you should be wishy-washy and hedge everything you say with maybes and perhapses? Does it mean that to be a critical thinker you must forsake convictions? The answer to both questions is an emphatic *no!* It means only that you should value firm, bold statements so much that you reserve them for occasions when the evidence permits. Similarly, you should value convictions so highly that you embrace them only when you have sufficient knowledge to do so and modify them whenever intellectual honesty requires.

APPLICATIONS

1. Evaluate the following arguments as you did the arguments in Chapter 2, application 7. First identify the argument's component parts (including hidden premises) and ask relevant questions, as shown in that chapter. Then check the accuracy of each premise, stated or hidden, and decide whether the conclusion is the most reasonable one. Note that checking the accuracy of the premises may require obtaining sufficient evidence to permit a judgment—distinguish carefully between, on the one hand, what you know and, on the other, what you do not know and need to find out. If you find a premise to be inaccurate or a conclusion to be less than completely reasonable, revise the argument accordingly.

   a. *Background note: The ancient religion known as Santeria is still practiced by a number of people in the United States. One of its beliefs is that the sacrifice of animals is pleasing to the god Olodumare. Thus as part of their ritual, Santerian priests slit the throats of chickens, doves, turtles, and goats, drain the blood into clay pots, and prepare the animals' flesh for eating. Many other Americans complain to the authorities about this practice.*

Argument: The United States Constitution guarantees the free exercise of religion. It does not exclude religions that displease the majority. However displeasing ritual animal sacrifice may be to other citizens, the law should uphold Santerians' constitutional rights.

   b. *Background note: In recent years many cities have experienced an increase in aggressive panhandling—the practice of approaching passersby and begging for money. Some panhandlers block people's paths and otherwise intimidate them. A number of cities have outlawed panhandling.*

The following argument has found expression in some court decisions: Panhandling is a form of speech. Speech is protected by the Constitution. Therefore, panhandling is a right that cannot be abridged.

2. In each of the following cases someone believes he or she knows something. In light of what you learned in this chapter, discuss whether the person really does.

   a. Ted reads in the morning newspaper that a close friend of his has been arrested and charged with having burglarized a number of stores. Ted is shocked. "It's impossible. The police have made a mistake," he tells his mother. "Bob and I have been as close as brothers. I just *know* he's not guilty."

   b. *Ralph:* Here, Harry, try my deodorant. It really stops wetness.
   Harry: No thanks. I'm suspicious of antiperspirants. It seems to me that anything designed to block a normal body function may do a lot of harm. I wouldn't be surprised if it caused cancer.
   Ralph: Don't be foolish. I *know* it doesn't cause cancer. Products like these are carefully tested before they're allowed to be sold. If it caused cancer, it would be banned.

   c. *Jane:* I just read there's some evidence that aspirin can prevent heart attacks.

Jenny: That's a lot of nonsense. I *know* it can't. My uncle took lots of aspirin and he died of a heart attack last year.

3. "Man Is Released in Wrong Rape Charges," "Traditional Idea Debunked," "Ex-Aide Admits Lying About Lawmakers"—daily newspapers contain numerous stories like these, stories showing how what was "known" a week, a month, or years ago has been found to be false. Find at least three examples of such stories in current or recent newspapers.

4. "It ain't what a man doesn't know that makes him a fool, but what he does know that ain't so," wrote Josh Billings, the nineteenth-century American humorist. Recall as many occasions as you can in which your own experience confirms his words.

5. A court case pitting the U.S. government against the American Indian Movement was conducted quietly in South Dakota in late 1982. The government sought to end the Indian group's twenty-month occupation of public land in the Black Hills National Forest. The Indians claimed the area is a holy land to them—their birthplace, the graveyard of their ancestors, and the center of their universe—and therefore should be turned into a permanent, religion-based Indian community.[13] The government maintained the Indians have no legal claim to the land. What factors do you think should be considered in a case like this, and what solution would best serve the interests of justice? In answering, be sure to distinguish carefully between what you know and what you assume, guess, or speculate. If your knowledge is very limited, you may wish to do some research.

6. The Equal Rights Amendment (ERA) failed to gain the legislative support necessary to be passed into law. Its opponents believe that wisdom prevailed. Its sponsors, however, attribute its defeat to apathy and ignorance. What is your position? Do you believe the ERA is a worthy addition to the U.S. Constitution? In answering, be sure to distinguish carefully between what you know and what you assume, guess, or speculate. If your knowledge is very limited, you may wish to do some research.

7. In recent years there has been much discussion of the insanity plea as a legal defense. Many believe it should be abolished, but many others regard it as an essential part of any reasonable criminal justice system. What is your position? In answering, be sure to distinguish carefully between what you know and what you assume, guess, or speculate. If your knowledge is very limited, you may wish to do some research.

8.   *Group discussion exercise:* Decide if you know whether each of the following statements is accurate. Discuss your decisions with two or three classmates. Be sure to distinguish knowing from guessing or assuming.

    a.   Most criminals come from lower economic backgrounds.

    b.   Black people are victims of crimes more often than white people are.

    c.   The U.S. Constitution guarantees every citizen the right to own a handgun.

    d.   Violence in the media is responsible for real-life violence.

CHAPTER 5

How Good Are Your Opinions?

Opinion is a word that is often used carelessly today to refer to matters of taste, belief, and judgment. This casual use would probably cause little confusion if people didn't attach much importance to opinion. Unfortunately, most do attach great importance to it. "I have as much right to my opinion as you to yours" and "Everyone's entitled to his or her opinion" are common expressions. In fact, anyone who would challenge another's opinion is likely to be branded intolerant.

Is that label accurate? Is it intolerant to challenge another's opinion? It depends on what definition of opinion you have in mind. For example, you may ask a friend, "What do you think of the new Buicks?" And he may reply, "In my opinion, they're ugly." In this case, it would not only be intolerant to challenge his statement but foolish, for it's obvious that by "opinion" he means his *personal preference*, a matter of taste. And as the old saying goes, "It's pointless to argue about matters of taste."

However, consider this very different use of the term. A newspaper reports that the Supreme Court has delivered its opinion in a controversial case. Obviously the justices did not state their personal preferences, their mere likes and dislikes. They stated their *considered judgment*, painstakingly arrived at after thorough inquiry and deliberation.

Most of what is referred to as opinion falls somewhere between these two extremes. It is not an expression of taste. Nor is it careful judgment. Yet it may contain elements of both. It is a view or belief more or less casually arrived at, with or without examination of the evidence.

Is everyone entitled to his or her opinion? In a free country this is not only permitted but guaranteed. In Great Britain, for example, there is still a Flat Earth Society. As the name implies, the members of this organization believe that the earth is not spherical but flat. In this country, too, each of us is free to take as bizarre a position as we please about any matter we choose. When the telephone operator announces, "That'll be ninety-five cents for the first three minutes," you may respond, "No, it won't—it'll be twenty-eight cents." When the service station attendant notifies you, "Your oil is down a quart," you may reply, "Wrong—it's up three."

Being free to hold an opinion and express it does not, of course, guarantee favorable consequences. The operator may hang up on you. The service station attendant may threaten you with violence.

Acting on our opinions carries even less assurance. Consider the case of the California couple who took their eleven-year-old diabetic son to a faith healer. Secure in their opinion that the man had cured the boy, they threw away his insulin. Three days later the boy died. They remained unshaken in their belief, expressing the opinion that God would raise the boy from the dead. The police arrested them, charging them with manslaughter.[1] The law in such matters is both clear and reasonable. We are free to act on our opinions only so long as, in doing so, we do not harm others.

◇ Opinions Can Be Mistaken

We may be tempted to conclude that, if we are free to believe something, it must have some validity. That, however, is not the case. Free societies are based on the wise observation that people have an inalienable right to think their own thoughts and make their own choices. But this fact in no way suggests that the thoughts they think and the choices they make will be reasonable. It is a fundamental principle of critical thinking that ideas are seldom of equal quality. Solutions to problems vary from the practical to the impractical, beliefs vary from the well-founded to the ill-founded, arguments from the logical to the illogical, and opinions from the informed to the uninformed. Critical thinking serves to separate the more worthy from the less and, ultimately, to identify the best.

Evidence that opinions can be mistaken is all around us. The weekend drinker often has the opinion that as long as he doesn't drink during the week, he is not an alcoholic. The person who continues driving her gas guzzler with the needle on Empty may have the opinion that the problem being signaled can wait for another fifty miles. The student who quits school at age sixteen may have the opinion that an early entry into the job market ultimately improves job security. Yet, however deeply and sincerely such opinions are held, they are wrong.

Research shows that people can be mistaken even when they are making a special effort to judge objectively. Sometimes their errors are caused by considerations so subtle they are unaware of them. For example, before Taster's Choice coffee was introduced, it was tested and sampled with three different labels—brown, yellow, and red. People who sampled the coffee in the container with the brown label reported that it was too strong and kept them awake at night. People who sampled the yellow-labeled coffee found it weak and watery. Those who sampled the red-labeled coffee judged it just the right strength and delicious. All this even though the coffee in all the jars was exactly the same. *The people had been subconsciously influenced by the color of the label.*[2]

◇ EVEN EXPERTS CAN BE WRONG

History records numerous occasions when the expert opinion has been the wrong opinion. In ancient times the standard medical opinion was that headaches were caused by demons inside the skull. The accepted treatment ranged from opening the skull to let the demons out to giving medicines derived from cow's brain and goat dung. (Some native American tribes preferred beaver testicles.)[3]

When the idea of inoculating people against diseases such as smallpox first arrived in the colonies in the early 1700s, most authorities regarded it as nonsense. Among them were Benjamin Franklin and a number of the men who later founded Harvard Medical School. Against the authorities stood a relatively unknown man who didn't even have a medical degree, Zabdiel Boylston. Whose opinion was proved right? Not the experts' but Zabdiel Boylston's.[4]

In 1890 a Nobel Prize–winning bacteriologist, Dr. Robert Koch, reported that he had found a substance that would cure tuberculosis. When it was injected into patients, though, it was found to cause further illness and even death.

In 1904 psychologist G. Stanley Hall expressed his professional opinion that when women engage in strenuous mental activity, particularly with men, they experience a loss of mammary function and interest in motherhood, as well as decreased fertility. If they subsequently have children, the children will tend to be sickly.[5]

Between 1919 and 1922 the Metropolitan Museum of Art in New York City bought seventeen gold vessels that experts determined were authentic treasures from a 3,500-year-old Egyptian tomb. In 1982 they were discovered to be twentieth-century fakes.[6]

In 1928 a drug called thorotrast was developed and used to outline certain organs of the body so that clearer X rays could be taken. Nineteen years later, doctors learned that even small doses of the drug caused cancer.

In 1959 a sedative called thalidomide was placed on the market. Many physicians prescribed it for pregnant women. Then, when a large number of babies were born deformed, medical authorities realized that thalidomide was to blame.

In 1973, using refined radar mapping techniques, scientists decided that their earlier claims about the surface of Venus were wrong. It is not smooth, as they had thought, but pockmarked with craters.[7]

Psychiatrists often agree on the symptoms of particular mental disorders and have little difficulty reaching very similar professional opinions about particular cases. In some cases, however, those opinions may not be completely trustworthy. One man, Garrett Trapnell, has committed numerous crimes without ever spending a day in prison. His secret? He learned how to fool psychiatrists by playing the role of a paranoid schizophrenic, getting judged incompetent and assigned to a mental institution, and then escaping.

When he revealed his trickery, of course, some psychiatrists claimed he really was insane and his story merely sounded believable. But soon afterward the possibility that he was correct was underlined when three men and five women conducted an experiment to determine whether the sane could be distinguished from the insane in psychiatric hospitals. They succeeded in faking symptoms of mental disorders and were admitted to a number of mental hospitals in five eastern and western states.[8]

It is impossible to know what expert opinions of our time will be overturned by researchers in the future. But we can be sure that some will be. And they may well be views that today seem most unassailable.

◇ KINDS OF ERROR

Opinion can be corrupted by any one of four broad kinds of error.* These classifications, with examples added for clarification, are:

*The classifications noted here are adaptations of Francis Bacon's well-known "Idols," *Novum Organum*, Book I (1620).

1. Errors or tendencies to error common among all people by virtue of their being human. (For example, the tendency to perceive selectively or rush to judgment or oversimplify complex realities)

2. Errors or tendencies to error associated with one's individual habits of mind or personal attitudes, beliefs, or theories. (For example, the habit of thinking the worst of members of a race or religion against which one harbors prejudice)

3. Errors that come from human communication and the limitations of language. (For example, expressing a thought or feeling inadequately and leading others to form a mistaken impression)

4. Errors in the general fashion of an age. (For example, the tendency in our grandparents' day to accept authority unquestioningly; or the tendency in ours to recognize no authority but one's self)

Some people, of course, are more prone to errors than others. John Locke observed that these people fall into three groups. He described them as follows:

> Those who seldom reason at all, but think and act as those around them do—parents, neighbors, the clergy, or anyone else they admire and respect. Such people want to avoid the difficulty that accompanies thinking for themselves.
> Those who are determined to let passion rather than reason govern their lives. Those people are influenced only by reasoning that supports their prejudices.
> Those who sincerely follow reason, but lack sound, overall good sense, and so do not look at all sides of an issue. They tend to talk with one type of person, read one type of book, and so are exposed to only one viewpoint.[9]

To Locke's list we should add one more type—people who never bother to reexamine an opinion once it has been formed. These people are often the most error-prone of all, for they forfeit all opportunity to correct mistaken opinions when new evidence arises.

◇ INFORMED VERSUS UNINFORMED OPINION

If experts can, like the rest of us, be wrong, why are their views more highly valued than the views of nonexperts? In light of the examples we have considered, we might conclude that it is a waste of time to consult the experts. Let's look at some situations and see if this conclusion is reasonable.

What are the effects of hashish on those who smoke it? We could ask a person who never saw or smelled it, let alone smoked it. But it would make better sense to get the opinion of a smoker or to take a poll of a large number of smokers. Better still would be the opinion of one or more *trained* observers, research scientists who have conducted studies of the effects of hashish smoking. (At least one such group, a team of army doctors, has found that heavy use of hashish leads to severe lung damage. Also, if the smoker is predisposed to schizophrenia, it can cause long-lasting episodes of that disorder.[10])

A giant quasar is positioned on what may be the edge of our universe, 10 billion light-years away from us.[11] (To calculate the distance in miles, just multiply the speed of light, 186,000 miles per second, times the number of seconds in a day, 86,400; next multiply that answer times the number of days in a year, 365; finally, multiply that answer by 10,000,000,000.) The pinpoint of light viewed by the astronomers has been streaking through space for all those years and has just reached us. The quasar may very well have *ceased to exist* millions and millions of years ago. Did it? It may take millions and millions of years before we can say. If we wanted to find out more about this quasar or about quasars in general, we could stop someone on a street corner and ask about it, and that person would be free to offer an opinion. But it would be more sensible to ask an astronomer.

Can a whale communicate with another whale? If so, how far can he transmit his message? Would our auto mechanic have an opinion on this matter? Perhaps. And so might our grocer, dentist, banker. But no matter how intelligent these people are, chances are their opinions about whales are not very well informed. The people whose opinions would be valuable would be those who have done some research with whales. (They would tell us that the humpback whales can make a variety of sounds. In addition to clicking noises, they make creaking and banging and squeaking noises. They've been found to make these sounds for as long as several minutes at a time, at an intensity of 100 to 110 decibels, and for a distance of 25,000 miles.[12])

Similar examples could be cited from every field of knowledge: from antique collecting to ethics, from art to criminology. All would support the same view that by examining the opinions of informed people before making up our minds, we broaden our perspective, see details we might not see by ourselves, consider facts we would otherwise be unaware of, and lessen our chances of error. (It is foolish to look for *guarantees* of correctness—there are none.) No one can know everything about everything; there is simply not enough time to learn. Consulting those who have given their special attention to the field of knowledge in question is therefore not a mark of dependence or irresponsibility but of efficiency and good sense.

To be considered informed, an opinion must be based on something more substantial than its familiarity to us or the length of time we have held it or our presumed right to think whatever we wish. It must be based on careful consideration of relevant evidence. And when we express an opinion in formal speaking or writing, we should support it adequately. Authors Ray Marshall and Marc Tucker, for example, asserted that the reason teaching in the United States has not been a highly respected profession is the fact that most teachers have been women. To support this contention, they traced the relevant historical development, citing administrative directives and statements of philosophy, presenting hiring patterns (from 59 percent women in 1870 to 86 percent in 1920), detailing significant shifts in curriculum, contrasting male and female salary statistics, and demonstrating the relative powerlessness of women to negotiate professional salaries and working conditions.[13]

As this example illustrates, in most responsible expressions of opinion, the statement of opinion takes up only a sentence or two, whereas the supporting detail fills paragraphs, pages, even entire chapters.

◇ Forming Sound Opinions

Forming opinions is natural. We are constantly receiving sensory impressions and responding to them, first on the level of feelings, then on the level of thought. Even if we wanted to escape having opinions, we couldn't. Nor should we want to. One of the things that makes human beings vastly more complex and interesting than trees or cows is their ability to form opinions.

This ability has two sides, however. It can either lift us to wisdom or topple us to absurdity. Here are three helpful tips to ensure that your opinions will be sound:

1. Base your opinions on careful observation rather than on habit or impulse, on evidence rather than whim or personal preference. In particular, use your critical thinking skills in forming them.

2. From time to time, reexamine old opinions in the light of new knowledge. If you find that an opinion is no longer reasonable, modify it accordingly.

3. Do not mistake familiarity for soundness. Once you've formed an opinion, it's bound to seem solid to you—the very act of forming it shapes it to your outlook. The test to apply is not how comfortable you feel having the opinion but how well it fits the reality it is supposed to represent.

✥ APPLICATIONS

1. Imagine that you are the senior librarian for your college. A faculty member sends you the following list of recommended magazines, with a brief description of each quoted from a standard guide, *Magazines for Libraries* by Bill Katz and Linda Sternberg Katz:[14]

> *The Nation.* "This is the foremost liberal/left-wing journal, and the standard by which all other liberal publications should be judged . . . unabashedly partisan . . . ."
>
> *Human Events.* "The editor makes no claims about impartiality. . . . The editorial tone is decidedly conservative, particularly when discussing Congress."
>
> *Free Inquiry: A Secular Humanist Magazine.* "The articles in this journal strongly reflect the position of CODESH [the Council for Democratic and Secular Humanism] and tend to be more anti-organized religion than positively secular humanist."
>
> *Paidika: the Journal of Paedophilia.* "*Paidika* is a journal intended for academics studying human sexuality as well as for pedophiles and pederasts discovering a history and an identity."
>
> *Lesbian Connection.* "LC is sort of a national bulletin board for lesbian culture. Probably best known for its 'Contact Dykes' listing of lesbian 'welcome wagoneers' in cities around the nation and the world."

Explain which magazines you would subscribe to for the library, which you would not, and which you would need more information about before you decided. If you would need more information, explain what it would be and how you would obtain it. (*Note:* Your library may have a copy of *Magazines for Libraries.*)

2. Which of the following individuals is likely to be most successful at persuading the public to buy a certain brand of running shoes?

    a. an experienced trainer

    b. an Olympic running champion

    c. a podiatrist

    d. a physician in general practice

    e. the Surgeon General of the United States

Explain your reasoning.

3. Of the individuals listed in application 2, who is likely to be the most reliable source of information on running shoes?

4. What factors might possibly compromise the endorsements of the various people listed in application 2? Which one is likely to be the most reliable source of information? Explain the reasoning underlying each answer.

5. When the author uses the word *opinion*, his major emphasis is on

    a. a statement of preference

    b. a considered judgment

    c. a view or belief casually arrived at

    d. a bigoted position

    e. an unsupportable position

    f. none of the above

Explain your reasoning.

6. Which of the following would the author be likely to rate as most important in forming a reliable opinion? Explain your reasoning.

    a. Seek reasons to support your opinions.

    b. Distinguish between input from experts and input from others.

    c. Reject others' opinions.

    d. Subject opinions to ongoing reexamination based on new evidence.

7. Evaluate the following argument as you did the arguments in Chapter 2, application 7. First identify the argument's component parts (including hidden premises) and ask relevant questions, as shown in that chapter. Then check the accuracy of each premise, stated or hidden, and decide whether the conclusion is the most reasonable one. Note that checking the accuracy of the premises may require obtaining sufficient evidence to permit a judgment. (Remember that it is a judgment that is required and *not* an uninformed opinion.) If you find a premise to be inaccurate or a conclusion to be less than completely reasonable, revise the argument accordingly.

> *Argument:* The schoolyard practice of "choosing up sides" is embarrassing, even humiliating, to children who are unskilled in sports. Therefore, it should be discouraged on the playground and outlawed in physical education classes.

8. Read the following dialogue carefully. Then decide whether anything said violates the ideas in the chapter. Identify any erroneous notions and explain in your own words how they are in error:

Fred: There was this discussion in class today that really bugged me.

Art: Yeah? What was it about?

Fred: Teenage sex. The question was whether having sex whenever we please with whomever we please is harmful to teenagers. Some people said yes. Others said it depends on the circumstances.

Art: What did you say?

Fred: I said it doesn't do any harm to anybody, that parents use that story to scare us. Then the teacher asked me what evidence I had to back up my idea.

Art: What did you tell him?

Fred: I said I didn't need any evidence because it's my *opinion*. Sex is a personal matter, I said, and I've got a right to think anything I want about it. My opinions are as good as anybody else's.

9. Think of an instance in which you or someone you know formed an opinion that later proved incorrect. State the opinion and explain in what way it was incorrect.

10. Each of the following questions reflects a controversial issue—that is, an issue that tends to excite strong disagreement among people. State and support your opinion about each issue applying what you learned in this chapter.

    a. In divorce cases, what guidelines should the courts use in deciding which parent gets custody of the children?

    b. Until what age should children be spanked (if indeed they should be spanked at all)?

    c. Should the minimum drinking age be sixteen in all states?

    d. In what situation, if any, should the United States make the first strike with nuclear weapons?

    e. Do evil spirits exist? If so, can they influence people's actions?

    f. Does the end ever justify the means?

11. A high school junior invited his thirty-five-year-old neighbor, the mother of four children, to his prom. The woman was married and her husband approved of the date. However, the school board ruled that the boy would be denied admission to the dance if he took her.[15] What is your opinion of the board's decision?

12. *Group discussion exercise:* Read the following dialogue carefully. Then discuss it with two or three of your classmates. Determine which opinion of the issue is more reasonable. Be sure to base your decision on evidence rather than mere preference.

Background note: A Rochester, New York, lawyer has issued a court challenge to the practice of charging women half-price for drinks during "ladies' nights" at bars. He argues that the practice is a form of sex discrimination against men.[16]

Henrietta: That lawyer must be making a joke against feminism. He can't be serious.

Burt: Why not? It's clearly a case of discrimination.

Henrietta: Look, we both know why ladies' nights are scheduled in bars: as a gimmick to attract customers. The women flock to the bars to get cheap drinks, and the men flock there because the women are there. It's no different from other gimmicks, such as mud-wrestling contests and "two for the price of one" cocktail hours.

Burt: Sorry, Hank. It's very different from two-for-one cocktail hours, where a person of either sex can buy a cocktail at the same price. Ladies' nights set a double standard based on sex and that's sex discrimination, pure and simple.

Henrietta: So now you're a great foe of discrimination. How come you're not complaining that men haven't got an equal opportunity to participate half-naked in mud-wrestling contests? And why aren't you protesting the fact that women are paid less for doing the same jobs men do? You're a phony, Burt, and you make me sick.

Burt: Name calling is not a sign of a strong intellect. And why you should get so emotional over some lawyer's protest, I can't imagine. I guess it goes to show that women are more emotional than men.

II

THE PROBLEMS

CHAPTER SIX

THE BASIC PROBLEM: "MINE IS BETTER"

It's natural enough to like our own possessions better than other people's possessions.* Our possessions are extensions of ourselves. When first graders turn to their classmates and say, "My dad is bigger than yours" or "My shoes are newer" or "My crayons color better," they are not just speaking about their fathers or their shoes or crayons. They are saying something about themselves: "Hey, look at me. I'm something special."

Several years later those children will be saying, "My car is faster than yours," "My football team will go all the way this year," "My marks are higher than Olivia's." (That's one of the great blessings of students—though they may have to stoop to compare, they can always find someone with lower grades than theirs.)

Even later, when they've learned that it sounds boastful to *say* their possessions are better, they'll continue to *think* they are: "My house is more expensive, my club more exclusive, my spouse more attractive, my children better behaved, my accomplishments more numerous."

All of this, as we have noted, is natural, although not especially noble or virtuous or, in many cases, even factual. Just natural. The tendency is

---

*One exception to the rule occurs when we are *envying* others. But that is a special situation that doesn't contradict the point here.

probably as old as humanity. History records countless examples of it. Most wars, for example, can be traced to some form of "mine is better" thinking. Satirists have pointed their pens at it. Ambrose Bierce, for instance, in his *Devil's Dictionary*, includes the word *infidel*. Technically, the word means "one who is an unbeliever in some religion." But Bierce's definition points up the underlying attitude in those who use the word. He defines *infidel* this way: "In New York, one who does not believe in the Christian religion; in Constantinople, one who does."[1]

For many people, most of the time, the "mine is better" tendency is balanced by the awareness that other people feel the same way about their things, that it's an unavoidable part of being a person to do so. In other words, many people realize that we all see ourselves in a special way, different from everything that is not ourselves, and that whatever we associate with ourselves becomes part of us in our minds. People who have this understanding and are reasonably secure and self-confident can control the tendency. The problem is that some people do not understand that each person has a special viewpoint. For them, "mine is better" is not an attitude that everyone has about his or her things. Rather, it is a special, higher truth about their particular situation. Psychologists classify such people as either egocentric or ethnocentric.

◇ EGOCENTRIC PEOPLE

Egocentric means centered or focused on one's own self and interested only in one's own interests, needs, and views. Egocentric people tend to practice "egospeak." The term was coined by Edmond Addeo and Robert Burger in their book of the same name. Egospeak, they explain, is "the art of boosting our own egos by speaking only about what we want to talk about, and not giving a hoot in hell about what the other person wants to talk about."[2] More important for our discussion is what precedes the outward expression of self-centeredness and energizes it: egocentric people's habit of mind. Following Addeo and Burger, we might characterize that habit as egoTHINK.

Because the perspective of egothink is very limited, egocentric people have difficulty seeing issues from a variety of viewpoints. The world exists for them and is defined by their beliefs and values: What disturbs them should disturb everyone; what is of no consequence to them is unimportant. This attitude makes it difficult for egocentric people to observe, listen, and understand. Why should a person bother paying attention to others, including teachers and textbook authors, if they have nothing valuable to offer? What incentive is there to learn when one already knows everything worth knowing? For that matter, why bother with the laborious task of investigating controversial issues, poring over expert testimony, and evaluating evidence when one's own opinion is the final, infallible arbiter? It is difficult, indeed, for an egocentric to become proficient in critical thinking.

◇ ETHNOCENTRIC PEOPLE

Ethnocentric means centered or focused on one's group. Unlike egocentric people, ethnocentrics are not absorbed in themselves but rather in their race, religion, ethnic group, or culture, which they believe is superior to all others. This belief they consider above the normal processes of examination and questioning. Faced with a challenge to it or even a situation in which they are called on to explain it, they will resist. In their minds there is no point in examining or questioning it. The matter is settled.

Ethnocentric people, of course, are not born but made. Their early training in the home creates the habits of mind that characterize them. As children, they tend to expect and need strong leadership and strict discipline from their parents and teachers. Also, they are rigid and inflexible in their views, unable to face problems for which the outcomes or answers are not clear. They have no patience with complex situations and meet their daily affairs with oversimplifications.

As adults, ethnocentric individuals tend toward inflexible categorizing. They recognize no middle ground to issues. Things are either all one way or all the other. If such people are not completely *for* something, they are completely *against* it. The political party or candidate of their choice, for example, is the savior of the country; the opposition can only lead the country to destruction.[3]

For ethnocentrics, the measure of any person or idea, of course, is the person's or idea's similarity to their race, their religion, their culture, their value system. Whatever blends with their outlook is worthy. Whatever differs from it is suspect, threatening, dangerous. This is a sad and undesirable attitude to take. But ethnocentric people find it quite satisfying. Psychologist Gordon Allport offers this explanation:

> By taking a negative view of great groups of mankind, we somehow make life simpler. For example, if I reject all foreigners as a category, I don't have to bother with them—except to keep them out of my country. If I can ticket, then, all Negroes as comprising an inferior and objectionable race, I conveniently dispose of a tenth of my fellow citizens. If I can put the Catholics into another category and reject them, my life is still further simplified. I then pare again and slice off the Jews . . . and so it goes.[4]

Ethnocentric people's prejudice has an additional function. It fills their need for an out-group to blame for real and imagined problems in society. Take any problem—crime in the streets, the drug trade, corruption in government, the assassination of a leader, a strike in a major industry, pornography, a rise in food prices—and there is a ready-made villain to blame it on: The "kikes" are responsible—or the "wops," "niggers," "spics," or "polacks." Ethnocentrics achieve instant diagnosis—it's as easy as matching column A to column B. And they get a large target at which they can point their anger and fear and inadequacy and frustration.

◇ CONTROLLING "MINE IS BETTER" THINKING

It's clear what the extreme "mine is better" attitude of egocentric and ethnocentric people does to their judgment. It twists and warps it, often beyond correction. The effect of the "mine is better" tendencies of the rest of us is less dramatic, but no less real.

Our preference for our own thinking can prevent us from identifying flaws in our own ideas, as well as from seeing and building upon other people's insights. Similarly, our pride in our own religion can lead us to dismiss too quickly the beliefs and practices of other religions and ignore mistakes in our religious history. Our preference for our own political party can make us support inferior candidates and programs. Our allegiance to our own opinions can shut us off from other perspectives, blind us to unfamiliar truths, and enslave us to yesterday's conclusions.

Furthermore, our readiness to accept uncritically those who appeal to our preconceived notions leaves us vulnerable to those who would manipulate us for their own purposes. Historians tell us that is precisely why Hitler succeeded in winning control of Germany and very nearly conquering the world.

"Mine is better" thinking is the most basic problem for critical thinkers because, left unchecked, it can distort perception and corrupt judgment. The more mired we are in subjectivity, the less effective will be our critical thinking. Though perfect objectivity may be unattainable, by controlling our "mine is better" tendencies, we can achieve a significant degree of objectivity. One way to gain that control is to keep in mind that, like other people, we too are prone to "mine is better" thinking and that its influence will be strongest when the subject is one we really care about. As G. K. Chesterton observed,

We are all exact and scientific on the subjects we do not care about. We all immediately detect exaggeration in an exposition of Mormonism or a patriotic speech from Paraguay. We all require sobriety on the subject of the sea serpent. But the moment we begin to believe in a thing ourselves, that moment we begin easily to overstate it; and the moment our souls become serious, our words become a little wild.[5]

The second way to control "mine is better" thinking is to be alert for signals of its presence. Those signals can be found both in our feelings and in our thoughts:

In feelings: Very pleasant, favorable sensations, the desire to embrace a statement or argument immediately, without appraising it further. Or very unpleasant, negative sensations, the desire to attack and denounce a statement or argument without delay.

In thoughts: Ideas such as "I'm glad that experts are taking such a position—I've thought it all along" and "No use wasting time analyzing this evidence—it must be conclusive." Or ideas such as "This view is outrageous because it challenges what I have always thought—I refuse to consider it."

Whenever you find yourself reacting this way, you can be reasonably sure you are being victimized by "mine is better" thinking. The appropriate response is to resist the reaction and force yourself to consider the matter fair-mindedly.

▧ APPLICATIONS

1. Some people claim that contemporary American culture tends to *increase* rather than diminish egocentrism and ethnocentrism. If this is true, then the ability to think critically is being undermined. Study the media for evidence that supports or refutes this charge and write a report on your findings. (Be sure to look for subtle, as well as obvious, clues—for example, the advice offered on talk shows and the appeals used in advertisements, as well as the formal statements of agencies promoting policy changes in government and elsewhere.)

2. Recall an occasion when you observed someone demonstrating one or more of the characteristics of ethnocentrism in his or her behavior. Describe the occasion, the way in which the characteristics were revealed, and the effect they had on the person's judgment.

3. Compose a summary of this chapter for the person whose ethno-centrism you described in application 2. Make it as persuasive as you can for that person. That is, focus on the particular occasion of his or her "mine is better" thinking and the effects of that thinking on his or her judgment.

4. Think of two illustrations of your own "mine is better" thinking. Describe that thinking and the way in which you first became aware of it. If you can, determine what caused you to develop that way of thinking.

5. Evaluate the following arguments as you did the arguments in Chapter 2, application 7. First identify the argument's component parts (including hidden premises) and ask relevant questions, as shown in that chapter. Then check the accuracy of each premise, stated or hidden, and decide whether the conclusion is the most reasonable one. Note that checking the accuracy of the premises may require obtaining sufficient evidence to permit a judgment. (Be alert to your own "mine is better" thinking. Don't allow it to influence your analysis.) If you find a premise to be inaccurate or a conclusion to be less than completely reasonable, revise the argument accordingly.

    a. *Background note: Many schools around the country are experiencing significant budget reductions. Forced to cut activities from their programs, they must decide where their priorities lie. Some follow the reasoning expressed in this argument.*

Argument: Interscholastic sports programs build character and pre-pare young athletes to meet the challenges of life. In addition, com-petition with other schools provides the student body with entertainment and an opportunity to practice school spirit and loy-alty. Therefore, in all budget considerations, interscholastic sports programs should be given as high a priority as academic programs.

    b. *Background note: Concerned with the rise in teenage pregnancy, the Baltimore, Maryland, school system became the first in the nation to offer Norplant, a surgically implanted contraceptive, to teenagers. School offi-cials' reasoning was probably, at least in part, as follows:*

Argument: Teenage pregnancy continues to rise despite efforts to educate students about the use of condoms. Norplant will effective-ly prevent pregnancy. Therefore, the school system should make Norplant available.

6. State and support your position on each of the following issues. Be sure to recognize and overcome your "mine is better" tendencies and base your response on critical thinking.

a. Carl F. Henry, a leading evangelical theologian, warns that the widespread attitude that there are no moral standards other than what the majority approves is a threat to our country. The survival of democratic society, he suggests, depends on recognizing definite moral standards, such as the biblical criteria of morality and justice.[6]

b. Allen B. Ballard, Professor of Political Science at City College of New York, argues that Mark Twain's *Huckleberry Finn* should not be taught in high school classes because hearing "nigger" read aloud often causes acute embarrassment to black students. He reasons, "Why should a learning experience intended to make children love literature instead end up inflicting pain upon black children?" He suggests the book be used as an optional choice for additional reading in high school or deferred until college.[7]

c. A Hasidic rabbi serving a three-year term (for bank fraud) in a federal prison petitioned a U.S. district court to order the prison to provide a kosher kitchen, utensils, and diet for him. He argued that his health was failing because the food served at the prison did not meet his kosher requirements. He could eat only lettuce, oranges, apples, carrots, and dry rice cereal.[8]

d. "Heavy metal" music has drawn pointed criticism from a number of social critics. They argue that it at least aggravates (and perhaps causes) antisocial attitudes and thus can be blamed for the increase in violent crime.

e. Some people believe the penalty for driving while intoxicated should be stiffened. One provision they are urging be added to the law is mandatory jail sentences for repeat offenders.

7. Read the following dialogues carefully. Note any evidence of "mine is better" thinking. Then decide which view in each dialogue is more reasonable and why. (Be sure to guard against our own "mine is better" thinking.)

a. *Background note: On a trip to Spain in November 1982, Pope John Paul acknowledged that the Spanish Inquisition, which began in 1480 and lasted for more than 300 years and resulted in many people's being imprisoned, tortured, and burned at the stake, was a mistake.*[9]

Ralph: It's about time the Catholic church officially condemned the Inquisition.

Chester: The pope shouldn't have admitted that publicly.

Ralph: Why? Do you think five hundred years after the fact is too soon? Should he have waited for one thousand years to pass?

Chester: Don't be sarcastic. I mean that his statement will

undoubtedly weaken the faith of many Catholics. If you love someone or something—in this case, the Church—you should do nothing
to cause it shame or embarrassment. Of course the Inquisition was
wrong, but it serves no good purpose to say so now and remind people of the Church's error.

b. *Background note: When an unmarried high school biology teacher in
a Long Island, New York, school became pregnant, a group of parents petitioned the school board to fire her. They reasoned that her pregnancy was
proof of immorality and that allowing her to remain a teacher would set a
poor example for students. The school board refused to fire her.*[10]

Arthur: Good for the school board. Their action must have taken
courage. Pious hypocrites can generate a lot of pressure.

Guinevere: Why do you call them hypocrites? They had a right
to express their view.

Arthur: Do you mean you agree with that nonsense about the
pregnant teacher's being immoral and a poor example to students?

Guinevere: Yes, I suppose I do. Not that I think everybody
deserves firing from her job in such circumstances. I think teachers
are in a special category. More should be expected of them. They
should have to measure up to a higher standard of conduct than
people in other occupations because they are in charge of young people's education, and young people are impressionable.

8. *Group discussion exercise:* Reflect on the following quotation. Does it
make sense? Does anything you read in this chapter help to explain it?
If so, what? Discuss your ideas with two or three classmates.

It doesn't matter if everyone in the world thinks you're wrong. If you
think you're right, that's all that counts.

CHAPTER SEVEN

RESISTANCE TO CHANGE

One day a woman was about to cook a roast. Before putting it in the pot she cut off a small slice. When asked why she did this, she paused, became a little embarrassed, and said she did it because her mother had always done the same thing when she cooked a roast. Her own curiosity aroused, she telephoned her mother to ask why she always cut off a little slice before cooking her roast. The mother's answer was the same: "Because that's the way my mother did it." Finally, in need of a more helpful answer, she asked her grandmother why she always cut off a little slice before cooking a roast. Without hesitating, her grandmother replied, "Because that's the only way it would fit in my pot."[1]

This story is told by Harvard Professor Ellen J. Langer. She classifies it as three generations of "mindlessness." That designation is not inappropriate, though a kindlier classification would be the tendency to continue doing things as we have always done them, or resistance to change. This tendency is probably as old as humankind, so examples abound: earlier in this century, "If people were meant to fly, they'd have wings" and "Women voting? Nonsense—voting is men's business"; and in our time, "I've never worn a seatbelt in my life so I'm not going to start now." Even slight changes upset our routine, threaten our established habits, challenge the familiar. They demand that we reconsider old responses and that's unpleasant. After all, we may find that they were ill-conceived. (Or even mindless.)

Just as we prefer patterns of acting that we know, so we prefer ideas that are not strange or foreign sounding, ideas we're comfortable with. When Galileo said, "The earth moves around the sun," people were upset, partly because thousands of sunrises and sunsets had told them the *sun* did the moving, but also partly because they simply had never before heard of the earth's moving. The new idea threatened their fixed belief that the earth was the center of the solar system. They had that idea neatly packaged in their minds. It was a basic part of their understanding of the universe; it was intertwined with their religion. And now this upstart Galileo was demanding no less than that they untie the package, reopen the issue.

When the astronauts first landed on the moon, at least one elderly man expressed total disbelief. "It's a trick thought up by the TV people," he said. "It's impossible for man to reach the moon."

◇ INSECURITY AND FEAR

Why do we resist change? Mainly because the new and unfamiliar challenge our "mine is better" thinking and threaten our sense of security. In many of us that sense is very fragile. Insecurity is the reason some people will go to elaborate lengths to explain away new ideas they cannot cope with. For example, the child whose father is in jail and whose mother steals to support him may believe "all cops are bad." Once that idea becomes fixed, he may cling to it. As a result, even years later he may reject the police officer who offers him genuine concern and friendship.

Another reason people resist change is that they're afraid of the unknown. In some ways this fear may be caused by insecurity; in others it may itself cause insecurity. "Who knows what will happen if . . . ?" they wonder, and they are inclined to suspect the worst. Fired by that suspicion, they fight the new idea. This kind of fearful reaction is everywhere in evidence—in education and government, in religion, in law, science, and medicine.

As late as 1948, California law prohibited the marriage of an Oriental man and a Caucasian woman. Many people are still mumbling vague warnings about the unspeakable dangers that the racial integration of schools will bring. And a sizable number of Americans react to the gay liberation movement somewhat like this: "If we allow them to parade their perversion in public, our young people will be corrupted and our value system destroyed."

We might be inclined to think that the problem is peculiar to the United States, but examples of fear-inspired behavior fill the history books. After all, what drove the early settlers of North America from their European homelands was one form or another of intolerance for different ideas and beliefs. Torturing and killing heretics and witches was an established practice at innumerable times and places.

◇ FEAR AND TRADITION

It is probably because of the interaction between insecurity and fear that people hold tradition in such high regard. Many traditions, of course, are worthwhile. They help keep intact the valuable lessons of the past. In many cases, they assist us in defining our loyalties and, indeed, our own identities. However, like most good things, respect for tradition can be shortsighted and unwise. This is the case whenever clinging to tradition represents not careful judgment that something deserves preservation but rather some internal panic. "Anything is worth clinging to, so long as we cling" is not a reasonable attitude.

Surely some such panic was partly responsible for the centuries-long prohibition of dissection of the dead. Despite the entreaties of medical people, who wished only to learn the secrets of the human body for the fight against disease, religious and secular authorities refused to allow autopsies. Why? Because being unheard of, the practice was considered outrageous, sacrilegious.

Similarly, the furor that arose over Darwin's theory of evolution in the nineteenth century was fired by the fear that the theory would undermine belief in God and the Christian religion. The beliefs that Adam and Eve were actual people and that the earth was only five thousand years old were time honored. Any suggestion that the book of Genesis might be interpreted symbolically rather than literally seemed to challenge nothing less than the entire Christian perspective on life.

So great were the shock and fear that greeted Darwin's theory, in fact, that almost three quarters of a century after it was first advanced, a teacher named Scopes in a small Tennessee town could be brought to trial for teaching evolution in his biology class. His trial pitted two famous Americans against each other—the prosecutor, a gifted orator, William Jennings Bryan; the defender, a brilliant lawyer, Clarence Darrow. When their historic confrontation was over, Scopes paid merely a token fine, and the teaching of the theory of evolution was vindicated. Soon after that, the law he had been tried under was repealed.

Yet the resistance to this change has not passed so easily. Half a century later, a poll of high school students in the same Tennessee town revealed that 75 percent of them still interpreted the biblical story of creation literally, and many townspeople believed Darwin's theory causes "corruption, lust, immorality, greed . . . , drug addiction, war, and atrocious acts of genocide."[2] To this day, despite their previous failure, supporters of "creation science" around the country are working to get equal time for their view in the nation's classrooms.

The task of guarding the established ways of viewing things has always been regarded by many as a sacred task. This is true even in primitive cultures. For example, the Trobriand Islanders considered sexual success a praiseworthy accomplishment. The man who was unusually successful with women was much admired and honored. Yet it was assumed that such success would be achieved only by the favored social class. If a common islander became too successful, he was resented. As one observer, Robert K. Merton, suggested, this reaction was not due to any conspiracy on the part of the Trobriand chiefs: "It is merely that the chiefs had been indoctrinated with an appreciation of the proper order of things, and saw it as their heavy burden to enforce the mediocrity of others."[3]

Of course, it isn't always panic that makes us cling to established patterns. The man in Robert Frost's poem "Mending Wall" kept repairing the wall between his land and his neighbor's not because there was still any good purpose in doing so but only because his father had done so before him. Consider this case of uncritical dependence on past ways. A girl was told by her mother, "Never put a hat on a table or a coat on a bed." She accepted the direction and followed it faithfully for years. One day, many years later, she repeated the direction to her own teenage daughter, and the daughter asked, "Why?" The woman realized that she had never been curious enough to ask her own mother. Her curiosity at long last aroused, she asked her mother (by then in her eighties). The mother replied, "Because when I was a little girl some neighbor children were infested with lice and my mother explained I should never put a hat on a table or a coat on a bed." The woman had spent her entire adult life following a rule she had been taught without once wondering about its purpose or validity.[4]

At times a tradition may seem relatively unimportant and yet in a subtle way hold tremendous significance for people. In the late 1960s, for instance, the tendency of many young people to think and act and dress differently from their parents drew surprisingly angry responses from many adults. To them it represented much more than an assertion of young people's independence. In some vague way it threatened the idea of order itself, for the parent–child relationship represented only one aspect of a whole network of higher–lower relationships: God–

human, leader–follower, master–servant, employer–employee, rich–poor, teacher–student. To challenge one was to challenge all. And to challenge all was to attack the very fabric of civilized society. Given this perspective, the rabid rejection of hippies and communes and peace signs was understandable. To the traditionalist, long hair and bare feet were not just matters of appearance; they were symbols of anarchy.

Despite such resistance to change, however, many new ideas do manage to take hold. We might think that when they do, those who fought so hard for them would remember the resistance they had to overcome in others. Ironically, they often forget very quickly. In fact, they sometimes display the same fear and insecurity they so deplored in others. An example occurred in psychiatry. Sigmund Freud and his followers were ostracized and bitterly attacked for suggesting that sexuality was an important factor in the development of personality. The hostility toward Freud was so strong, in fact, that his masterwork, *The Interpretation of Dreams*, was ignored when it was first published in 1900. It took eight years to sell 600 copies of the book.[5]

Yet when Freud's ideas became accepted, he and his followers showed no greater tolerance—they ostracized and attacked those who challenged any part of his theory. Karen Horney, for example, challenged Freud's view of woman as being driven by "penis envy." She believed, too, that neurosis is caused not only by frustrated sexual drives but also by various cultural conflicts and that people's behavior is not determined by instinctual drives but can in many instances be self-directed and modified. For these theories (today widely accepted), she was rewarded with rebuke and ostracism by the Freudian dogmatists.[6]

◇ OVERCOMING RESISTANCE TO CHANGE

Change does not come with a guarantee of progress. Not infrequently, the one large step forward promised by proponents of change actually represents several giant steps backward. Living in an era of unprecedented technological change, we are sometimes too quick to embrace new ideas merely because they are new and different or because we are bored with the old ones. We then suffer, at best, inconvenience and, at worst, harm to people and institutions. A case could be made that this tendency to embrace change uncritically will eventually displace the tendency to resist change uncritically. Nevertheless, the latter is deeply enough rooted in human behavior that it remains the dominant tendency.

It is important to overcome resistance to change for two reasons. The first is that all creative ideas are by definition new and unexpected departures from the usual and the accepted. Resisting change therefore means opposing creativity and the progress it brings about. The second reason is that resistance to change blocks the impartial judgment essential for critical thinking. Here are three tips for overcoming your resistance to change:

1. Expect yourself to react negatively to new ideas. In addition, expect your reaction to be especially strong when the new idea challenges a belief or approach you have become attached to.

2. Refuse to let your initial negative (or, for that matter, positive) reaction be the measure of the new idea. Force yourself to set aside that reaction long enough to appraise the idea fairly.

3. Judge the idea on the basis of your critical appraisal and not your initial reaction. If there are good and sufficient reasons for rejecting part or all of the idea, by all means do so. However, be honest with yourself. If your "reasons" are only excuses in disguise, acknowledge (at least to yourself) that you are too prejudiced to judge the idea fairly.

▦ APPLICATIONS

1. Evaluate the following arguments as you did the arguments in Chapter 2, application 7. First identify the argument's component parts (including hidden premises) and ask relevant questions, as shown in that chapter. Then check the accuracy of each premise, stated or hidden, and decide whether the conclusion is the most reasonable one. Note that checking the accuracy of the premises may require obtaining sufficient evidence to permit a judgment. (Be sure that you make your judgment on the evidence and not on the basis of the argument's familiarity or unfamiliarity.) If you find a premise to be inaccurate or a conclusion to be less than completely reasonable, revise the argument accordingly.

a. *Background note: One reason the court system is clogged with cases is that prisoners are filing what some regard as frivolous lawsuits against the state or federal government—for example, suits claiming their rights are being violated because the prison food doesn't meet their dietary preferences. Lawbooks are available in the prison library for prisoners to use in preparing their lawsuits.*

Argument: Frivolous lawsuits clog the court system. The availability of law books in prison libraries encourages prisoners to file such suits. Therefore, law books should be removed from prison libraries.

b. *Argument:* The duties of the president of the United States are too numerous and complex for one individual to fulfill, so the office of the presidency should be changed from a one-person office to a three-member board.

2. Describe a tradition in your family, religion, or ethnic group that continues to be significant for you. Then describe a tradition that has lost its meaning for you. What could have contributed to that loss other than conscious evaluation and choice?

3. To what extent do you tend to resist change? The following ideas will give you an opportunity to reach a tentative conclusion. Read each one, react to it, and observe your reaction. If you notice yourself resisting it at all, examine the reaction more closely and determine what parts of the chapter shed light on your resistance:

a. A federal law should be passed requiring women to retain their maiden names when they marry (that is, forbidding them from adopting their husbands' names).

b. Cemeteries should open their gates to leisure-time activities for the living. Appropriate activities would include cycling, jogging, fishing, nature hiking, and (space permitting) team sports.

c. The United States should never send troops to a foreign country without a formal declaration of war.

d. Federal and state penitentiaries should allow inmates to leave prison during daytime hours to hold jobs or attend college classes. (The only ones denied this privilege should be psychopaths.)

e. Colleges should not admit any student who has been out of high school for less than three years.

f. To encourage a better turnout at the polls for elections, lotteries should be held. (Voters would send in a ballot stub as proof that they voted. Prizes would be donated by companies.)[7]

g. Retired people should be used as teachers' aides even if they lack college degrees.[8]

h. Everyone should be issued and required to carry a national identity card, identifying him or her as a U.S. citizen.[9]

i. Churches and synagogues should remove all restrictions on women's participation in liturgical and counseling services, thus permitting women to serve as priests, ministers, and rabbis.

j. Colleges should charge juniors and seniors higher tuition than that charged to freshmen and sophomores.

4.   Test the reactions of three other people to one or more of the ideas in the previous application. Be selective, choosing people you believe may be shocked by the ideas. Observe their reactions. Have them explain their positions. Decide to what extent, if any, they seem to be resistant to change. (Keep in mind that it is possible for people to disagree with the idea not because they resist a change but because they see real weaknesses in it.)

5.   Read the following dialogue carefully. Note any instances of resistance to change. Decide which view is more reasonable. (Be sure you avoid resisting change yourself and judge the issue fair-mindedly.)

Background note: In past decades college officials debated whether to censor student newspapers that published stories containing four-letter words and explicit sexual references. The debate continues, but the issue has changed. Some student papers are publishing articles that make fun of blacks, women, and homosexuals. And others are urging students to paint graffiti on campus buildings and take up shoplifting to combat conformity.[10]

    Ernest: Such articles may be childish and tasteless, but that's no reason to censor them.

    Georgina: Are you kidding? Minorities pay good money to go to college. And on most campuses, I'm sure, their student activity fee pays for the student newspaper. Where's the fairness in charging them for articles that insult them or that encourage lawbreaking, which ultimately costs them as taxpayers?

    Ernest: Why is everything a money issue with you? So a buck or so from every student's activity fee goes to the newspaper. Big deal. That doesn't give every student the right to play fascist and set editorial policy. The articles are written in a spirit of fun or for shock value. Censorship is not the answer. If a pesky fly buzzes around your head, you don't fire an elephant gun at it. Well, maybe *you* do, but no sensible person does.

6.   Bill Beausay, a sports psychologist, suggests that sports be rated much as films are: X, R, or G, depending on the amount of danger and/or violence in them. He urges that children not be allowed to take part in any X-rated sport at an early age. Such sports include motorcycle and auto racing, hockey, football, boxing, and horse racing.[11] Decide whether his suggestion has merit. Be sure to avoid resistance to change.

7.   Decide whether you accept or reject the following arguments. Be careful to avoid both "mine is better" thinking and resistance to change, and judge the issues impartially. You may wish to research the issues further before judging.

a. Beer and wine commercials should be banned from television because they glamorize drinking, leading people to associate it with love and friendship and happiness. Such associations are every bit as misleading as those used to sell cigarettes. Alcohol commercials surely are a contributing factor in the current increase in alcohol abuse by adults and children.

b. Beauty pageants today give somewhat more attention to talent than pageants did in the past. But the underlying message is the same—"Beauty in a woman is strictly a surface matter. Only those with ample bosoms, pretty faces, and trim figures need apply." These pageants make a mockery of the truth that inner beauty, character, is the real measure of a woman (or of a man).

8. *Group discussion exercise:* Discuss with two or three classmates one of the issues you examined in application 7. Be careful that your views are not affected by resistance to change. Be prepared to present your group's view to the class.

CHAPTER EIGHT

CONFORMITY

Conformity is behaving the way others around us do. In many ways conformity is desirable. Children are conforming when they stay away from the hot stove and look both ways before crossing the street. Automobile drivers are conforming when they obey traffic signs and signals. Hospital workers are conforming when they sterilize the operating room. These cases of conformity make living safer. Conformity can also make daily activities more productive. When the employees of a department store arrive at their workplaces at the specified time each day, the store can open promptly without inconveniencing its customers. When supermarket stock clerks stock the various items in their designated places, customers can shop more efficiently.

Similarly, in a hundred different ways, from using the "up" escalator to go up, to not parking by a fire hydrant, to using the door on the right to enter a building and the door on the left to exit, conformity makes life less confusing for ourselves and others. And by conforming to the rules of etiquette, we make it more pleasant.

Without a measure of conformity people would never learn to hold a pencil, let alone write. More complex skills, like flying a plane or operating a computer, would be impossible to acquire. How much nonconformity, after all, does the job of driving a car permit? Can we drive facing sideways or to the rear? Can we accelerate with our left hand and blow the horn with our right foot? Certainly not without some frustration. Yet these limitations are hardly cause for complaint. The safety and comfort such conformity brings us far outweigh the crimp in our creativity.

Unfortunately, conformity does not always work to our advantage. Sometimes going along with others does not so much increase our safety or serve our convenience as it reinforces our dependency on others. Some situations require careful evaluation and judgment. In such situations, to conform with the views or actions of others out of conviction, after we have thought and decided, is reasonable. However, to conform *instead* of thinking and deciding is irresponsible.

◇ INTERNAL AND EXTERNAL PRESSURES TO CONFORM

As human beings, we are social creatures. We must live with others and relate to them. From our earliest moments of consciousness, we learn the importance of getting along with others. Few things are more painful to most children than separation from the group. Parents sending us to our room, teachers keeping us in while friends went out to play—these were hard punishments to bear. Even more difficult was rejection by the group itself.

As we grow older the desire to be included does not go away. It merely takes different forms. We still yearn for the recognition, acceptance, and approval of others. That yearning is intensified by the bombardment of thousands of advertisements and TV commercials. "Join the crowd—buy this." "Don't be left out—everyone who is someone has one." Young teenagers trying to be sophisticated, and middle-aged people trying to be "relevant," have in common the urge to fit some prefabricated image. Conformity promises them *belonging*.

In addition to the urge to conform that we generate ourselves, there is the external pressure of the various formal and informal groups we belong to, the pressure to endorse their ideas and attitudes and to imitate their actions. Thus our urge to conform receives continuing, even daily, reinforcement. To be sure, the intensity of the reinforcement, like the strength of the urge and the ability and inclination to withstand it, differs widely among individuals. Yet some pressure is present for everyone. And in one way or another, to some extent, everyone yields to it.

It is possible that a new member of a temperance group might object to the group's rigid insistence that all drinking of alcoholic beverages is wrong. He might even speak out, reminding them that occasional, moderate drinking is not harmful, that even the Bible speaks approvingly of it. But the group may quickly let him know that such ideas are unwelcome in their presence. Every time he forgets this, he will be made to feel uncomfortable. In time, if he values their fellowship, he will refrain from expressing that point of view. He may even refrain from *thinking* it.

This kind of pressure, whether spoken or unspoken, can be generated by any group—Friday night poker clubs, churches, political parties, committees, fraternities, unions—regardless of how liberal or conservative, formal or casual it may be. The teenage gang that steals automobile accessories may seem to have no taboos. But let one uneasy member remark that he is beginning to feel guilty about his crimes and the wrath of the rest of the gang will descend on him.

Similarly, in high school and college, the crowd a student travels with has certain (usually unstated) expectations for its members. If members drink or smoke, they will often make the member who does not do so feel that she doesn't fully belong. If a member does not share their views on sex, drugs, studying, cheating, or any other subject of importance to the group, the other members will communicate their displeasure. The *way* they communicate, of course, may be more or less direct. They may tell her she'd better conform "or else." They may launch a teasing campaign against her. Or they may be even more subtle and leave her out of their activities for a few days until she asks what is wrong or decides for herself and resolves to behave more like them.

Ironically, even groups pledged to fight conformity can generate strong pressure to conform. As many young people in the 1960s learned to their dismay, many "hippie" communes were as intolerant of dissenting ideas, values, and styles of dress and living as the "straight" society they rebelled against.

The urge to conform on occasion clashes with the tendency to resist change. If the group we are in advocates an idea or action that is new and strange to us, we can be torn between seeking the group's acceptance and maintaining the security of familiar ideas and behavior. In such cases, the way we turn will depend on which tendency is stronger in us or which value we are more committed to. More often, however, the two tendencies do not conflict but reinforce each other, for we tend to associate with those whose attitudes and actions are similar to our own.

◇ "GROUPTHINK"

The urge to conform can cripple thought. Yale psychologist Irving L. Janis intensively analyzed several important actions by U.S. government leaders, actions that later were shown to be unwise. The actions were Franklin D. Roosevelt's failure to be ready for the Japanese attack on Pearl Harbor, Harry S Truman's decision to invade North Korea, John F. Kennedy's plan to invade Cuba, and Lyndon B. Johnson's decision to escalate the Vietnam War. In each case Janis found that the people who made the decision exhibited a strong desire to concur in the group decision. Janis named this conformist tendency "groupthink."[1]

More specifically, Janis identified a number of major defects in decision making that could be attributed to this conformity. The groups he analyzed did not survey the range of choices but focused on a few. When they discovered that their initial decision had certain drawbacks, they failed to reconsider those decisions. They almost never tested their own thinking for weaknesses. They never tried to obtain the judgments of experts. They expressed interest only in those views that reinforced the positions they preferred, and they spent little time considering the obstacles that would hinder the success of their plans. In each of the cases Janis studied, these defects in thinking cost untold human suffering.

In other areas, the harm caused by the urge to conform is perhaps less dramatic but no less real. A single example will suggest the extent of that harm. For two or three decades many educational psychologists argued that failure in school is traumatic and students should be passed from grade to grade even if they have not mastered the required knowledge and skills. Many grade and high schools operated on this principle. The few psychologists and teachers who disputed it were classified as unprogressive. Yet now it is being recognized that the struggle to acquire basic reading, writing, and arithmetic skills is much more traumatic at age eighteen than at age eight.

◇ Avoiding Mindless Conformity

Some people believe the way to avoid conformity is simply to oppose the majority view. It is not. *Opposing* a particular view because the majority endorses it is no different from *endorsing* the view because the majority endorses it. In both cases our judgment is determined by what others think. And that makes us conformists.

Other people believe the way to avoid conformity is to ignore what everyone else thinks and decide on the basis of our own ideas alone. This, too, is a mistake. It protects us from other people's foolishness, but it leaves us prey to our own. Consulting informed people, either in person or through their public statements in interviews, articles, and books, is an important part of the process of examining an issue. Other people's views are thus part of the *evidence* we must consider in forming a judgment.

The secret of avoiding mindless conformity is neither to prefer the majority or the minority view nor to be selective in the evidence we consider. It is to apply our critical thinking to all the evidence and endorse the most reasonable view regardless of who or how many endorse that view.

⊞ Applications

1.   List some desirable conforming behaviors. List some undesirable ones. In each case, explain your classification of the behavior.

2.   Describe one or more examples of groupthink that you have observed. Explain what factors were responsible for the people abandoning their individuality.

3.   Think of *two* significant ways in which you have conformed with the ways of others. Examine each separately and determine what motivated you to conform. Evaluate the effects of your conformity on you and others.

4.   Advertising frequently plays on our urge to conform. Describe at least three advertisements or commercials that do so, and explain how they do it.

5.   Evaluate the following argument as you did the arguments in Chapter 2, application 7. First identify the argument's component parts (including hidden premises) and ask relevant questions, as shown in that chapter. Then check the accuracy of each premise, stated or hidden, and decide whether the conclusion is the most reasonable one. Note that checking the accuracy of the premises may require obtaining sufficient evidence to permit a judgment. (Be sure that you make your judgment on the evidence and not on the basis of what you feel comfortable saying to your professor or classmates.) If you find a premise to be inaccurate or a conclusion to be less than completely reasonable, revise the argument accordingly.

Background note: Though once allowed everywhere, smoking is now being banned in a growing number of places—on airlines and buses, in public buildings, in many restaurants. Many smokers feel they are the victims of discrimination.

Argument: Unnecessarily restricting people's right to choose is a violation of their constitutional rights. Restrictions on smoking unnecessarily restrict people's rights. Therefore, restrictions on smoking are a violation of smokers' constitutional rights.

6.   In each of the following situations the person is conforming. Study each situation and determine what effects the conformity will have on that person and on other people. On the basis of those effects, decide whether the conformity is desirable. If your decision depends on the degree of the conformity or the circumstances in which it occurred, explain in what situations you would approve and why.

a.   Bert is thirteen. His friends are insensitive to other people. They even look for opportunities to ridicule other people. If a classmate is overweight or homely or unusually shy or not too intelligent, they will taunt the person about it. If the person shows signs of being bothered by the cruelty, they will consider this a sign of weakness and increase the abuse. Bert knows this behavior is wrong and he derives no pleasure from it, but he goes along with it and even indulges in it from time to time so as not to appear weak to his friends. He realizes that in their eyes if he is not with them completely, he is against them.

b.   Rose works in a dress factory. Shortly after she began work, she realized that the other workers' output was unrealistically low, that it was possible for her to complete twice as much work as the others without straining. Then in subtle ways the other workers let her know that if she worked at a reasonable pace, the employer would become aware of their deception and demand more work from them. Knowing she would at the very least be ostracized if she did not conform to their work pace, she decided to do so.

c.   Alex is a freshman representative in the state legislature. When an important issue is being debated, he is approached by a powerful lobbyist who informs him that his political career will stand a better chance of surviving if he votes a certain way. The lobbyist mentions the names of half a dozen other representatives and suggests that Alex ask them about the wisdom of voting that way. He contacts them and they say, in effect, "We're supporting the position of that lobbying group; if you value your career, you'll do the same." He takes their advice and conforms.

d.   Emma and Homer are a young married couple. They become acquainted with a group of couples in their neighborhood. After they have been accepted in the group, they realize that the group's main diversion is mate swapping. It becomes clear to Emma and Homer that the price they must pay for the group's friendship and association is involvement in their diversion. Both of them find the idea repulsive, but they like the people and value their friendship, so they decide to become involved in the mate swapping.

7.   Analyze each of the following issues carefully, and then decide what judgment is most reasonable. Be sure to apply what you learned in this chapter about avoiding mindless conformity.

    a.   Christian churches have traditionally regarded homosexuality as a sin. Some theologians and church leaders have begun to question that view.[2] What is your position? In other words, do you think homosexuality is immoral?

    b.   Reports of human rights violations (such as imprisonment without formal charges or trial, torture, and even murder) continue to come from a number of countries that receive foreign aid from the United States. Many people believe the United States should demand that those countries end such violations as a condition of receiving foreign aid. Do you agree?

    c.   When people are stopped on suspicion of drunken driving, they are often asked to submit to a breathalyzer test. If they refuse, their refusal can be used as evidence against them in court. Some lawyers believe such evidence amounts to testifying against oneself and is therefore unconstitutional. What is your view?

    d.   The Georgia Supreme Court ruled that a church founded by a woman who calls herself "a pagan and a witch" is entitled to a property tax exemption on the building her group uses for worship.[3] Do you endorse that court ruling?

8.   *Group discussion exercise:* Discuss the following idea with two or three classmates. Decide how reasonable it is.

> Many men view pornography as a harmless sexual stimulant. But it is not harmless at all. It exploits women by presenting them as objects rather than persons, and it creates the impression that women are "looking for it." This impression tends to make men more tolerant of rape and, in some cases, prompts men to rape.

9.   After your group discussion (application 8), consider what pressure to conform you felt before or during the discussion. Be sure to consider subtle pressure, such as the feeling that your family or friends might disagree with you or the discomfort of having someone in the group dispute your view. Determine what influence, if any, this pressure had on your final decision on the issue.

CHAPTER NINE

FACE-SAVING

Everyone has a self-image, and often it is a favorable one. It's perfectly natural to want to see ourselves affirmatively: as wise, responsible, intelligent, careful, observant, courageous, generous, thoughtful of others, and so on. Similarly, there's nothing wrong with wanting to project a good image to others. This desire is part of the larger desire to be good people, people of character, and to live up to the demanding standards that are required.

Unfortunately, those natural and healthy desires often prompt us to resort to face-saving maneuvers. Face-saving is attempting to preserve our self-image or the image we project to others when some unpleasant reality threatens it. The child who loses his temper and punches his playmate, for example, will say, "It's not my fault; she made me do it by laughing at me." The adult who makes a costly mistake at work will explain, "I couldn't help it; the directions I was given were misleading." Both are trying to save face, to find an excuse for their behavior. Most people are quick to accept praise but slow to accept blame. (A good example of these twin characteristics is the way many students speak of their grades: They'll say, "*I got* a B," but "*The professor gave* me a D.")

Fully mature, emotionally balanced individuals should be able to draw the line at these relatively modest, face-saving maneuvers and not go beyond them. That is, they should be able to resist projecting onto others the share of blame they themselves deserve. Most people undoubtedly do resist most of the time, yet no one behaves maturely in every situation.

◇ FACE-SAVING SITUATIONS

All of us have moments when we strive unreasonably, and often unconsciously, to protect our image. For some of us, those moments occur when a particular aspect of our image is involved. Individuals who pride themselves on being good judges of people may be mature and balanced about many things, but when the candidate they voted for is found guilty of misusing his or her office, they may persist in denying the evidence, scream about the hypocrisy of the opposing party, and predict that in years to come the judgment will be reversed. They may do all of this merely to preserve the image of their perceptiveness in judging people.

Similarly, people who believe they possess unusual self-control may deny that they are slaves to smoking or drinking and strain good sense in defending their habit. ("No one has really *proved* smoking is harmful; besides, it relieves tension" or "I don't drink because I have to but because I enjoy it; I can stop any time I want to.") When people who think of themselves as totally self-sufficient are reminded that they owe someone money, they may find fault with that person for reminding them. Those who see themselves as sensitive to others and completely free of prejudice may denounce anyone who points, however innocently and constructively, to evidence that suggests otherwise. In each of these cases, the people may act to maintain their favorable self-image.

For many people the need to save face centers around a particular role in their lives:

Sam thinks of himself as a very devoted father who sacrifices for his children and has a close relationship with them. One day during an argument, his son blurts out that for years Sam has been more concerned with his business and his own leisure pursuits than with his children; he has in fact ignored and rejected them. Sam turns to his wife and demands that she tell the boy his charge is untrue. His wife slowly and painfully replies that the charge is essentially *true*. Sam storms out of the house, angry and hurt, convinced that he has been grievously wronged.

Agnes regards herself as an excellent homemaker. One day her husband suggests that the stove is overdue for cleaning. She becomes angry and accuses her husband of a host of offenses, from insensitivity to her, to selfishness, to rudeness to her parents.

Jackie sees herself as an unusually bright and conscientious student. Whenever the teacher returns a test paper that Jackie has done poorly on, she challenges the fairness of the questions. If this fails to get her grade changed, she paces the corridors and lounges of the campus complaining to her classmates and friends that the teacher is incompetent or dislikes her because of her clothes or religion or point of view. Those courses from which she absents herself regularly, she tells herself, are boring or useless.

For still others, it is neither the particular aspect of the image nor the role involved that triggers the face-saving reaction. It is the people who are observing. Are they friends or strangers? Parents or peers? Employers or co-workers? What some people think of us we may not care about at all; what others think of us we may care about beyond reasonableness.

◇ CAUSES AND EFFECTS OF FACE-SAVING

Different theories attempt to explain why people feel the need to save face. One plausible theory, proposed by psychologist Alfred Adler, is that to some extent everyone suffers from feelings of inferiority. Building on this theory, Thomas A. Harris suggests that the early childhood experience, with the feeling of being dominated by adults, leaves everyone feeling somewhat insecure and unconfident in later life.[1] This theory helps explain why some people feel such a need to maintain a favorable image that they become defensive about various situations, including not only those in which they do look bad but also those in which they might possibly look bad and even those in which their suspicion of their own inferiority makes them *imagine* they might.

As the foregoing examples clearly indicate, the face-saving process can impede growth in self-awareness by locking us into a rigid and wishful view of our personalities. Less obvious but equally unfortunate, it can pose a serious obstacle to clear thinking. By indulging our fears of unpleasant facts, face-saving leaves us indisposed to inquiry. And by limiting us only to the conclusions that reinforce our self-image, it blocks out the full range of conclusions that deserve consideration.

Just how do these effects occur in real situations? Let's consider three actual cases. In the first, I was discussing a thought-provoking article on marijuana with a college instructor friend. The article, which appeared in the *Journal of the American Medical Association*, reported the results of a clinical study of marijuana use.[2] The authors concluded that "contrary to what is frequently reported, we have found the effect of marijuana to be not merely that of a mild intoxicant which causes a slight exaggeration of usual adolescent behavior, but a specific and separate clinical syndrome. . . ." The principal effects they noted were "disturbed awareness of the self, apathy, confusion and poor reality testing." They presented the details of thirteen actual cases to demonstrate these effects.

My friend remarked that his own experiences with marijuana while in college showed all these signs and that the changes in his behavior closely paralleled those described in the thirteen cases. That is, he had become careless in his appearance, irritable, and forgetful; had experienced difficulty concentrating on his studies and paying attention in class; and had developed frequent headaches. Yet at that time, he explained, he succeeded in convincing himself that nothing had changed in his behavior, that his courses had merely become less interesting and meaningful, others were annoying him, and so on. Why? Apparently because his self-image—a self-possessed person, very much in control of himself and his behavior, unaffected by his pot smoking—was so important to him that he was willing to *deny his own perceptions and the obvious logic of the situation rather than threaten that image.* So effective were his face-saving maneuvers, he explained, that more than five years passed before he could accept the truth.

The second case concerns a student who was enrolled in a critical thinking class a few years ago. One of the topics for analysis in the course was abortion. A number of exercises were used to identify the various strengths and weaknesses found in the arguments on both sides of the issue. (For example, the tendency of many on the "pro" side to ignore the question of at what point, if any, the fetus acquires human rights; and the tendency of many on the "anti" side to minimize the emotional harm often caused by having an unwanted baby.) One of the later assignments was to observe a televised debate on abortion between two professors and identify the strengths and weaknesses of their arguments.

This student's written analysis said, in effect, that the "pro" professor's argument had no weaknesses at all and that the "anti" professor's was riddled with weaknesses. The student maintained this position in class discussion even though his classmates found significant strengths and weaknesses in both positions. (In fact, a clear majority gave the edge not to the "pro" professor but to the "anti.") Even after the class listened to a tape of the debate that demonstrated that this student had heard wrong in several important instances, he remained convinced that his analysis was correct. The more the evidence mounted against his position, the more strongly he advanced it. "Not giving in" had become a last-ditch device to save face.

The third case involves a college professor. While reading a book that discussed effective teaching, she encountered a chapter that examined a particular classroom practice and showed how it was not only ineffective but actually harmful to learning. As soon as the approach was identified, she recognized it as one of her own favorite approaches. As she read further into the author's criticism of it (she recounted to me later), she began to feel defensive, even angry. "No," she mumbled to herself, "the author is wrong. The approach is a good one. He just doesn't understand." The professor had nothing rational to base these reactions on—just the impulse to save face. No one else was around. She was alone with the author's words. Yet defending the approach, and saving herself the embarrassment of admitting she didn't know as much as she thought she did, became more important than knowing the truth.

It's a mark of the professor's strength of character that as soon as she recognized what she was doing, she checked the tendency and forced herself to consider the author's arguments calmly and reasonably. Surely the temptation not to do so must have been powerful.

◇ CONTROLLING FACE-SAVING TENDENCIES

The harm face-saving does to critical thinking is significant. By prompting us to misinterpret our perceptions and substitute wishful thinking for reality, it leads us to rationalize. Rationalizing is the very opposite of reasoning; whereas reasoning works from evidence to conclusion, rationalizing works from conclusion to evidence. That is, rationalizing starts with what we *want* to be so and then selectively compiles "evidence" to prove that it *is* so. Thus face-saving undermines the very process by which we think critically.

Unfortunately, there is probably nothing we can do to eliminate our face-saving tendency. It is too much a part of being human to be disposed of entirely. Nevertheless, we can learn to control it and thereby greatly reduce its effect on our critical thinking. To control your face-saving tendency, begin by admitting that you have it. In addition, persuade yourself that there is no shame in having it because it is a natural tendency; there is only shame in being dishonest with yourself and denying its existence. Then become more aware of your reaction to unpleasant ideas that you hear or read. Try to anticipate occasions of face-saving. Finally, whenever you catch yourself saving face, stop and say, "OK, that's what I want to be so, but what really is so? Where does the truth lie?" By refusing to cooperate with the irrationality within you and demanding that your thinking be uncompromisingly honest rather than merely self-congratulatory, you will soon have your face-saving under control.

⊞ APPLICATIONS

1. Which of the following statements are consistent with the view detailed in the chapter? Explain your choices and, if you reject any, give your reasons for doing so.

    a. Face-saving is unavoidable.

    b. Face-saving is a normal tendency.

    c. Face-saving is dishonest.

    d. Face-saving is harmful.

2. Evaluate the following argument as you did the arguments in Chapter 2, application 7. First identify the argument's component parts (including hidden premises) and ask relevant questions, as shown in that chapter. Then check the accuracy of each premise, stated or hidden, and decide whether the conclusion is the most reasonable one. Note that checking the accuracy of the premises may require obtaining sufficient evidence to permit a judgment. If you find a premise to be inaccurate or a conclusion to be less than completely reasonable, revise the argument accordingly.

Background note: More and more communities are trying to do something about the growing problem of litter, which is not only unsightly but in many cases unsanitary and dangerous. Here is an argument addressing one aspect of the problem.

Argument: Things that have monetary value are less likely to be discarded (or at least more likely to be recovered) than things that don't have such value. For that reason a ten-cent deposit on bottles and cans would virtually eliminate that part of the litter problem.

3. Recall an occasion in which you observed someone else resorting to (or at least *seeming* to resort to) face-saving devices. Explain what happened. Decide what triggered the face-saving behavior. Was it the particular aspect of the person's image that was threatened, the specific role involved, or the people who were observing?

4. Recall two situations in which you resorted to face-saving devices. For each, follow the directions for application 3. If you have difficulty recalling any situations, look back at the group discussion exercises in previous chapters. (Chances are good that during one of those conversations someone will have challenged your idea and prompted you to resort to face-saving.)

5. Sherri is a sophomore in college. While she is home for spring vacation, she is very irritable with her parents. She seizes every opportunity to criticize them and their values and manages to take offense at their every comment to her. Just before she returns to college, she causes a row in which she accuses them of never having given her enough attention and love. Her parents are at a loss to understand her behavior. What they do not know is that for the past several months she has been living off-campus with her boyfriend and using the money her parents send her to help support him. Explain how this fact may have influenced her behavior toward her parents.

6. Read the following dialogue carefully. Identify any indications of face-saving and explain what might have prompted it.

Teresa: Abortion is always wrong. There is no such thing as a case in which it is justified.

Gail: I just read of a case in which I believe it is justified. I think even you'd agree.

Teresa: No way.

Gail: It happened in New York. The woman was a twenty-five-year-old ward of the state with the mental capacity of an *infant*. The doctor she was referred to said she was totally incapable of understanding who she was, let alone what it means to be pregnant. The experience of delivery would have been so traumatic and the consequences so tragic, in the doctor's view, that abortion was the only reasonable course of action.[3] Even though I'm against abortion, in a case like this, I'm convinced it's justified.

Teresa: The issue in that case is not whether the woman should be allowed to have an abortion but what should be done to the insensitive slob who took advantage of her retardation and got her pregnant. Capital punishment is too good for creeps like that.

7. A number of communities around the nation have enacted legislation banning the sale or possession of handguns. Many people hail such legislation as an important step toward public safety and the prevention of crime. Many others, however, believe it is a violation of the constitutional guarantee of every citizen's "right to bear arms." Examine this issue critically, taking special care to control your face-saving tendencies. State and support your view of the issue.

8. The U.S. Supreme Court has ruled that state, city, and county governments may not hand over their decision-making power to churches. The Court's decision nullified a Massachusetts law giving churches a veto power over the (liquor) licensing of any bar or restaurant that would be established within 500 feet of church buildings.[4] Examine this issue critically, taking special care to control your face-saving tendencies. State whether or not you agree with the court's decision and why.

9.   *Group discussion exercise:* Discuss the following dialogue with two or three classmates. Decide the merits of Quentin's view. Be sure to check any tendency to face-saving that arises during discussion.

Quentin: There'd be a lot less ignorance in the world today if parents didn't pass on their views to their children.

Lois: How can they avoid doing so?

Quentin: By letting children form their own views. There's no law that says Democrats have to make little Democrats of their children, or that Protestants have to pass on their Protestantism.

Lois: What should they do when their children ask them about politics or religion or democracy?

Quentin: Send them to the encyclopedia, or, if the parents are capable of objective explanation, explain to them the various views that are possible and encourage them to choose their own.

Lois: How can you ask a three-year-old to make a choice about religion or politics or philosophy?

Quentin: In the case of young children the parents would simply explain as much as the children could understand and say that when they get older they can decide for themselves.

Lois: How would all this benefit children or society?

Quentin: It would make it possible for children to grow up without their parents' prejudices and would help control the number of ignoramuses in the world.

CHAPTER TEN

STEREOTYPING

Stereotypes are a form of generalization. When we generalize, we group or classify people, places, or things according to the traits they have in common. For example, we may say most Masai tribesmen are unusually tall or Scandinavians are usually fair-skinned. If our observations are careless or too limited, the generalization may be faulty, as when someone says, "Hollywood hasn't produced any quality movies in the past fifteen years."

But stereotypes are more serious than mere faulty generalizations. They are *fixed, unbending* generalizations about people, places, or things. When a stereotype is challenged, the person who holds it is unlikely to modify or discard it, because it is based on a distortion of perception. As Walter Lippmann explains, when we stereotype, "we do not so much see this man and that sunset; rather we notice that the thing is man or sunset, and then see chiefly what our mind is full of on those subjects."[1]

The most common kinds of stereotyping are ethnic and religious. Jews are shrewd and cunning, clannish, have a financial genius matched only by their greed. Italians are hot-tempered, coarse, and sensual. The Irish, like the Poles, are big and stupid; in addition, they brawl, lust after heavy liquor and light conversation. Blacks are primitive and slow-witted. (Often each of these stereotypes includes a virtue or two—Jews are good family members, Italians artistic, Poles brave, the Irish devout, blacks athletic.)

Beyond these stereotypes are numerous other, less common ones, about Swedish women, foreign film directors, Southern senators, physical education instructors, fundamentalist clergymen, agnostics, atheists, Democrats, Republicans, Mexicans, scientists, prostitutes, politicians, English teachers, psychiatrists, construction workers, black militants, college dropouts, homosexuals, and society matrons. There are stereotypes of institutions as well: marriage, the church, government, the military, the Founding Fathers, Western culture, the Judeo-Christian tradition. (A full list would include even God and mother.)

◇ Facts Don't Matter

It is pleasant to assume that when the facts are known, stereotypes disappear. However, that is seldom the case. The late Harvard psychologist Gordon Allport, in *The Nature of Prejudice*, pointed out that "it is possible for a stereotype to grow in defiance of *all* evidence. . . ."[2] People who stereotype don't just accept the facts that are offered to them. They measure those facts against what they already "know." That is, they measure them against the *stereotype itself*. Instead of seeing that the stereotype is false and therefore dismissing it, they reject the unfamiliar facts.

People who think in terms of stereotypes tend to be selective in their perceptions. They reject conditions that challenge their preformed judgment and retain those that reinforce it. Thus a person can notice the Jewish employer promoting another Jew but ignore a dozen occasions when that employer promotes a gentile. Where the risk of embarrassment or criticism prevents them from ignoring details that challenge, they can, as Bruno Bettleheim and Morris Janowitz point out, employ the exception-to-the-rule argument.[3] "I agree O'Toole is shy, introverted, and doesn't drink," they might admit, and then add, "He really isn't very Irish in his manner, is he?"

On occasion, though, stereotypers can be surprisingly flexible. They can move from the most narrow oversimplifications to remarkably fair and sensible judgments and then back again. An example of this phenomenon occurred in a series of interviews Harvard psychiatrist Robert Coles had with a police sergeant. At one point the sergeant made this statement: "I'm not prejudiced when I say that colored people have a lot of violence in them, like animals. The Irishman will get sloppy drunk and pass out. The Italian will shout and scream his head off. The Jew will figure out a way he can make himself a little more money, and get even with someone that way. But your nigger, he's vicious like a wild leopard or something when he's been drinking or on drugs. They throw lye at each other, and scalding water, and God knows what."[4]

Despite a generous helping of stereotypes in that passage, at other places in the transcript the same man who uttered those judgments is revealed as balanced, thoughtful, capable of insights *even in areas where he is given to stereotyping*. He can say things like, "I believe you should know the man, not where his grandfather came from" and "Most Negro people are too busy for demonstrations; they go to work, like the rest of us."

◇ CONTRADICTORY STEREOTYPES

Robert K. Merton has noted that the same set of characteristics can be used to support opposite stereotypes. He observed that though the identifying terms differ, Abraham Lincoln has been loved for precisely the same attributed qualities for which Jews have been hated: his thrift (their stinginess), his hard-working perseverance (their excessive ambition), his zeal for the rights of others (their pushiness for causes).[5] And James G. Martin comments on the ease with which a person can invoke the stereotype with the least of details. If we wish to have it so, he observes, "the minority group member who is quiet is 'conceited' or 'unfriendly.' And if he is talkative he is 'aggressive' or 'brash.'"[6]

Stereotyped thinking often reveals a technique common to all forms of prejudice: shifting responsibility for judgments from the judger to the judged. "The pattern of prejudiced judgment," as Martin explains, "is to ascribe a certain trait to a group with little or no evidence to support it; to judge the trait to be undesirable; and to hold the object-group responsible for the trait, and therefore blameworthy." When the prejudiced person says, "I dislike them because they are . . .," Martin concludes, "he really means "Because I dislike them, they are . . . ."[7]

◇ CAUSES OF STEREOTYPING

Among the most significant causes of stereotyping is "mine is better" thinking, especially in its extreme form, ethnocentrism. Ethnocentrism—the belief that one's nationality, race, or religion is superior to other people's—can be present in out-groups as well as in the majority, and in newcomers to a country as well as in "established" groups. For example, in the United States the heavy immigration of the past hundred years brought millions of people who had their own language and culture. These people understandably tended to remain for a time within their own groups. Later, when they became assimilated into the general culture, they retained many of their fixed views of outsiders. Traces of ethnocentrism can linger for generations and resurface in movements of ethnic pride. Despite the obvious value of such pride, particularly for groups whose rights have been denied and whose emotional well-being has been undermined, it can do great harm.

James G. Martin sees ethnocentrism as "the root of almost all the evil in intergroup relations." "We are almost constantly obligated to choose sides in human relations," he argues, "to identify ourselves with one group or another. There is often no room for neutralism. . . . One must be either for or against, enemy or patriot, in-group or out-group."[8]

Another cause of stereotyping is what Gordon Allport calls "the principle of least effort." Most of us learn to be critical and balanced in our thinking in some areas, he notes, but we remain vulnerable to stereotyped thinking in others. "A doctor," for example, "will not be swept away by folk generalizations concerning arthritis, snake bite, or the efficacy of aspirin. But he may be content with overgeneralizations concerning politics, social insurance, or Mexicans."[9] Will Rogers may have had a deeper insight than he knew when he observed how most people are fools when they venture from their areas of competence.

◇ EFFECTS OF STEREOTYPING

Stereotyping does a great injustice to those who are stereotyped. It denies them their dignity and individuality and treats them as nameless, faceless statistical units of a group. The effects of stereotyping on all who encounter it are similarly disturbing. It triggers their frustrations and anxieties, feeds their fears of conspiracies, and creates a network of suspicion and scapegoating.

Given the popular stereotypes, what is more natural than seeing the Jews as responsible for periods of economic instability, the Italians as responsible for organized crime, blacks as responsible for the decay of the inner city, and radicals and atheists as responsible for the erosion of traditional values and the loss of influence of organized religion. Stereotypes provide a ready supply of simplistic answers to whatever questions happen to be plaguing us at the moment.

Nor do the stereotypers themselves escape the crippling effects of their fixation. Indeed, they are often its most pathetic victims.

Stereotyping cuts them off from reality and cripples their thinking. Anton Chekhov was right in observing that people are what they believe. When they believe that others fit into neat categories, they believe a lie. In the sense in which Chekhov spoke, they *become* that lie.

A good many people see all police officers as corrupt "pigs," all college professors as impractical or misguided theorists, all sex education teachers as leering perverts, and all advocates of nuclear disarmament as subversives. It is difficult, sometimes impossible, for such people to deal with complex problems and issues when they have such preconceptions in their minds. Consider, for example, a plan that was advanced some years ago to meet the needs of unmarried pregnant women and the poor. Called "shepherding families," it provided homes for the pregnant women to live in until the babies were born (as an alternative to abortion) and guaranteed adoption. It also called for aid to the poor (as an alternative to welfare), in which churches would provide food, clothing, medical care, legal advice, plumbing, and in many cases, jobs. It was an interesting idea that deserved careful consideration. But anyone who accepted the negative stereotypes associated with the plan's author, Moral Majority founder Reverend Jerry Falwell, would be tempted to reject it automatically.[10]

Similarly, it would be difficult for people to deal fairly with questions of Native Americans' land claims when they see every Indian as a feathered savage, uttering bloodcurdling shrieks while burning settlers' homes and scalping women and children. And how can people be reasonable about the issue of welfare when they see the poor as scheming, lazy, irresponsible, filthy, immoral, wasteful, undeserving scoundrels?

◇ AVOIDING STEREOTYPING

It is not easy to set aside stereotypes that have been in your mind since childhood, particularly if they have been reinforced by ethnocentrism. Yet if you do not set them aside, you will never realize your capacity for critical thinking. Stereotypes will corrupt your observation, listening, and reading and therefore block your understanding.

Here are two tips for freeing yourself from stereotyping. First, remind yourself often that people and institutions and processes seldom fit into neat categories and that critical thinking demands that you evaluate each on who or what it is at the particular time and place and circumstance, not on preconceived notions. Second, whenever you begin observing, listening, or reading, be alert for the feeling that you needn't continue because you *know* what the correct judgment must be. If that feeling occurs early in the information-gathering process, you can be reasonably sure it is a sign of stereotyping and should be ignored.

❖ APPLICATIONS

1. Evaluate the following arguments as you did the arguments in Chapter 2, application 7. First identify the argument's component parts (including hidden premises) and ask relevant questions, as shown in that chapter. Then check the accuracy of each premise, stated or hidden, and decide whether the conclusion is the most reasonable one. Note that checking the accuracy of the premises may require obtaining sufficient evidence to permit a judgment. (Be sure that you resist being influenced by stereotypes associated with people who have advanced this or similar arguments in the media.) If you find a premise to be inaccurate or a conclusion to be less than completely reasonable, revise the argument accordingly.

> **a.** *Argument:* Taking animals from the wild and exhibiting them for human pleasure is a violation of their natural rights. Therefore, zoos should be outlawed.

> **b.** *Background note: In 1993 a gay organization took the Ancient Order of Hibernians (AOH), the organizers of New York's St. Patrick's Day Parade, to court. The charge was that the AOH illegally discriminated against the gay organization by excluding it from the parade. The reasoning of the AOH was as follows:*

> *Argument:* This parade honors one of the saints of our church. Our religion teaches that homosexuality is a sin. To require us to include gay organizations in the parade would be a violation of our rights.

2. Review the stereotypes mentioned in the chapter. Select *three* of them. For each, recall an occasion when that stereotype was revealed in the thinking of someone you know. Detail the circumstances in which you observed it. If there were other people present and they reacted to the stereotype in any noticeable way, explain their reactions. If possible, decide what prevented the person who stereotyped from seeing the reality in its complexity.

3. Compose a summary of the chapter for one of the people whose stereotyping you described in application 2. Make the summary as persuasive as you can. That is, make it focus on the particular occasion of that person's stereotyping and the effects of that error on her or his thinking.

4. List the stereotypes that you are most inclined to accept uncritically (or at least are not quick to challenge). Try to determine what has conditioned you to be vulnerable to those stereotypes. For example, it may have been something you were taught as a child or some traumatic experience you had.

5. Apply your critical thinking to each of the following cases. Be especially careful to avoid stereotyping.

a. A Monroe, Michigan, hospital has a policy that only members of a pregnant woman's immediate family can be present in the delivery room. An unwed couple, wishing to be together at the birth of their baby, challenged that policy in court. The judge upheld the hospital policy.[11] What would your decision have been?

b. Sixty-five percent of all school-age children have working mothers. (Twenty-two percent are "single-parent children.") A great many of these children are "latch-key kids," those who come home before their mothers, let themselves in, and amuse themselves, in some cases for several hours. Some of these children must also let themselves out in the morning because their mothers leave for work early. Many "latch-key kids" are as young as eight.[12] Do you think this is a desirable situation for a child? If not, what would you do to improve the situation or eliminate it altogether?

c. Some people believe that gays should be barred from certain jobs, such as military service and elementary school teaching. Do you agree?

6. Read each of the following dialogues carefully. Note any instances of positive or negative stereotyping. Decide which view of the issue in each dialogue is more reasonable. (Be sure you don't engage in stereotyping.)

a. *Background note: A born-again Texas businessman and a television evangelist smashed $1 million worth of art objects and threw them into a lake after reading the following verse from Deuteronomy in the Bible: "The graven images of their gods shall ye burn with fire: thou shalt not desire the silver and gold that is on them, nor take it unto thee, lest thou be snared therein: for it is an abomination to the Lord thy God." The objects, which belonged to the businessman, were mostly gold, silver, jade, and ivory figures associated with Eastern religions.*

Cecil: That's a real measure of faith, the willingness to discard earthly treasures out of spiritual conviction.

Ellie: It's more like an act of lunacy. It's a terrible waste of wealth. If he'd wanted to express his religious conviction, he could have done something to help his fellow human beings.

Cecil: By doing what?

Ellie: He could have sold the objects, taken the million dollars, and given it to the needy of the world. Or he could have donated it to a religious organization or a hospital. Instead, he threw it away and helped no one.

Cecil: You don't understand. Selling the objects would have corrupted others. He's a religious man. The Bible told him what to do, and he had no choice but to obey.

b. *Background note: A former Florida policewoman filed a federal discrimination suit, alleging that she was fired because of a sex-change operation. The officer, now a man, charged that the firing violated his constitutional rights and asked both monetary damages and reinstatement on the police force.*[13]

Christine: If the cause for the firing was as the officer describes it, then it was improper.

Renee: I disagree. A police officer is a public official and should not engage in behavior that disgraces that office.

Christine: What's disgraceful about having a sex-change operation?

Renee: It's sick, strange, abnormal, and it makes the police department the laughingstock of the community.

Christine: Wrong. The only concern of the police department and of the general public should be the officer's performance of his or her duty. Whether he or she decides to have a sex-change operation is no more their business than if the officer decides to take up stamp collecting as a hobby.

7. *Group discussion exercise:* Discuss one of the dialogues in application 6 with two or three of your classmates, being alert for any stereotyping that may occur during the discussion. Try to reach consensus on the issues. Be prepared to present the group's view (or the individual views) to the class.

□ CHAPTER ELEVEN □

OVERSIMPLIFICATION

Simplification is a useful, even necessary, activity. The world is complex. Thousands of subjects and millions of facts and interpretations of facts exist. No one can hope to be an expert in more than one or two subjects. Furthermore, as we have seen in previous chapters, even an expert's knowledge and understanding are limited.

Yet the job of communicating about these subjects is an everyday necessity. Circumstance forces those who know more about a subject to speak with those who know less. In industry, for example, supervisors must train new workers. In government, experienced employees must explain procedures to novices. In each of these cases the effectiveness of the training depends on the clarity of the instruction. Complicated matters can be made clear only by simplifying them.

Nowhere is the value of simplification clearer than in formal education. First-grade teachers cannot expect their pupils to grasp the lessons in science and math and English as the teachers learned them. They must phrase the lessons in a simpler way, a way suited to the pupils' level of understanding.

Similarly, if those first-grade teachers take graduate courses, their professors probably don't speak to them in quite the same way that they do with colleagues or in articles for professional journals. The professors simplify. (And people who attain such levels of intellectual penetration as Albert Einstein must probably simplify when they talk about their fields to *anyone.*)

◇ OVERSIMPLIFICATION DISTORTS

Although there is nothing wrong with simplification, *over*simplification (excessive simplification) is an obstacle to critical thinking. Oversimplification does not merely scale down a complex idea to more manageable proportions. It twists and distorts the idea so that it states, not truth, but error. Rather than informing others, oversimplification misleads them.

Let's consider a few examples. The first involves a rather common idea: "*If the students haven't learned, the teacher hasn't taught.*" This asserts that learning is the sole responsibility of the teacher. Are there poor teachers? Of course. Do such teachers confuse students and impede learning? Certainly. However, that is only part of the truth, for there are also lazy or uninterested students who can successfully resist the best efforts of the finest teacher. When they fail, the blame cannot fairly be assigned to the teacher.

In many cases, perhaps most, failure to learn is too complex to place the blame wholly on either side. The students' lack of effort may be a factor and so may the quality of instruction. Also significant may be the attitudes of both students and teacher and the responses these attitudes trigger in the other. In any particular situation, there are likely to be so many variables, in fact, that only a careful accounting of all relevant details will be satisfactory.

Here is another common idea: "*We know ourselves better than others know us.*" Now in a sense this is true. There is a side of our personalities that we keep to ourselves—many of our hopes and dreams and fantasies. Surely no one else can know all the experiences we have had and all our thoughts and feelings about those experiences. Even those closest to us cannot know everything about us.

Yet there is another sense in which others can know us better than we know ourselves. Surely the image we project to others is as much a part of us as our self-image. None of us can really know precisely how we "come through" to others. However objective we become, we remain hopelessly bound up in ourselves, unable to see our outer image apart from our intentions. It often happens that even our own deeper motivations are hidden from us. People who have undergone psychotherapy often learn something about themselves they didn't know before.

When that occurs, what precisely has happened? One way or another the therapist has probed into those people's thoughts and attitudes (and perhaps largely forgotten experiences), learned something about them, and then has shared it with them. In other words, for a time, however brief, the therapist has had an insight into the patients that the patients themselves did not have.

It's careless to judge on impressions alone. Many oversimplifications sound good. *"Give people a welfare handout and you make bums of them"* is accepted by many people as a profound truth. Yet it is an oversimplification. People whose problem is not misfortune but laziness will undoubtedly be made lazier by receiving welfare. But what effect will welfare have on a responsible person whose situation was caused by misfortune—say, a man stricken with a serious illness leaving him unable to work, or the mother of two small children deserted by her husband? Surely in such cases welfare can be a temporary helping hand that makes the person no less responsible.

Similarly, the idea that *"compulsory class attendance rules thwart students' maturation"* may seem sound to many college students. Yet it omits an important aspect of reality. Too many rules may hamper one's development, but so may too few. Rules requiring students to attend class do not really take away freedom to cut class. They only make the *exercise* of that freedom more significant. For many students that can be an added motivation to make wise, mature choices.

◇ CAUSES OF OVERSIMPLIFICATION

The most obvious causes of oversimplification are simple (unhabitual) error and unwillingness to invest the time necessary to probe the complexity of issues. But there are other, deeper causes as well. One is "mine is better" thinking, which can lead us to see issues in a biased way and thus ignore facts that don't support our view.

Another cause is insecurity. If we are intimidated by complexity, we may prefer superficial answers to questions because they make us feel comfortable. Some people need simple answers. Complex situations and those in which judgment can only be tentative and speculative leave such people disoriented.

Still another cause of oversimplification is the habit of seeing only what affects us. When the law of the land required that public restaurants serve any customer, regardless of race, religion, or national origin, some restaurant owners were angry. They reasoned that people who invest their hard-earned money in a business have the right to serve or not serve whomever they please. That side of the issue was so important to them that they regarded it as the only side. But there was another important side: the right of a citizen to have access to a public place.

Similarly, when the Federal Aviation Administration published regulations governing hang gliders and ultralight motorized aircraft, the U.S. Hang Gliders Association attacked the regulations. They argued that the government "has no business regulating an outdoor recreational sport that consists largely of people running and gliding down remote hills and sand dunes." The association was seeing one side of the issue, the side that affected them. Now if that were the only side, their position would be reasonable. But there is another important side to the issue: keeping the airspace safe for all who use it, including commercial and private planes. (The FAA reports that hang gliders have been observed as high as 13,000 feet.)[1] By ignoring that side, the association oversimplified the issue.

◇ AVOIDING OVERSIMPLIFICATION

Oversimplification occurs either as a simple assertion independent of any argument or as a premise of an argument. (In contrast, hasty conclusion, as we will see in the next chapter, occurs in the conclusion of an argument.) Avoiding oversimplification simply means refusing to overstate the case for an idea. Before you express any idea to others, first check it for accuracy. If it is not completely accurate, rephrase it. Here is how you might revise the oversimplifications discussed in the chapter. (In each case, of course, other effective revisions are possible.)

Oversimplification	*Balanced Statement*
If the students haven't learned, the teacher hasn't taught. (*The statement is categorical, allowing for no other causes of students' failure to learn.*)	Sometimes, when the students' haven't learned, the teacher hasn't taught. (*This statement makes essentially the same assertion, but without ruling out the possibility of other causes.*)
We know ourselves better than others know us. (*Lacking a qualification of frequency or circumstance, this clearly implies that self-knowledge is superior in all cases.*)	We know some things about ourselves better than others can know them. (*This is still a forceful statement, but its claim, unlike that of the first statement, is not excessive.*)

Give people a welfare handout and you make bums of them. *(Other, more favorable effects of welfare are ruled out altogether.)*	Welfare can develop a sense of dependency and a loss of confidence in solving one's own problems. *(This statement does not deny that in some cases welfare does not have these effects.)*
Compulsory class attendance rules thwart students' maturation. *(This statement denies the possibility of positive effects.)*	Attendance rules that are too numerous or too rigid can thwart students' maturation. *(This statement speaks of certain kinds of attendance rules, not all such rules.)*

The number of words in an assertion is no index of balance or lack thereof. A short assertion may be quite defensible. Consider these examples: "Astronauts receive intensive training," "Large doses of vitamin D are harmful," "Haste makes waste." On the other hand, a long assertion may be oversimplified—for example, "African-Americans who criticize affirmative action in the private or public sector are dishonoring the memory of Martin Luther King, Jr., and the countless others who have labored to achieve justice for their people." This assertion denies the possibility that criticism of affirmative action policy can be thoughtful or constructive, and that is unreasonable. (Supreme Court Justice Clarence Thomas terms this kind of assertion "the new intolerance," and argues that it is "an attempt to intimidate and silence those who dare to question popular political, social or economic fads.")[2] In checking for oversimplification, consider not the number of words but the scope of the assertion. If the scope is so broad that it rules out known realities or distinct possibilities, the assertion is an oversimplification.

In looking for oversimplification (or, for that matter, any other error in reasoning), you may be tempted to nitpick. When someone says, "Michael Jordan had a unique ability to maneuver in the middle of a soaring leap," you could respond, "Wait a minute. He not only had that ability—he still has it. After all, he's still a young man even if he's retired from the game, and one doesn't lose a gift like that so quickly." Similarly, if you read, "A series of tourist slayings in Florida in 1993 hurt the tourist industry there," you could say, "That's an oversimplification. The tourist industry was hurt mainly in the cities where those killings occurred. The rest of the state was less affected." In both cases, you'd have a point, but it would be so minuscule that you'd be wiser not to make it. Nowhere is it written that to be a critical thinker one must be a pest.

⊞ APPLICATIONS

1. Which of the following do you think the author would cite as caus-es of oversimplification? Explain why you think so, with references to the text, where appropriate.

mine is better thinking

peer pressure

unwillingness to be tentative

one-sided perspective

ineptness with complexity

intellectual laziness

2. Evaluate the following argument as you did the arguments in Chapter 2, application 7. First identify the argument's component parts (including hidden premises) and ask relevant questions, as shown in that chapter. Then check the accuracy of each premise, stated or hidden, and decide whether the conclusion is the most reasonable one. Note that checking the accuracy of the premises may require obtaining sufficient evidence to permit a judgment. (Be careful to avoid oversimplification.) If you find a premise to be inaccurate or a conclusion to be less than completely reasonable, revise the argument accordingly.

Background note: From time to time people have challenged the recitation of the Pledge of Allegiance in public schools. Their objection is usually to the words "under God." Their reasoning is as follows:

Argument: A public school recitation that claims the United States is "under God" is an endorsement of religion and thus violates the consti-tutional requirement that church and state be kept separate. Therefore, the recitation of the Pledge of Allegiance should not be permitted.

3. Analyze the following ideas. Decide whether each is an oversimpli-fication. Explain your reasoning carefully.

a. "I need only consult with myself with regard to what I wish to do; what I feel to be right is right, what I feel to be wrong is wrong." (Jean Jacques Rousseau)

b. Elected officials should be held accountable to a higher ethical standard than the average citizen is.

c. The scandals involving television ministries prove what many critics have noted for years—that televangelists are hypocrites.

d. Guns don't kill people; people kill people.

4. Apply your critical thinking to each of the following cases, being sure to avoid oversimplification.

a. The U.S. Supreme Court has ruled that states must provide free public education not only to all children of citizens and aliens legally residing in this country but to the children of *illegal* aliens as well.[3] Do you support this decision?

b. As many as 50 percent of those teaching high school math and science lack the proper qualifications. The problem is that qualified math and science teachers are leaving teaching for higher-paying jobs in industry. To attract qualified teachers, some experts propose that schools offer math and science teachers a special salary scale, higher than that offered to teachers in other disciplines. Do you support this proposal?

c. In some states the law now requires motorists to secure in an approved child restraint seat each young child riding in their cars. Do you support such mandatory restraint laws?

d. Some conservative Christian churches practice snake handling as a part of their religious rituals. That is, they pass poisonous snakes like moccasins and rattlers from one person to another as a test of their religious faith. This practice of snake handling, however, is illegal in all states but one: West Virginia. Should it be made illegal there too?

e. Women employees of the National Broadcasting Company are eligible for six months of maternity leave with job and seniority guarantees. However, when a male engineer with the company applied for paternity leave with the same guarantees (so that he could care for his baby and ease his wife's return to work), he was turned down.[4] Is the idea of paternity leave a reasonable one?

f. A minister in Hoffman Estates, Illinois, proposed some years ago that convicted murderers be executed publicly on prime time television. The shock of seeing such executions, he reasoned, would deter others from crime.[5] Do you agree?

g. Laboratories have traditionally used animals such as rats, dogs, and monkeys in experiments to develop safe cosmetics and to find cures for disease. The experiments sometimes cause the animals pain. Some animal-rights activists argue that causing animals pain is never justified. Do you agree?

5. *Group discussion exercise:* Select one of the cases you analyzed in application 4 and discuss it with two or three of your classmates. Try to reach a consensus, but be careful to avoid oversimplification. Be prepared to present your idea(s) to the class.

CHAPTER TWELVE

HASTY CONCLUSION

We have seen that oversimplification is an error that typically occurs in a simple assertion or in the premise of an argument. It distorts reality by misstatement or omission. Hasty conclusion, on the other hand, is an error that occurs only in the conclusion of an argument. It is a premature judgment—that is, a judgment made without sufficient evidence. Exactly what constitutes sufficient evidence, of course, varies from case to case. In general, we may say that evidence is clearly insufficient when there are two or more possible conclusions and the evidence does not clearly favor any one of them.

For example, consider a conclusion some people accept quite readily: *"The average American college student is in college to have a good time."* Most who accept this probably arrive at their position from a mixture of the stereotype of the carefree, fun-loving college student and some acquaintance with a few college students. They may know a neighbor who failed out of a couple of colleges, have heard stories about wild irresponsibility among other young people, and believe their own sons or daughters pay too little attention to their studies.

Is that enough evidence to support the conclusion? Hardly. The judgment may not even fit the known students. The neighbor may have been enrolled in programs beyond his capacity and failed despite arduous effort. The stories about the other students may be inaccurate or oversimplified. And the people's own children may be more conscientious than they appear to be. Yet even if the judgment fits all those individuals, that does not prove that their behavior is typical of the "average college student."

A close study of a wider sampling of college students would undoubtedly reveal that for many, perhaps a majority, no single motivation prompted them to attend college. Rather, they were driven by *several* motivations—for example, some degree of interest in their particular field of study, a hope for the added career security that a degree traditionally brings, the desire to please their parents, and the hope of meeting other young people with similar interests. In such cases, where the motivation to have a good time exists—and it is entirely normal for it to exist—having a good time is usually only a part of the overall motivation.

Of course, once the hasty conclusion is drawn, there is little chance that the person who has drawn it will go on to discover the facts.

◇ WEIGHING BOTH SIDES

Another example of a quite common hasty conclusion is this one: *"The overall effect of technology has been to dehumanize people."* Many arrive at this conclusion after reading an article or two lamenting the decline of craftsmanship or the rising rate of crime in cities. A wide array of additional evidence can be used to attack technology—from the character of many of the tasks workers are expected to perform to the development of sprawling suburbs, the emphasis on objects rather than human relationships, the increase in personal mobility, and the resulting erosion of family life and the values traditionally taught by the family.

However, even this impressive evidence would not be sufficient to support the conclusion. Any judgment about the "net or overall effect" demands a weighing of both sides, the plus and the minus. Specifically what is needed, then, is the other side of the issue—the *favorable* effects of technological advance. If we were to look for such balancing effects, we'd find that technology has decreased the burden of extreme physical labor for millions of people. It has cut the fourteen- to sixteen-hour workday in half and given people time to invest in the finer human pursuits. It has given us electric lights and central heating and the means to travel long distances quickly and comfortably. It has conquered plague and famine. Any judgment of technology that does not weigh these and other advantages against the shortcomings is unfair and shallow.

Hasty conclusions are not just an affliction of the uneducated. They are also found among the highly educated—even among serious scholars. The reason is that hasty conclusions are a consequence of the human condition. In other words, they are made possible by our own natural tendencies and the difficulty of obtaining evidence.

◇ CAUSES OF HASTY CONCLUSIONS

Some people's major concern in thinking is convenience. They are afraid of arduous analysis and rattled by complexity. As a result they leap at the first conclusion that occurs to them. They may hear someone say energy shortages are artificial, manufactured by the oil companies and corrupt government officials. And so they accept that conclusion uncritically. After repeating it a few times, they harden it into an article of faith.

Compounding this tendency is the desire to sound authoritative. Feeling some insecurity and wanting to compensate for it, or wanting to make their conversation livelier, many people have the habit of escalating every statement to a higher level of generalization. "A teenager was behaving very boisterously in the supermarket yesterday" becomes "Today's teenagers are very boisterous." "Mr. Easel, the art teacher at the local high school, gave my son an unfairly low grade" becomes "Teachers aren't fair in their grading." In a thousand different ways, "one" becomes "many" or "all," and "once" becomes "often" or "always."

Even people who have managed to get beyond convenience thinking to greater intellectual maturity cannot escape another normal tendency—the tendency to prefer, in certain matters, one idea over all others. People may be fully conscious of this tendency, even as it is exerting its pull on their thinking. Or they may be completely unaware of it. In the latter case, of course, they are more likely to be affected by it. But either way its attraction is powerful.

Many movie magazine and romance magazine readers fall prey to this tendency. They stand ready to embrace any report, however far-fetched, of scandalous behavior among celebrities. They accept as gospel the most incredible fictions, like "I Was Attacked by My Boyfriend's Brother's Uncle." Undoubtedly, many of the conclusions they eagerly accept reinforce their own deep desires and fantasies. Almost certainly, their conclusions support their view of life and human nature.

Here's how one's preferences can influence one's judgment. Two businessmen have just concluded an extended conference and are having a late dinner in a crowded restaurant. Across the room they notice an acquaintance dining with a woman. They realize she is not the man's wife. The first businessman has had several extramarital affairs himself and assumes other people behave similarly. He is also erotically stimulated by the idea that the couple are cheating on their mates. He concludes that they are.

The second businessman likes to think well of people. He is also very disturbed by the thought of any kind of dishonesty, including marital infidelity. He concludes the couple are innocent of any wrongdoing.

Which conclusion is reasonable? Neither. In the absence of additional evidence, both are hasty conclusions. It may be that the couple are having an affair. Or it may not. (Any number of other reasons could explain their being together.) So the only reasonable reaction is not to draw any conclusion at that time.

◇ THE DIFFICULTY OF OBTAINING EVIDENCE

The difficulty of obtaining evidence can prompt even careful thinkers to draw conclusions hastily. Examples occur in every field of thought and work. One good example is a problem that drug manufacturers face. Every new drug must be thoroughly tested and proved safe for people to take before it can be released on the market. But testing is expensive and time-consuming. Furthermore, competition with other firms in the industry encourages speedy research. For these reasons it is tempting to judge a drug prematurely.

In the 1960s the most tragic example of this tendency involved the drug thalidomide, which was branded safe and sold to thousands of pregnant women around the world. Only when hundreds of babies were born deformed, some grotesquely so, was the harm of the drug recognized. In the 1970s the "safe" drug Innovar began to be used as an anesthetic. It was soon discovered that a number of people apparently suffered extensive paralysis and brain damage from it.[1]

How much drug testing is enough? It is a difficult question. A drug called Intal has been effective in controlling the symptoms of asthma. An aerosol, it is sprayed into the bronchial passages. It desensitizes these passages so they no longer constrict when allergens (pollen, for instance) are inhaled. During the early testing of this drug, one group of monkeys developed kidney lesions after being administered the drug. Was the reaction coincidental to the use of the drug, or did the drug cause the lesions? More testing was done, but the kidney lesions did not occur, so the conclusion was drawn that the lesions in the early testing had probably been coincidental.

It is possible that the conclusion about the drug Intal may be proved incorrect in the future. However, that would not mean that the original conclusion had been hasty. Rather, it would mean that new evidence was discovered that did not exist earlier and could not reasonably have been anticipated.

◇ AVOIDING HASTY CONCLUSIONS

We should avoid hasty conclusions because they are insupportable and because, once we form any conclusion, our curiosity in the matter is diminished. In other words, we make up our mind, and before we can even entertain a different conclusion, we must first *unmake* our mind. Doing that is difficult. "Mine is better" thinking, resistance to change, and face-saving weigh heavily against us.

Here are three suggestions that can help you avoid hasty conclusions in your thinking:

1. Before you draw any conclusion, be sure you have identified *and answered* all important questions pertaining to the issue.

2. Where you cannot obtain sufficient evidence, either withhold judgment or (if circumstances require an immediate judgment) use the "If . . . then" approach. For example, if the issue concerns what punishment would be most appropriate for a murderer and you lack some important details about the case, you might say, "*If* the murderer acted in the heat of anger, without any premeditation, *then* I believe he deserves leniency. However, *if* he visited the victim with the clear intention of harming her, *then* I believe his punishment should be severe."

3. Where the evidence will support probability but not certainty, make your conclusion reflect that fact. That is, admit that it is impossible to say for sure what the right conclusion is, and explain why that is so. Then say what the right conclusion *probably* is.

⊞ APPLICATIONS

1. In late August, the Lees, a Chinese-American family, move into Louise's neighborhood and Louise becomes acquainted with one of the children, Susan, a girl her own age. A week later, during school registration, Louise passes Susan in the hall, but Susan doesn't even look at her. Which of the following conclusions is Louise justified in drawing? (You may select more than one or reject all of them.) Explain your answer with appropriate references to the chapter.

   a. Susan behaved rudely.

   b. Susan is a rude person.

   c. The Lees are a rude family.

   d. Chinese-Americans are rude.

   e. The Chinese are rude.

   f. Asians are rude

2. Evaluate the following argument as you did the arguments in Chapter 2, application 7. First identify the argument's component parts (including hidden premises) and ask relevant questions, as shown in that chapter. Then check the accuracy of each premise, stated or hidden, and decide whether the conclusion is the most reasonable one. Note that checking the accuracy of the premises may require obtaining sufficient evidence to permit a judgment. (Be careful to avoid forming a hasty conclusion.) If you find a premise to be inaccurate or a conclusion to be less than completely reasonable, revise the argument accordingly.

   Background note: Despite the fact that Cuba's AIDS policy has been much more successful than the U.S. policy, it remains controversial. When Cuban citizens test positive for the AIDS virus, they are taken to a sanitarium, where they are fed and housed very well, and given the best AIDS medicine; however, they are not allowed to leave.[2] This policy is based on the following reasoning.

   Argument: AIDS is an easily transmitted—at present, incurable—disease, so the suspension of victims' freedom of movement and association is necessary for the good of the Cuban people as a whole.

3. Examine each of the following conclusions. Decide the specific kind and amount of information that would be necessary to obtain before the conclusion would be justified. Determine whether another possible conclusion might be more supportable than this one.

   a. Why are there so many broken homes today? Why are crimes of violence increasing at an alarming rate? Why is pornography flooding our country? Because religion has been shut out of the schools.

   b. Many people have spoken out in recent years for a reduction in U.S. military spending. This is madness. We need to spend every dollar we are spending to maintain our national security.

c. What makes people willing to speak out against lawful authority? What makes them attack the representatives of that authority—police officers, judges, members of Congress, presidents? Only one thing: lack of respect for authority.

d. Have you ever wondered why European and American cultures have been so opposed to premarital sex? The answer is simple: *prudishness*.

4. While reading her evening newspaper, Jean notices that her congressional representative has voted against a highway proposal that would bring revenue to the area. She recalls that a recent poll of the voters in the district revealed that 63 percent favor the proposal. Concluding that the representative has violated the people's trust, Jean composes an angry letter reminding the representative of his obligation to support the will of the majority. Is Jean guilty of drawing a hasty conclusion? Explain your answer.

5. Ramona and Stuart are arguing over whether their ten-year-old son should have certain duties around the home, such as taking out the garbage and mowing the lawn. Ramona thinks he should. Stuart's response is as follows: "When I was a kid, a close friend of mine was so busy with household chores that he could never play with the rest of the guys. He always had a hurt look on his face then, and as he got older, he became increasingly bitter about it. I vowed a long time ago that I would never burden my son with duties and responsibilities. He'll have more than enough of them when he grows up." Evaluate Stuart's conclusion in light of the chapter.

6. Apply your critical thinking to the following cases. Be especially careful to avoid hasty conclusions.

a. An Oklahoma man was sentenced to ninety-nine years in prison for indecent exposure. The prosecutor was able to ask for and get such a long sentence because the man had eleven prior convictions for burglary. The district attorney explained, "People are just tired of crime—they want the repeat offenders off the streets."[3] Do you support the sentence in this case?

b. A Connecticut teenager who stabbed a neighbor to death argued that he had not been responsible for his actions because at the time he had been possessed by demons. Despite that defense he was found guilty.[4] Do you agree with the verdict in this case?

c. A New York woman was having an argument with her neighbor over their children. In anger she used an anti-Semitic obscenity.

Because it is a misdemeanor in New York to harass others with racial or ethnic slurs, the woman was sentenced to thirty-five hours of community service.[5] Do you think such a law makes sense?

d. A high school anatomy class in Agoura, California, dissects human cadavers as well as cats and frogs. The teacher obtains the bodies from a university medical school.[6] Do you approve of this practice?

e. Some people believe the college degree should be abolished as a job requirement. They reason that because it is possible to be qualified for many jobs without formal academic preparation (or, conversely, to be unprepared for many jobs even with a college degree), the only criterion employers should use for hiring and promoting is ability. Do you agree?

7. *Group discussion exercise:* Discuss one of the cases in application 6 with two or three of your classmates. Try to reach a consensus on the issue, taking special care to avoid hasty conclusions. Be prepared to present your group's view (or the individual views) to the class.

CHAPTER THIRTEEN

UNWARRANTED ASSUMPTION

As we saw in Chapter 12, a conclusion is a judgment made after thinking. (It may be carefully or hastily formed.) We reach conclusions through reasoning. An assumption, on the other hand, is an idea we have in mind without having thought about it. It is not arrived at by reasoning but is merely *taken for granted*.

It is natural to make assumptions. Every day we make hundreds of them. Students walking across campus to class assume that the building is open, that the teacher is still alive and sufficiently motivated to be there, that their watches are accurate in indicating that it is time for class, and that going to class will help them learn the subject (or at least not hinder them from learning it). Without assumptions we would have to ponder every word we utter, every move we make every single moment of every day. Obviously, that would represent an enormous output of energy. The net effect would be to increase our fatigue to an intolerable level and hinder progress.

Fortunately, many of the assumptions we make are warranted. That is, they are justified in the particular circumstances. In the case of the students walking to class, probably every one of the assumptions they make is warranted. The experience of walking to class day after day and finding the building open and the teacher there with a helpful lecture to deliver has made those assumptions reasonable. In fact, even on the first day of class those assumptions would undoubtedly be warranted if the school were accredited and had published a schedule saying that class would be held at that time. (In that case, the justification to assume would not be quite so strong as later in the semester, but the assumptions would still be warranted.)

But what if something unexpected happened? If the class were at 8:00 A.M., the custodian may have neglected to open the door to the building. Or the teacher may have become ill that morning and stayed home. Would that make the students' assumptions that the building would be open and the teacher there unwarranted? No. In such cases we would say that the students were justified in assuming that those things would happen, but they just did not happen. What makes an assumption unwarranted is taking *too much* for granted. For example, if the students had heard on the previous evening's news that the teacher had just been seriously injured in an automobile accident, it would be unwarranted for them to assume he would be in class the next day.

◇ ASSUMPTIONS REFLECT OUTLOOK

All the assumptions discussed so far have concerned relatively routine matters. Yet the network of assumptions people make goes far beyond the routine. It is intimately bound up with their outlook on a large and diverse number of subjects. People may assume that the elected officials of their city, state, and nation are honest and work for the interests of their constituents. Or they may assume the reverse. They may go to the polls each November confident that their vote matters, or they may stay at home on the assumption that it does not. When a world crisis develops that involves the nation (an outbreak of armed conflict is the most dramatic example), people may assume that their country is entirely in the right, or that it is entirely in the wrong, or that some fault lies on each side.

Many people take it for granted that the teachers in their local schools are adequately trained in the subjects they teach, have carefully and fairly worked out their grading systems, and have painstakingly developed meaningful lessons. They may also assume that the school's administrators are aware of what is happening in the various classrooms, have developed precise methods of evaluating faculty performance, and are applying those methods to identify the most and least effective performances. Others, of course, assume exactly the opposite.

Most people hold similar assumptions about other areas of endeavor: about medicine, law, and other professions, about industry, about small and large businesses, about the numerous organizations found in society. And their general assumptions usually govern their particular ones. The person who assumes that all doctors are quacks will be inclined to assume that the particular doctor she visits is also a quack.

Which of those assumptions are warranted? Those supported by sufficient experience. What constitutes "sufficient" depends on the situation; the more general and sweeping the assumption, the more experience is needed. Unfortunately, it is very easy to take too much for granted, to assume something even if we have little or no experience to support it or if our experience leads equally well to an entirely different view.

◇ POPULAR UNWARRANTED ASSUMPTIONS

Many viewers of the Dracula movies assume the main character is purely a fiction. They do so casually, with little or no warrant. But the assumption is unwarranted, for the character could easily have been patterned after a real-life villain. In fact, it was. His name was Vlad Tepes, nicknamed "Draculya." Tepes was a fifteenth-century Rumanian nobleman who ruled so cruelly that peasants of the time regarded him as a human vampire. Though he never bit people's necks and drank their blood, he once invited the poor and sick people of his domain to a large feast and then set fire to the banquet hall. Another time a Turkish ambassador who was visiting him explained that it was the custom of his people not to remove their hats to anyone, so Tepes had the hats of the ambassador and his party nailed to their heads. Certainly his most horrible deed was to have the heads of *twenty thousand* of his victims cut off and mounted on stakes for display.[1]

For decades many Americans assumed that China was a medically backward country. The basis of their assumption was little more than the more general assumption that the Chinese were socially backward. Because China was closed to Westerners, no substantial evidence was obtainable to support *any* assumption about Chinese medicine. So no assumption was warranted. (Since the early 1970s, when visitors were permitted in China, reports have suggested not only that their health care is quite advanced but that in general it is better for the average person than what is available in the United States.[2])

Similarly, the traditional assumption of most Americans about Native American medicine men and women has been that they are charlatans, dispensing superstition that certainly can't help anyone who is really sick. This assumption is not based on any knowledge but merely on a generally derogatory view of Native Americans. Only in the past several decades have people begun to learn the value of their treatments. The National Institute of Mental Health, for example, established a scholarship program to help Navajo Indians study "curing ceremonials" under tribal medicine men and women. One of the supporters of this program, psychiatrist Robert Bergman, knows a medicine man who "apparently cured a psychotic woman after a modern psychiatric hospital had failed to help her."[3]

When the sexual liberation movement was launched in modern America, it was rather widely assumed that sexually promiscuous people are more emotionally healthy and stable than their "straight" neighbors—in other words, that the former do not need the crutch of traditional morality but can choose their behavior freely and independently. Actually, though supported by the existence of sexually oriented magazines, books, and films and by the mood of the time that sexual "rules" are narrow and restricting, there was no evidence linking promiscuity to emotional health. The assumption was probably grounded more in wishful thinking or acceptance of others' wishful thinking than in any experience or evidence. In other words, it was unwarranted. (At least one study suggested that sexual promiscuity is the reverse of what was assumed: not a sign of strength but of deficiency. Dr. I. Emery Breitner claimed the eighty-eight promiscuous people he studied were lonely people looking for companionship and approval and using sex as the means to find it. He termed them "love addicts."[4])

One of the most common unwarranted assumptions is that the present European and American concept of childhood has always existed. However, the only reason why Europeans and Americans take the concept for granted is that they have been familiar with it since their own earliest years. That, of course, is not sufficient reason. Naturally the concept is familiar to them. But they did not experience living and thinking in 3000 B.C. or in A.D. 1500, so they have no warrant to assume that people in those times shared all their concepts and values. Indeed, the barest contact with history gives ample suggestion that concepts and values do change over time.

Was this concept of childhood shared by their ancestors back to the beginning of humanity? No. On the contrary, it is a relatively recent idea, dating back only a few centuries. Before that, children were not considered different from adults in their nature and needs. Examination of the historical accounts, painting, and sculpture of earlier centuries reveals that children were thought of and depicted as little adults. They were expected to perform adult roles and meet adult standards of behavior. Moreover, they were included in adult society.[5] The concept of adolescence as an extended period of emotional upheaval and self-searching is a twentieth-century idea that the ancestors of contemporary Europeans and Americans, as well as people from very different cultures, would find strange and perhaps amusing.

Very likely much of the tension between young people and their parents could be eliminated by a clearer understanding of how dramatically attitudes toward children have changed. As in so many situations, however, such understanding can be reached only when the prevailing assumption is recognized and found unwarranted.

◇ Recognizing Unwarranted Assumptions

It is not too difficult to evaluate an assumption and decide whether or not it is warranted. The real difficulty is in identifying it in the first place. The reason for this is that, unlike the other problems in thinking we have discussed, assumptions are usually *unexpressed*. To recognize the assumptions in your thinking and the thinking of others, develop the habit of reading (and listening) between the lines. In other words, become sensitive to ideas that are not stated but are nevertheless clearly implied. Consider this dialogue:

Cloris: I really don't understand why people make such a fuss about violence in films.
Mavis: They say that violent films harm viewers.
Cloris: That's silly. I've watched them all my life, and I've never done anything violent.

Cloris reasons that if she has watched violent films all her life yet hasn't done anything violent, violence in films can't be harmful. That reasoning reveals two assumptions Cloris may be unaware of. The first is that the only conceivable way for film violence to harm people is by making them violent. Is that assumption warranted? No. There is another way that film violence could conceivably do harm: by making people insensitive to others' pain and complacent about violence in real life. The second assumption is that Cloris's experience is necessarily typical. This assumption is also unwarranted. The possibility exists that Cloris is an exception—in other words, that most people are more affected by vicarious screen experiences than Cloris is.

One final consideration. You may from time to time experience some difficulty deciding whether you are dealing with an oversimplification, a hasty conclusion, or an assumption. The following comparison should help you minimize confusion:

Oversimplification	Hasty Conclusion	Assumption
stated directly	stated directly	unstated but implied
occurs as a simple assertion or as the premise of an argument	occurs as the conclusion of an argument	often is a hidden premise in an argument
distorts reality by misstatement or omission	fails to account for one or more significant items of evidence	may be either warranted (supported by the evidence) or unwarranted

Of course, the conclusion of an argument may be expressed as a simple assertion. How can you be sure that any assertion is not a conclusion (hasty or otherwise) in disguise? Fortunately, the question isn't worth agonizing over. If the context in which you encounter the flawed assertion is not an argument, call it an oversimplification. Reserve the term "hasty conclusion" for situations in which there has been a rush to judgment without proper attention to the evidence. And keep in mind that though precise terminology is laudable, it is not your most important concern. That concern is recognizing errors and being able to explain why they are errors.

❖ APPLICATIONS

1. Evaluate the following argument as you did the arguments in Chapter 2, application 7. First identify the argument's component parts (including hidden premises) and ask relevant questions, as shown in that chapter. Then check the accuracy of each premise, stated or hidden, and decide whether the conclusion is the most reasonable one. Note that checking the accuracy of the premises may require obtaining sufficient evidence to permit a judgment. (Be careful to avoid making unwarranted assumptions.) If you find a premise to be inaccurate or a conclusion to be less than completely reasonable, revise the argument accordingly.

Background note: During his presidency, Ronald Reagan formally proposed a constitutional amendment permitting prayer in the public schools. The wording was as follows: "Nothing in this Constitution shall be construed to prohibit individual or group prayer in public schools or other public institutions. No person shall be required by the United States or by any state to participate in prayer." Though the proposal was not adopted, many people continue to support it. Their reasoning, like Mr. Reagan's, is as follows:

Argument: Prayer should be allowed in public schools because its abolition was a violation of citizens' rights.[6]

2. Examine each of the following dialogues. Identify any assumptions made by the speakers. Be precise. If possible, decide whether the assumptions are warranted.

a. *Olaf:* Did you hear the good news? School may not open on schedule this year.

Olga: How come?

Olaf: The teachers may be on strike.

Olga: Strike? That's ridiculous. They're already making good money.

b. *Janice:* What movie is on at the theater tonight?

Mike: I don't know the title. It's something about lesbians. Do you want to go?

Janice: No thanks. I'll wait for a quality film.

c. *Boris:* Boy, talk about unfair markers. Nelson's the worst.

Bridget: Why? What did he do?

Boris: What did he do? He gave me a D– on the midterm, that's all—after I spent twelve straight hours studying for it. I may just make an appointment to see the dean about him.

d. *Mrs. Smith:* The Harrisons are having marital problems. I'll bet they'll be separating soon.

Mr. Jones: How do you know?

Mrs. Smith: I heard it at the supermarket. Helen told Gail and Gail told me.

Mr. Jones: I knew it wouldn't work out. Jeb Harrison is such a blah person. I can't blame Ruth for wanting to leave him.

3. Apply your critical thinking to the following cases. Be sure to identify all your assumptions and decide whether they are warranted.

a. A Cambridge, Massachusetts, man got tired of looking at his neighbor's uncut lawn and untrimmed shrubs, which reached above the second-story window, and took his grievance to court. The neighbor admitted to the judge that he hadn't cut the lawn in fourteen years, but he argued that he preferred a natural lawn to a manicured one and untrimmed to trimmed shrubs. The judge decided he was perfectly within his legal rights in leaving his lawn and shrubs uncut, regardless of what his neighbor felt.[7] Do you think the judge's decision was fair?

b.   Should parents who feel their college-age sons and daughters are being brainwashed by religious cults be allowed to kidnap their children and have them deprogrammed?

c.   Should parents be allowed to keep their children out of school if they believe they can educate them better at home?

d.   Many motorcyclists object to the laws of some states that require them and their passengers to wear helmets. They believe they should be free to decide for themselves whether to wear a helmet. Do you agree?

4.   *Group discussion exercise:* Discuss one of the cases in application 3 with two or three of your classmates. Try to reach consensus on the issue, taking care to avoid unwarranted assumptions. Be prepared to present your group's view (or the individual views) to the class.

CHAPTER FOURTEEN

LOGICAL FALLACIES

Logical fallacies are errors in reasoning. Logicians have identified dozens of specific fallacies. We have already considered some of the most common ones in previous chapters. In this chapter, we discuss others you are likely to encounter and describe the contexts in which they generally occur.

◇ ERRORS OF PERSPECTIVE

Strictly speaking, errors of perspective are not committed in the process of analyzing an issue or developing a line of thought (though they may manifest themselves then). Rather, they are omnipresent convictions about reality. These errors shape the attitudes we bring to problem solving and decision making, creating expectations that influence our thinking. The fact that errors of perspective tend to exist at the level of assumptions rather than at the level of articulated convictions makes them especially difficult to identify and correct.

ABSOLUTISM

The absolutist perspective is characterized by rigidity, inflexibility, and impatience with ambiguity. Absolutists demand clear-cut, tidy answers.

Because of this, when confronted with complex situations demanding acknowledgment of exceptions and carefully qualified language, they are tempted to oversimplify and reach hasty conclusions.

RELATIVISM

The relativist perspective is the opposite of absolutism. Relativists are committed to subjectivism—the belief that we live in a world of different viewpoints on issues, none of them more worthy than the others. Because of this, when confronted with a problem needing a solution or an issue needing resolution, relativists are forced to choose between contradicting their core belief and indecision.

EITHER-OR THINKING

The either-or perspective holds that the only views one can take of an issue are extreme views: total affirmation or total rejection. It denies us the opportunity even to consider moderate views. However, the most reasonable response to complex issues is very often just such a moderate view, one that incorporates the insights of the various conflicting positions. Thus, either-or thinking condemns us to unreasonableness on many, perhaps most issues.

Whereas absolutists are tempted to ignore the differences in cases, relativists tend to ignore the similarities. Either-or thinkers may see either differences or similarities, but not both. All three perspectives are unreasonably narrow and restricting and therefore inimical to critical thinking.

◇ ERRORS OF PROCEDURE

Errors of procedure occur in the process of analyzing an issue or developing a line of thought. They are generally committed independently of errors of perspective though, as we have noted, they may be influenced by those errors. Two of the errors explained in previous chapters—oversimplification and hasty conclusion—are among the most common errors of procedure.* Here are some others.

---

*The other errors discussed in previous chapters may be variously classified. "Mine is better" thinking is essentially an error of perspective, but can also be an error of procedure or an error of reaction. The same is true of resistance to change, conformity, and stereotyping. Unwarranted assumptions may be errors of either perspective or procedure.

OVERGENERALIZATION

A generalization is a judgment about a class of people or things made after observing or studying a number of members of that class. Overgeneralization exceeds the limitation of the observation or study. The following continuums depict visually the contexts in which overgeneralization usually occurs:

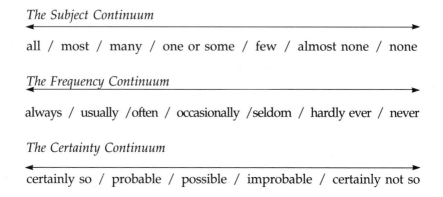

The Subject Continuum

all / most / many / one or some / few / almost none / none

The Frequency Continuum

always / usually /often / occasionally /seldom / hardly ever / never

The Certainty Continuum

certainly so / probable / possible / improbable / certainly not so

On each continuum the center position requires the least supporting evidence. *The amount of evidence needed increases with each division to the right of the center or to the left of the center.* (That, of course, is not to say that the center position always has the weight of probability in its favor or is a safe choice. That may not be the case.)

DOUBLE STANDARD

The double standard consists of using one set of criteria for judging issues that do not concern us or arguments we agree with, and another standard for judging other issues and arguments. This error involves viewing evidence selectively or twisting it to serve our own purposes. Double standard is especially common in situations in which we have a strong commitment to a certain view or action, often because we have chosen it ourselves in similar situations and wish to avoid retroactive self-condemnation.

IRRATIONAL APPEALS

Irrational appeals urge us to accept ideas at face value or on some other basis than reasonableness. They are considered logical fallacies because they say, in effect, "You don't have to think about this matter—there is no danger of error here." And that is itself a serious error. The danger of error always exists, and thinking critically is the best way to minimize that danger.

Irrational appeals usually take one of the following forms:

Appeal to Emotion. This appeal urges the uncritical acceptance of strong feelings—for example, love of family or country, fear, resentment, guilt.

Appeal to Tradition or Faith. This appeal urges maintaining past customs or beliefs not because they are applicable to the present situation, but merely because they have always been maintained.

Appeal to Moderation. An appeal to moderation urges a moderate view not because it is the most reasonable view, but merely because it is inoffensive to anyone.

Appeal to Authority. This appeal urges the unquestioning acceptance of an authority's view. The authority may be a person, a book or document, or an agency (such as the Supreme Court).

Appeal to Common Sense. This appeal is often accompanied by such phrases as "everyone knows that," "no reasonable person would deny that," and "it's common sense." (Many ideas that were at one time accepted as common sense—such as sacrificing young virgins to ensure a good harvest and abandoning deformed babies to die—are now recognized as uncommon nonsense or worse.)

Appeals to emotion, tradition, faith, moderation, authority, or common sense are not *necessarily* irrational. In many cases they are rational— that is, they invite, rather than discourage, critical thinking. Be sure to distinguish between rational and irrational appeals whenever you evaluate issues.

FALSE CAUSE

It is perfectly natural to wonder "Why did this happen?" In fact, one mark of a critical thinker is that she asks this question more frequently than others do. However, she realizes that mere closeness in time does not prove a cause and effect relationship. In other words, one event can follow another by coincidence and thus be entirely unrelated to it.

The fallacy of false cause occurs when coincidence is ignored. It consists of thinking, "If B occurred after A, A must have caused B." This error is undoubtedly the basis of most superstitions. Misfortune befalls someone shortly after he walks under a ladder, or breaks a mirror, or has a black cat cross his path, and he judges that event to be responsible for the misfortune.

Sam is in the habit of arriving late to English class. Yesterday the professor told him that the next time he was tardy, he would be refused admission. Today Sam got a composition back with a grade of D. He reasons that the professor gave him a low grade out of anger over Sam's lateness. Sam has committed the fallacy of false cause. Maybe the professor did lower the grade for that reason, maybe not. Without additional evidence, Sam should withhold judgment.

FALSE ANALOGY

An analogy is a line of reasoning suggesting that things alike in one respect are also alike in other respects. Analogy is acceptable as long *as the similarities claimed are real.* An analogy that suggests similarities that are not real is a faulty analogy. An infamous example is the analogy traditionally invoked by revolutionaries and terrorists around the world to justify killing people: "If you want to make an omelette, you've got to break some eggs." Critical thinking responds "But people are very unlike eggs!"

◇ ERRORS OF REACTION

Errors of reaction occur some time after we have completed the thought process, reached a conclusion, presented our views to others, and received unfavorable criticism and/or a counterargument. These errors are characterized by face-saving defensiveness and unwillingness to accept criticism, even when it is well-intentioned and merited. One error of reaction, rationalization, was discussed in Chapter 9.

ATTACKING THE PERSON

At times, the character of a person is the issue under discussion—for example, in cases where a member of Congress is being investigated for alleged lawbreaking or ethical violations. In such cases, it is appropriate to focus our argument on the person. However, in cases where the issue is an idea, it is inappropriate to focus on the person.

Consider the issue of whether nuclear power plants are a danger to human beings and the environment. Among the supporters of those plants (as among the opponents) there are, presumably, informed people and uninformed, honest and dishonest, emotionally balanced and emotionally unbalanced. If we find a supporter who is uninformed, dishonest, and emotionally unbalanced, what does that tell us about his side of the issue? Nothing at all. It might still be the most reasonable view. The only way to make a decision about an issue is to analyze the issue itself.

STRAW MAN

As the term implies, straw man is an argument without substance. This fallacy consists of pretending one's adversary has said something false, and then proceeding to demonstrate that it is false. Suppose you are debating whether legislation should be enacted restricting the sale of assault weapons. You state that you support such legislation because assault weapons are designed, not for hunting or even for self-defense, but for killing people, often indiscriminately. Your opponent responds, "So *you* believe you should decide what weapons are acceptable and what weapons aren't. It's exactly this kind of arrogance by self-appointed social reformers that everyone who values the Constitution should fear."

Your opponent has committed the straw man fallacy. Perhaps she did so consciously to put you on the defensive. (The best response is to point out what she has done: "First you put irresponsible words in my mouth and then you say I'm irresponsible. I'd prefer to hear your reaction to what I really said.")

SHIFTING THE BURDEN OF PROOF

The error of shifting the burden of proof is also known as the argument from ignorance. It consists of demanding that others disprove our assertions. Let's say Bill asserts, "The greatest single cause of exploding health care costs in this country is unnecessary referral of patients for costly medical testing." Barbara then asks Bill to explain why he believes that to be the case. And he responds, "Can you cite any evidence to disprove it? If you can't, then say so." Bill is guilty of shifting the burden of proof. He made an assertion—he should be ready to support it if asked and not demand that others refute it. The rule is that whoever makes the assertion bears the burden of supporting it, and the more the assertion departs from what knowledgeable people believe, the greater the responsibility of the person making the assertion to support it.

Whenever you are examining your own or other people's arguments critically, searching for fallacies, remember the admonition offered at the end of Chapter 13: Though precise classification of errors is laudable—

"this one is a hasty conclusion," "that one an oversimplification," and so on—it is not your most important concern. That concern is recognizing where reasoning has gone awry and being able to explain why in terms of the issue before you.

⬚ APPLICATIONS

1. Evaluate the following argument as you did the arguments in Chapter 2, application 7. First identify the argument's component parts (including hidden premises) and ask relevant questions, as shown in that chapter. Then check the accuracy of each premise, stated or hidden, and decide whether the conclusion is the most reasonable one. (Be alert for the errors described in this chapter.) Note that checking the accuracy of the premises may require obtaining sufficient evidence to permit a judgment. If you find a premise to be inaccurate or a conclusion to be less than completely reasonable, revise the argument accordingly.

Background note: When lawyers accept a case on a "contingency basis," they charge their clients nothing to initiate the case. Their fee is a percentage of the amount they win by bringing suit. (If they lose the case, the clients pay nothing.)

Argument: One way to reduce the cost of health care in the United States is to ban the legal practice of taking cases on a contingency basis.

2. Examine each of the following arguments carefully. If you are uninformed about the issue it addresses, do some research. Then decide which view of the issue is most reasonable. Be alert for logical fallacies in the arguments themselves and avoid committing fallacies in your reasoning.

a. I never vote in national elections. I figure that my vote will be canceled by someone else's. Besides, all politicians are going to rob the public so it doesn't matter who gets elected.

b. Dogfighting is a sport in which two specially trained dogs (often, but not always, pitbull terriers) do combat until one is killed or badly maimed. It is illegal in most states. But should it be? I say no. If I own a dog, it's my property and I should be able to do whatever I wish with it.

c. Affirmative action originated as a system to overcome the effects of years of prejudice against minorities. But it has created discrimination against the majority. I favor eliminating affirmative action requirements and returning to the old system. For all its imperfections, it's far better than what we have now.

d. Whenever Americans buy automobiles, clothing, and electronic equipment from other countries, they undermine American business and hurt American workers. Patriotism demands that we refrain from buying from foreign competitors even when their prices are lower and their quality is higher.

e. It's absurd to believe in life after death because no one has ever returned from the grave.

f. Women in the military should be required to undergo the same physical training men do. They should also not be exempted from frontline duty.

g. In 1982, New York State Social Services officials directed local adoption agencies not to reject applicants solely because they are homosexual or have a history of alcoholism or drug abuse, a criminal record, a dependency on welfare, or a severe emotional or physical handicap.[1] I think this is outrageous. People who fall into any of these categories are obviously not fit to be parents, and child welfare agencies have an obligation to protect children from them.

h. Every knowledgeable person agrees that the nation's court system is seriously bogged down with cases and that something must be done to alleviate that condition. The best way to do so, I am convinced, is to dispense with the outdated concept of "innocent until proven guilty" and make all those charged with a crime prove their innocence.

i. It's ironic that during the very time when Pete Rose was being castigated for his alleged gambling on sports events, newspapers were filled with stories about the Illinois and Pennsylvania lotteries and their respective $62.5 and $115 million jackpots. Millions of people were placing bets on those lotteries, and dozens of other state lotteries, and that was regarded as perfectly legitimate. And yet a great baseball star was being threatened with disgrace and expulsion from the game he loved. The whole fiasco can be explained only in terms of monumental ignorance or hypocrisy.

j. For the last few decades most Americans have swallowed the liberal line that everyone deserves a college education. As a result, college courses have been watered down and the college degree has been rendered meaningless. It's high time we adopt a more realistic view. College should be reserved for those who have not only taken a demanding high school program, but have excelled in it.

3. *Group discussion exercise:* Select one of the cases you analyzed in application 2 and discuss it with two or three of your classmates. Try to reach a consensus, but be careful to avoid committing logical fallacies. Be prepared to present your idea(s) to the class.

CHAPTER FIFTEEN

THE PROBLEMS IN COMBINATION

We have seen how each of the problems discussed in Chapters 6 through 14 occurs in isolation. Although it is common to find them that way, it is at least as common to find them occurring in various *combinations*. For example, "mine is better" thinking may lead us to resist new ideas that challenge our cherished beliefs. Similarly, the urge to conform may lead us to accept stereotyped images of people and institutions, and these in turn may lead us to make unwarranted assumptions or oversimplify complex situations. The possible combinations that may occur are innumerable, yet they all have one thing in common: Cumulatively they obstruct critical thinking more than any one of their component problems does singly.

◇ EXAMINING THE PROBLEMS IN COMBINATION

Let's examine several combinations of problems closely and determine the specific ways they affect the thinking of the people involved.

- Claude is an active worker for his political party. Because he feels a strong personal identification with the party and is therefore convinced that its platform and its candidates represent the salvation of the country, he is unusually zealous in his efforts. One day he is having lunch with Nell, a business acquaintance. The discussion predictably turns to politics. Claude delivers a few pronouncements on his candidate and the opposition. His candidate, he asserts, is a brilliant theorist and practitioner. Her opponent, in Claude's view, is a complete fool. Claude volunteers harsh judgments of the opponent's political record and of his family and associates and rattles on about how the country will be ruined if he is elected.

After listening for a while, Nell challenges Claude. She quietly presents facts that disprove many of Claude's ideas and points up the extravagance of Claude's assertions. Though there is nothing personal in Nell's challenge, and it is presented in a calm, objective way, Claude becomes angry. He accuses Nell of distorting his words, denies having said certain things that he did say, and stubbornly clings to others despite the facts Nell has presented.

Let's reconstruct what happened in terms of the problems we have been studying. Claude's initial problem was his "mine is better" attitude, which blinded him to the possibility that his candidate and platform were not perfect and that the opposition had some merit. In other words, it made him overvalue the things he identified with and undervalue those he did not. Accordingly, when he spoke about the candidates and the platforms, he was inclined to oversimplify. Then when Nell called his errors to his attention (as someone sooner or later was bound to do), Claude was driven to relieve his embarrassment through face-saving devices. Because the stronger one's commitment, the greater one's reluctance to admit error, Claude undoubtedly learned little from the incident.

- Alma is very conservative in her dress. She strongly resists any fashion change. When miniskirts came back into style, she was scandalized. She was fond of remarking, "Today's designers are nothing but perverts intent on destroying the very idea of modesty and promoting moral decay."

  Like Claude, Alma was the victim of a combination of problems. Her resistance to change led her to see only the worst possibilities in the new and to exaggerate the importance of the matter. This perspective caused her to form a hasty conclusion about the character and intentions of miniskirt designers and to overgeneralize that conclusion to *all* designers.

- Ten years ago, Sam fell in with a group of sexually promiscuous people. At first he had some reservations about becoming involved with them. After all, their attitudes toward sex and marriage were very unlike those he had grown up with. But the group seemed so exciting, so modern, so "relevant." Sam wanted very much to be accepted and approved by them. Once he was part of the group, he began buying books that glorify group sex and attack traditional attitudes toward sexuality and attending lectures calling sexual promiscuity an enlightened, liberated practice. Now Sam assumes that all sexually promiscuous people are intellectually courageous and emotionally healthy, and that monogamous people are unthinking, frightened, and repressed. Furthermore, he believes that warnings about AIDS are based on a puritanical aversion to sexual expression.

Sam's urge to conform was too strong for his own good. His desire to be popular, to belong to the "in" crowd, overrode his individuality. He did not join the group out of conviction, after thinking carefully about its good and bad points and weighing its values. He joined merely out of a desire to be included. This conformist urge also led him to suspend his critical sense. Instead of remaining reasonably open-minded after joining the group and reading both favorable and unfavorable analyses of promiscuity, he ignored all unfavorable, and even all mixed, views. This narrow, sheltered perspective eventually resulted in his making unwarranted assumptions about the promiscuous and non-promiscuous alike, based on stereotyped views of both. It also caused him to adopt a foolish position concerning the danger of AIDS.

◇ Avoiding the Problems in Combination

When combinations of problems occur, the effect is to multiply the obstacles to critical thinking. One error reinforces another, triggers a third, and so on. Moreover, though such chain reactions usually occur in one area—with Claude it was politics, with Alma fashion, with Sam sex—they often spread and influence our thinking in other areas as well. A person who indulges unthinking reactions to one aspect of life will very likely become more unthinking, not less. The reason is simple. Given the complexity of many everyday problems and the general temptation to deal with them in the easiest, quickest way possible, ready-made pat answers have a certain undeniable appeal.

The first and most important step in solving these problems in combination, like the first step in solving them individually, is to recognize that you are prone to them. They are not the "other person's" problems. Nor do they afflict only the uneducated or less intelligent. They can be found in varying degrees in all people.

Another helpful step is to remind yourself from time to time what each problem consists of and how you can most effectively deal with it. To help you do this, here is a brief summary of all the problems discussed in Chapters 6 through 14.

The Problems	*How to Recognize and Deal with Them*
"Mine is better"	Preferring your own ideas for no other reason than that they are yours. Remind yourself that all people tend to regard their ideas that way, but critical thinking demands that you examine your ideas as you would other people's.
Bias toward change	Preferring innovative to traditional ideas (or vice versa). Expect your first reaction to new ideas to be favorably (or unfavorably) biased. Set aside that reaction and judge the idea on the basis of your critical appraisal.
Conformity	Thinking the way others do because of the group or your desire to belong. (Or, conversely, thinking the way others do *not*, simply because they do not.) Base your thinking on the evidence and not on how others do or don't think.
Face-saving	Attempting to preserve your self-image or the image you project to others when some unpleasant reality threatens it. Distinguish between what you wish were so and what is so. Be honest with yourself.
Stereotyping	Making fixed, unbending generalizations about people, places, or things. Remind yourself that most

things do not fit into neat categories. In addition, resist the feeling that you *know* what the correct judgment is when that feeling arises early in the information-gathering process.

Oversimplification	Simplifying that does not merely scale down complex matters to more manageable proportions but twists and distorts them. Be sure your views are an accurate representation of reality.
Hasty conclusions	Judgments made before sufficient evidence is obtained. Withhold judgment until you have answered all important questions pertaining to the issue. If you must answer without sufficient evidence, use the "If . . . then" approach. If the evidence will support probability but not certainty, limit your conclusion to one that is merely probable.
Unwarranted assumptions	Erroneous ideas that you have in mind and that influence your reasoning without your being conscious of that influence. Develop the habit of reading (and listening) between the lines for ideas that are unexpressed but nevertheless clearly implied. Decide whether they are warranted.
Logical fallacies	Specific errors that occur in your reasoning about issues. Monitor your thinking for signs of these errors, especially when you are planning an oral or written presentation of your views.

⌗ APPLICATIONS

1. Evaluate the following arguments as you did the arguments in Chapter 2, application 7. First identify the argument's component parts (including hidden premises) and ask relevant questions, as shown in that chapter. Then check the accuracy of each premise, stated or hidden, and decide whether the conclusion is the most reasonable one. (Be alert for the errors summarized in this chapter.) Note that checking the accuracy of the premises may require obtaining sufficient evidence to permit a judgment. If you find a premise to be inaccurate or a conclusion to be less than completely reasonable, revise the argument accordingly.

> **a.** *Background note: In recent years an increasing number of people have complained about the level of violence and the amount of sexual material on television. Television industry spokespeople have generally dismissed the complaints, reasoning as follows:*
>
> *Argument:* Contemporary shows depict life more realistically than shows of twenty or thirty years ago. Our position is that such depiction does not cause or aggravate social problems, so until research proves otherwise, we will continue to produce programming that tells the truth about life, honestly and fearlessly.
>
> **b.** *Background note: In recent years a number of states have considered enacting "hate crime statutes," which assign harsher penalties for crimes in which the motivation was hatred of the victim's race, religion, or sexual orientation. In other words, the penalty for beating and robbing a black (or Jewish) victim while shouting racial (or anti-Semitic) epithets would be greater than that for the same act perpetrated against a white (or gentile) victim minus the epithets.*
>
> *Argument:* The law is a good one because greater emotional harm is done to the victim when the crime is motivated by hatred.

2. Analyze each of the following cases as the chapter does with the cases of Claude, Alma, and Sam:

> **a.** A middle-aged couple, Ann and Dan, learn that their twenty-two-year-old daughter, a senior in college, is a lesbian. They are appalled. They were raised to believe that lesbianism is willful moral degeneracy. Struggling to cope with their new awareness, each begins to blame the other—Ann suggests Dan has always been cold and aloof with the girl, and Dan is sure Ann has been too close to her, has smothered her with affection. After many hours of arguing, they decide that there is a more direct cause of her deviance—the

college. "You'd think educated people would be alert to the danger of degeneracy with all the girls crammed into dorms," Ann cries. Dan shouts, "Damn it, I'm going to send a letter to the chairman of that college's board of trustees. I want the dean of students fired."

b. Stephen enrolls as a freshman at Progress Technical College. He notices that he has an eight o'clock English class three days a week. Because he's a late riser, this disturbs him. But when he attends the first class, he notices that the instructor's name is Stein. "Wow," he thinks to himself, "what better break could a Jewish kid who likes to sleep in the morning have than a Jewish instructor!" Over the next few weeks, he seizes any excuse to stay after class, talk with Mr. Stein, and win his favor. For his first two compositions, Stephen chooses subjects that will permit him to stress his Jewishness (and thereby impress Mr. Stein). Soon he decides that Mr. Stein "understands" him. He begins to miss class occasionally and hands in about one assignment out of four. When he sees Mr. Stein, Stephen plies him with pathetic tales of misfortune. His mid-term grade is D, but he tells himself that Mr. Stein is just trying to scare him and will raise his grade in the end. Thus he attends class even less frequently and does less work. Eventually the semester ends, and he receives an F in English. His first reaction is disbelief. He rushes to see Mr. Stein, who says, "I made clear on the first day of class that students could expect to pass only if they attended class and did their homework faithfully. I'm sorry about the grade, but you deserve it." From that moment on, Stephen refuses to speak to Mr. Stein when he passes him on campus. And whenever the conversation in the snack bar or dorm turns to teachers, he loudly denounces Mr. Stein as a phony.

3. Three Southern California professors of medicine devised a hoax as an experiment. They paid a professional actor to lecture three groups of educators. Armed with a fake identity, "Dr. Myron L. Fox of the Albert Einstein University," false but impressive credentials, and a scholarly sounding topic, "Mathematical Game Theory as Applied to Physical Education," the actor proceeded to present one meaningless, conflicting statement after another. His words were a combination of double-talk and academic jargon. During the question and answer period, he made even less sense. *Yet not one of the fifty-five educators in his audience realized they had been tricked.* Virtually all of them believed they had learned something. Some even praised the impostor in this manner: "Excellent presentation, enjoyed listening. Has warm manner . . . lively examples. . . extremely articulate."[1] Explain what combination of the problems in Chapters 6 through 14 may have accounted for the audience's gullibility.

4. Determine your position on each of the following cases, being sure to avoid all the problems reviewed in this chapter.

a. When Alabama prisons and jails became seriously overcrowded, a U.S. district judge ordered that more than 300 convicts be granted early release. The group included murderers, rapists, and repeat offenders. The judge's argument was that serious overcrowding in prisons and jails is a violation of prisoners' rights against "cruel and unusual punishment."[2] Do you share the judge's view?

b. U.S. law has accorded most charitable and educational groups tax-exempt status as long as they refrain from lobbying activities. However, veterans groups like the American Legion and the Veterans of Foreign Wars were traditionally regarded as exceptions; that is, they were permitted to lobby extensively on such issues as the ratification of the Panama Canal treaties, Alaskan national parks, national security, and Saturday mail delivery (as well as issues more directly involving veterans) without jeopardizing their tax-exempt status. Then in 1982 a federal appeals court eliminated special treatment for veterans groups, arguing that it violated the equal protection guarantees of the Constitution.[3] Do you agree with this court decision?

5. Evaluate each of the following arguments carefully. Determine what the most reasonable position is and what makes it so. Avoid the problems in thinking reviewed in this chapter. (Be careful not to assume that the view expressed here necessarily contains errors. It may be error-free!)

a. For years criminals have sold the rights to their life stories to publishers and movie producers. The more terrible their crimes, the more money publishers and producers have usually been willing to pay. This practice in effect rewards criminals for their crimes. This practice should be ended. The profits criminals receive in this manner should be placed in a fund to be distributed among the victims of their crimes.

b. The New Testament contains these words from St. Paul: "Let every person be in subjection to the governing authorities. For there is no authority except from God, and those which exist are established by God. Therefore he who resists authority has opposed the ordinance of God; and they who have opposed will receive condemnation upon themselves. For rulers are not a cause of fear for good behavior, but for evil. Do you want to have no fear of authority? Do what is good, and you will have praise from the same. . . . Wherefore it is necessary to be in subjection, not only because of wrath, but also for conscience' sake."[4] It is clear from these words that all Christians have an obligation to be loyal to their country's government and not to challenge it. Therefore, Christians who live in the United States do wrong when they join any protest movement and even when they support protest movements in foreign countries—for example, the Solidarity movement in Poland.

c. There is a widespread notion in the United States that the censorship of books and other materials that are found objectionable is an undemocratic action. That notion is false. If a book or magazine or stereo record or videotape contains ideas that are philosophically alien to the American way of life, it is not only the right but the duty of responsible citizens to remove it from circulation. This duty is especially strong in the case of our children. We would not stand idly by and allow our children or our neighbor's children to drink poison. We would take it from them and dispose of it. Why should we be any less vigilant about what is poison to the mind than what is poison to the body?

d. In recent years, restrictions on smoking have increased. Whereas smokers used to be free to light up anywhere at any time, the anti-smoking lobby has managed to eliminate smoking on most airline flights, in many offices, and in a variety of public places. In addition, it has brought about the segregation of smokers in restaurants. All these actions are a denial of smokers' rights. The health risks of smoking have been overstated, but even so, if I choose to take risks with my health, that is my business and no one else's. If a co-worker doesn't want my smoke to drift her way, she has only to buy a small air purifier. If airline passengers want a special nonsmoking section for themselves, I won't object—but they have no business objecting when I demand a smoking section.

e. In 1983 the U.S. Supreme Court ruled that a driver's refusal to take a blood alcohol test can be used as evidence against him or her.[5] I believe the Court erred in making that decision. One reason for refusing to take a blood alcohol test is knowledge of one's drunken condition. But that is not the only possible reason. It's possible for a sober person to refuse the test because he sees it as an invasion of privacy. In such a case the "evidence" would probably be interpreted by the judge and the jury as a sign of guilt and an innocent person would be convicted.

f. A woman wrote to "Dear Abby," complaining that her son was taking his fiancée's name when they married. Abby replied that the young man was an adult and free to make his own decision, so the mother should accept the situation gracefully. In my opinion, this was terrible advice. When a man caves in to his fiancée's pressure in this way, the marriage gets off to a bad start. Besides, there's something bizarre and unmanly about a man's giving up his family name. His family has a right to expect that he will maintain the family name. It has always been so and should continue to be.

g.   On some campuses, when damage occurs on a dormitory floor and the person responsible is not identified, repair costs are charged to all those who live on the floor. This policy is unjust. Sometimes damage is done by strangers who are visiting the dormitory. And even in cases where the guilty party lives on the floor, it is unfair to charge innocent people, many of whom may not even know when or by whom the damage was done. If college authorities cannot determine who is responsible, no one should be charged.

6.   *Group discussion exercise:* Select one of the cases you analyzed in application 5 and discuss it with two or three of your classmates. Try to reach a consensus on the issue, but be careful to avoid committing the errors reviewed in this chapter. Be prepared to present your idea(s) to the class.

III

A STRATEGY

CHAPTER SIXTEEN

KNOWING YOURSELF

Western philosophy virtually began with Socrates' advice, "Know thyself." Ever since, thoughtful men and women have realized that knowing oneself is the key to wisdom. Why is self-knowledge so important? Because so many of the obstacles to clear thinking are found not in the problems we must deal with, but in ourselves.

Of course, innumerable factors contribute to how we feel and think and act. To be complete, any inventory of them would have to include answers to the following questions:

Am I quiet or talkative? Generally optimistic or pessimistic? Hardworking or lazy? Fearful or brave? Serious or easygoing? Modest or proud? Competitive or noncompetitive? Am I nervous or at ease with strangers? Do I retain my poise and presence of mind in emergencies? Am I confident in everything I do? Do I resent certain types of people (the popular classmate, for example)? Would I be more accurately classified as a leader or a follower?

How trustworthy am I? Can I keep a secret or must I reveal it to at least one or two others? Am I loyal to my friends? Do I ever "use" people? How sensitive am I to the feelings of others? Do I ever purposely hurt others? Am I jealous of anyone? Do I enjoy causing trouble, sowing seeds of suspicion and dissension among people? Do I rush to spread

149

the latest gossip? Do I talk behind friends' backs? Are my comments about others usually favorable or unfavorable? Do I criticize others' real or imagined faults as a means of boosting my own ego? Do I keep my promises? How tolerant am I of people's faults and mistakes?

Am I truthful with other people? With myself? How objective am I in assessing my skills and talents? How intelligent am I? How studious am I in school? How many different roles do I play with other people? Which of those roles are authentic? Which are masks designed to hide parts of myself I would be ashamed or embarrassed to have others see? How reasonable are my plans for the future? Do I work well under pressure?

◇ CRITICAL THINKING INVENTORY

In addition to the foregoing questions, numerous questions are suggested by the previous fifteen chapters. The following questions will help you take inventory of the habits and attitudes that affect your thinking:

1. Exactly what influences have shaped my identity? How have they done so? How has my self-image been affected? In what situations am I less an individual because of these influences?

2. In what ways am I like the good thinker (as outlined in Chapter 2)? In what ways like the poor thinker? What kinds of situations seem to bring out my best and worst qualities?

3. To what extent has my perspective on truth tended to be reasonable? (See Chapter 3 again, if necessary.)

4. How careful am I about separating hearsay and rumor from fact? About distinguishing known from assuming or guessing? How difficult is it for me to say "I don't know"?

5. How consistent am I in taking the trouble to make my opinions informed?

6. To what extent do I think that "mine is better" (not only the personal "mine," but the ethnocentric "mine," as well)? In what ways has this kind of thinking affected my view of personal problems and public issues? To what extent does it affect my ability to listen to those who disagree with me, my ability to control my emotions, my willingness to change my mind and revise a judgment?

7. In what matters am I most biased toward change? Am I overly accepting or resistant to change? What is the cause of this tendency? Insecurity? Fear? If fear, of what?

8. To what or whom do I feel the strongest urge to conform? In what situations has this conformist tendency interfered with my judgment?

9. How strong is my need to save face? What aspect of my image is most precious to me? Which of my roles am I most sensitive about? Which people am I most anxious to have think well of me? In what situations have my face-saving maneuvers corrupted my thinking?

10. Do I tend to make hard generalizations (stereotypes) about members of my own race or other races? Religions? Political or social organizations? Any of the other people, places, or ideas mentioned in Chapter 10? What caused me to first form those stereotyped views? In what ways have those views interfered with my evaluation of particular people, places, or ideas?

11. To what extent do I tend to oversimplify complex matters? Am I just unwilling to take the trouble to learn the truth in its complexity? Or do I feel threatened by answers that are not neat and tidy? What has made me this way?

12. To what extent do I tend to jump to conclusions? Do I tend to do so in some areas but not in others? If so, which areas? And why the difference? Do I draw my conclusions prematurely out of convenience? If so, is my purpose to sound authoritative and impress people? In what recent situations have I formed hasty conclusions?

13. Am I aware of the degree to which I assume certain things to be so? In what matters am I most inclined to assume too much, to take too much for granted?

14. Which of my beliefs have been influenced by the various logical fallacies?

   Errors of perspective—absolutism, relativism, either-or thinking

   Errors of procedure—overgeneralization, double standard, irrational appeals, false cause, faulty analogy

   Errors of reaction—attacking the person, straw man, shifting the burden of proof

15. To what extent have the above problems combined to undermine my thinking about important personal and public issues?

16. Which of the problems in questions 1 through 15 interfere with my thinking most frequently and significantly?

◇ USING YOUR INVENTORY

As important as the foregoing questions are, there is one question that is considerably more important: *How can you most effectively use your per-*

sonal inventory to improve your critical thinking performance? The answer is by following these steps:

> First, answer all the questions in the critical thinking inventory honestly and thoroughly, acknowledging not only the pleasant facts about yourself, but also the unpleasant ones. (If you ignore the latter, they will influence you no less; in fact, your refusal to face them may intensify the harm they do.)

> Next, reflect on your answers, noting the areas in which you are especially vulnerable. Don't expect to be equally vulnerable in all circumstances; it is common for some to be more troublesome than others. Your goal here is to know your intellectual habits so well that you can predict exactly which thinking problem will arise for you in any particular situation.

> Finally, whenever you are addressing an issue, anticipate what problems are likely to undermine your thinking, and make a conscious effort to resist their influence.

◇ CHALLENGE AND REWARD

It is one thing to understand the steps to improving your thinking and quite another to use them effectively. The latter task is a formidable challenge. It will take continuing effort over a long period of time.

Is the challenge worth the effort? Let's consider what is known about the role of thinking in everyday life. The most respected educators stress the importance of getting beyond mere memorizing and reflecting on the significance and application of facts. Thinking skill is necessary to understand and profit from college courses. Business and professional leaders stress that proficiency in thinking is necessary to solve problems and make decisions on the job. (All the books written in recent years about excellence underline the value of thinking skills.)

In addition, more and more psychologists affirm that thinking skills play a crucial role in our personal lives. The leading form of psychotherapy in this country, in fact, is cognitive therapy. This therapy is based on the idea that most mental problems (neuroses) result from faulty thinking habits. Noted psychologist Albert Ellis, founder of the Institute of Rational-Emotive Therapy, claims, "Man can live the most self-fulfilling, creative, and emotionally satisfying life by intelligently organizing and disciplining his thinking."

Like other famous psychologists before him, Ellis notes that to organize our thinking we must wrestle with our own negative tendencies. "As Freud and his daughter Anna accurately observed," he says, "and as Adler agreed, humans are prone to avoid focusing on and coping with their problems and instead often sweep them under the rug by resorting to rationalization, denial, compensation, identification, projection, avoidance, repression, and other defensive maneuvers."

In short, though the challenge of improving your thinking is great, no other kind of self-improvement can affect every area of your life so positively.

▨ APPLICATIONS

1. Examine yourself in light of the questions presented in the chapter. Don't settle for things you already know about yourself. Try to expand your self-awareness. And don't ignore your less favorable characteristics. Discuss the results of your self-examination.

2. Evaluate the following arguments as you did the arguments in Chapter 2, application 7. First identify the argument's component parts (including hidden premises) and ask relevant questions, as shown in that chapter. Then check the accuracy of each premise, stated or hidden, and decide whether the conclusion is the most reasonable one. (Be alert for any problems noted in your personal inventory.) Note that checking the accuracy of the premises may require obtaining sufficient evidence to permit a judgment. If you find a premise to be inaccurate or a conclusion to be less than completely reasonable, revise the argument accordingly.

   a. *Background note: The increase in juvenile crime around the nation has led many concerned people to consider more effective ways of addressing the problem.*

   Argument: Children's behavior is a direct reflection of the quality of their upbringing, so when a juvenile commits a crime, his or her parents should be held equally responsible. In other words, the parents should be co-defendants in any civil or criminal action brought against a juvenile.

   b. *Argument:* Animals and the environment—including rivers, lakes, oceans, forests, and beaches—are as entitled to an undisturbed existence as humans. Therefore, the government should enact laws acknowledging and protecting the rights of animals and the environment.

3. Apply your critical thinking to each of the following cases. Make a conscious effort to apply your new self-knowledge, anticipate the problems in thinking to which you will be vulnerable, and resist their influence on your judgment.

a. Some educators are urging that colleges become more selective than they have been in the past few decades. Specifically, these people propose that remedial courses be eliminated and entrance requirements tightened. This would mean that students who are deficient in basic skills, had poor marks in high school, or did poorly on admissions tests would not be accepted for college. Do you agree with this view?

b. The San Francisco Board of Supervisors approved an ordinance that would allow "live-in lovers" to qualify for the city's employee insurance programs. The measure was designed to allow homosexuals and unmarried heterosexuals to establish domestic partnerships and qualify for the same life and health insurance benefits traditionally limited to husbands and wives. Many people, including a majority of the gay community, endorsed the proposal. Others opposed it. The *San Francisco Examiner*, for example, editorialized against it, reasoning that "the notion that an unmarried relationship is the equivalent of marriage is an attack on social norms." The mayor vetoed the proposal.[1] Do you believe she was correct in doing so?

c. An outstanding senior English major (with a 3.7 grade point average out of a possible 4.0) at Princeton University submitted an analysis of a novel for her Spanish-American novel course. Her professor determined that the paper was plagiarized—that is, that it was copied, virtually word for word, from a scholarly reference work without proper acknowledgments. The student subsequently claimed she had committed only a "technical error." The case was referred to a faculty–student committee on discipline, which, after a hearing, recommended withholding the student's degree for one year and notifying the law schools to which she had applied of the details of the decision. Believing the penalty was too harsh, the student took the matter to court.[2] Do you believe the committee's decision was too harsh?

d. A federal court has ruled that Christmas (like Hanukkah, Easter, and Passover) may be observed in the public schools as a cultural event but not as a religious holiday. Educational lawyers interpret that as meaning that songs like *Silent Night* may be sung in a class learning about religious customs or in a music appreciation class but not as a religious celebration.[3] Do you support the idea of banning all religious celebrations from the schools in this manner?

e.   When Elizabeth Taylor learned that a TV movie based on her life was in preparation, she went to court to block its production, claiming that the so-called docudrama was "simply a fancy new name for old-fashioned invasion of privacy, defamation, and violation of an actor's rights." Some people would say her request should have been denied because it represents censorship. What do you think? (Would you think differently if the docudrama concerned the life of a deceased celebrity, like Elvis Presley?)[4]

f.   Shirley MacLaine, the well-known actress, is also a best-selling author. In her books she claims to have lived a number of former lives. For example, she says she once lived as a male teacher who committed suicide on the lost continent of Atlantis.[5] Do you find such claims believable?

4.   *Group discussion exercise:* Select one of the cases you analyzed in application 3 and discuss it with two or three of your classmates. Try to reach a consensus on the issue. Be prepared to present your idea(s) to the class.

CHAPTER SEVENTEEN

BEING OBSERVANT

French chemist Louis Pasteur once said, "Chance favors the prepared mind." True enough. He might have added that it also favors the observant eye. Many obvious things wait to be seen, and yet we never notice them. What color eyes does your father have? What is your mother's favorite color? What is the pattern of the wallpaper in your dining room? How many of the houses on your street have white roofs?

Being observant is not merely an interesting quality that livens our days. Clear and sound thinking often depends on subtleties that are revealed only by close observation. If there are gaps in our seeing and hearing, then there is less chance that the perceptions we base our judgments on will be complete and accurate. In addition, the keener our observation, the less likely it is that we will be slaves to stereotypes, oversimplifications, and unwarranted assumptions.

◇ OBSERVING PEOPLE

What people say and the way they say it (and sometimes what they *omit* saying) can be valuable clues to their unspoken views and attitudes. Noticing these things can help us decide which areas are sensitive to people, which their understanding seems weak in, and what approaches would be most fruitful in communicating with them.

When they are listening, people give certain signals to indicate approval or disapproval of what is being said. An occasional nodding of the head, an encouraging smile, even a low "uh-huh" of assent all signal "I'm in agreement with you." On the other hand, a slight shaking of the head, a raising of an eyebrow, a pursing of the lips as the eyes roll upward, a frown, all suggest at least partial disagreement. Similarly, people who are bored with a discussion will usually betray this feeling even if they are trying not to. The way they glance at their watches, sigh resignedly, turn their attention to someone or something outside the expected focus, nervously fidget with an article of their clothing, or shift position frequently communicates their wish to change the subject or their companions.

A great deal can be told from even a simple exchange of greetings by two people passing each other. Merely the tone in which the greeting is expressed can suggest whether the people like and respect each other and whether they consider each other equals. None of these reactions, however subtle, are missed by observant people. And, as may be obvious, aside from the benefits to their thinking, careful attention is a great aid in making people more sensitive to and thoughtful of others.

A student in a writing class raises his hand and asks the teacher if he can borrow a pen. (The class is in its ninth week and the in-class writing assignment was announced during the previous class.) The instructor gives him a long searching look, slowly reaches into her pocket and extracts a pen, walks in a labored step to the student's desk, and hands it to him. No words have been spoken. No obvious gestures have signaled the instructor's displeasure. But if the student is observant, he will have seen the displeasure in the look and the resigned, "what's the use" gait.

Good detectives are observant. They know that one small, easily overlooked clue can mean the difference between a solved and an unsolved case. Similarly, every good trial lawyer must be a studious observer of people. The nervous glance of a witness when a certain aspect of the case is mentioned can suggest the most productive line of questioning. Likewise, we can conduct our critical thinking more effectively if we observe other people's behavior carefully.

◇ OBSERVATION IN SCIENCE AND MEDICINE

We owe today's knowledge of the causes and treatments of heart attack in part to the careful observation of one doctor. Dr. James B. Herrick was the first physician ever to diagnose a heart attack in a living patient. He did so without benefit of blood tests or electrocardiograms. In doing so, he opened the door to the modern era in heart care. Until that time heart attacks were not recognized as a disease. The symptoms that even lay people have learned to recognize today were, until Herrick's discovery, regarded as "acute indigestion." Herrick established that most heart attacks are due to a clot in a coronary artery and that such an attack need not be fatal. (Interestingly, Herrick had earlier discovered the disease known as sickle-cell anemia.)[1]

Another well-known and extremely fortuitous occasion when the power of observation paid handsome dividends for humanity took place in 1929. Sir Alexander Fleming accidentally contaminated a staphylococcus culture with a mold. He noticed that the staph colonies began to undergo dissolution. Recognizing the great value of whatever substance in the mold had caused the dissolution, Fleming turned his attention to the mold. Eventually he isolated the substance that has since saved countless millions of lives—penicillin. A few years earlier, in 1922, Fleming had made another dramatic discovery. He had had a cold and a runny nose. As he was working with a glass plate on which bacteria were growing, a drop from his nose fell onto the plate. In a short time he noticed that the drop had destroyed some of the bacteria. Thus, he discovered a substance called lysozyme, a protein and enzyme also found in saliva and tears. Now some researchers believe that lysozyme may play a part in controlling cancer.[2]

The French Nobel Prize–winning molecular biologist Jacques Monod owes to his casual yet observant browsing through statistics his discovery that manic depression is genetically linked. He explains how it happened as follows:

> One day I was getting bored at one of the committee meetings we are always having to attend. I was leafing through some statistics from psychiatric hospitals, and I noted with amazement, under manic depressives, that women outnumbered men two to one. I said to myself, "That must have a genetic origin, and can mean only one thing; it is traceable to a dominant gene linked to sex."[3]

Note that though Monod's insight initially occurred to him as a conviction (it "can mean only one thing"), he did not treat it as such. Rather, he made it a scientific hypothesis and set about to test it. That was wise because—his positive phrasing notwithstanding—the idea could have turned out to be a fallacy of false cause (see Chapter 14).

◇ THE RANGE OF APPLICATION

Countless examples of the benefits of close observation could be cited in every occupation and activity in life. Two cases will serve to illustrate the range of application.

In a small upstate New York town, a steam foreman named Eric Houck was degreasing valves. One of the valves accidentally fell into a can of chemicals used to clean garbage cans. Houck grabbed an old stick and fished the valve from the can. As he did so, he noticed that the stick came out clean. The chemicals had stripped off the grime and paint. His curiosity aroused, Houck applied the chemicals to an old chair. It too came out clean to the bare wood. Since that happy discovery, Eric Houck has built a thriving furniture-stripping business, with more than 200 franchises operating in thirty-five states. All this has come from a chance happening that the average person would probably not even have noticed.

In the late 1950s, John T. Molloy was an instructor in a Connecticut prep school. He began to observe some connection between the kind of shoes a teacher wore and student performance. An instructor who wore laced shoes seemed to get consistently better results than one who wore penny loafers. Molloy was intrigued by this apparent connection. He began to conduct a number of experiments. He concluded that the light-colored work clothing worn by the Boston Strangler had apparently inspired trust in his victims. Molloy also found that secretaries more willingly follow the directions of people whose dress and manner suggest position and authority than they do those of people with a shabby appearance.

These observations have enabled Molloy to build a very successful "wardrobe engineering" consulting business (his services are sought by numerous executives) and to author the popular book *Dress for Success*.

For most of us, being observant may not have the dramatic results it did for Houck and Molloy. Nevertheless, it can help us relate more meaningfully to people and learn more about the things around us. Most importantly, it can aid our critical thinking.

◇ BECOMING MORE OBSERVANT

The way to be observant is to use all five of our senses to keep our minds from wandering aimlessly. Too often people are unobservant because they are too absorbed in themselves—their own thoughts and feelings. When they speak, they are so busy forming their words and enjoying the sound of their voices that they forget their listeners. Observant people, on the other hand, have learned how to get outside themselves, to be constantly in touch with what is happening around them.

A good way to start becoming more observant is to practice receiving sense impressions more attentively. At the next meeting of an organization you belong to or in the next discussion in your dorm, try to notice things you would normally miss—objects in the room, the arrangement of the furniture, the positions of the people in relation to one another, the subtle reactions of people during the discussion. The next time you are walking to the store or the movies, try to see how many things you've been missing. Which houses are best cared for? How many people smile and nod or otherwise greet you? What activities are people you pass engaged in? Do they seem to be enjoying what they are doing? How many different sounds do you hear? Which sounds dominate? Are they pleasant or harsh? How many different styles of walking can you detect among the people you pass?

When you are reading a magazine or newspaper or watching TV, look for the significance of things. Consider the connections between ideas, even among apparently unrelated ones. An article about an astronomer's location of a new phenomenon in the heavens may reveal something about concentration and mental discipline. A TV show about the effects of negligence and abuse on children may suggest a new perspective on marriage or divorce or the Hollywood image of romance.

◇ REFLECTING ON YOUR OBSERVATIONS

Observation will sometimes, by itself, bring valuable insights. But you can increase the number and quality of your insights by developing the habit of reflecting on your observations. The best way to do this is to set aside a special time every day—early in the morning, perhaps, or late in the evening (but not when you are exhausted). It needn't be long; ten or fifteen minutes may be enough. But be sure you are free of distractions. Review what you have seen and heard during the past twenty-four hours. Ask yourself what it means, how it relates to other important matters, and how you can use it to improve yourself or to spur achievement.

Let's say that you heard this proverb earlier today: "To be content with little is difficult; to be content with much, impossible." Reflecting on it might lead you to the conclusion that popular culture's emphasis on possessing things—new cars, stylish clothes, and so on—is a false value, that material wealth can never guarantee happiness.

Or you may have read the news that a Michigan court ruled that a fetus may be considered a person in a wrongful death lawsuit. A man's wife and sixteen-week-old fetus were killed after she swerved her car to avoid hitting an unleashed dog. The man sued the dog's owners. (This decision departed from previous court rulings in Michigan that a fetus is not a person until it can survive outside the uterus.)[4] Here your reflection might lead you to consider the implications of this ruling for the issue of abortion.

APPLICATIONS

1. Select a place where you can observe other people, as suggested in this chapter—the campus snack bar, for example, or a dormitory lounge. Go there and stay at least half an hour. Try to notice more than the obvious. Look for subtleties, things you'd normally miss. Take notes on what you observe.

2. Ask your instructor in this course or one of your other courses for permission to visit another of his or her sections. Go to that class and observe carefully the reactions of individual students—for example, the subtle indications they give of attention or inattention. Take notes.

3. Make yourself look as sloppy and scruffy as you can. Put on old, wrinkled clothes. Mess up your hair. Rub dirt on your face and arms. Then go into a store and ask a clerk for assistance. Speak to other customers. Check the clerk's reaction to you and the reactions of other customers. A day or so later return to the same store looking your very neatest and cleanest. Speak and act in the same manner. Note people's reactions. Compare them with those you got the first time.

4. How mannerly are the students, faculty, and staff at your college? To answer this question, observe their behavior in various campus situations, noting examples of courtesy and rudeness.

5. Many people have become so accustomed to advertisements that they no longer examine them carefully and critically. Look closely at the advertising you encounter in a typical day in newspapers and magazines, on television, and elsewhere. Determine what appeals are used to

elicit a favorable response from you and how much specific information about the products or services is presented in the advertisements. Record your observations.

6. Practice reflecting, as explained in this chapter, on the following quotations:

> If I am not for myself, who will be? But if I am only for myself, what am I?
> Rabbi Hillel

> Travel makes a wise man better but a fool worse.
> Thomas Fuller

> It is not easy to find happiness in ourselves, and it is not possible to find it elsewhere.
> Agnes Repplier

> You cannot really love God unless you love your neighbor.
> Anonymous

7. Evaluate the following arguments as you did the arguments in Chapter 2, application 7. First identify the argument's component parts (including hidden premises) and ask relevant questions, as shown in that chapter. Then check the accuracy of each premise, stated or hidden, and decide whether the conclusion is the most reasonable one. Note that checking the accuracy of the premises may require obtaining sufficient evidence to permit a judgment. If you find a premise to be inaccurate or a conclusion to be less than completely reasonable, revise the argument accordingly.

a. *Background note: Concern over the possibly damaging effects of pornography on children has led many people to lobby for laws banning the sale of pornography to anyone under eighteen. Others object to this, sometimes offering the following argument:*

Argument: Young people today are more sophisticated than any generation in this century. They know their own minds are able to decide better than anyone else, including their parents, what books and magazines they should read. The ban on the sale of pornography to anyone under eighteen is a denial of young people's right to think for themselves, and therefore should be opposed.

b. *Background note: The practice of infertile couples contracting with surrogate mothers to bear a child for them for a fee has given rise to thorny* *issues. For example, what should happen when the surrogate signs a contract, accepts a fee, is artificially inseminated, carries the baby to term, and then decides she will return the money and keep the child? Should she be held to the contract and be made to surrender the baby? Those who say no usually argue as follows:*

Argument: Although contracts should be honored in the vast majority of cases, this kind of case is an exception. The act of nurturing a new life within one's own body can establish the strongest of human bonds. No contract or legal ruling should ever be allowed to break that bond.

8. Apply your critical thinking to each of the following issues. Make a special effort to recall situations you have observed that are related to the issue, and ask yourself, "What conclusion do these observations point to?" (If your observations have been too limited, solicit the observations of other people.)

a. In recent years, books and articles have been written to warn people of the dangers of workaholism. During the same period there have been few, if any, warnings about chronic laziness. Which is more prevalent in this country today, workaholism or chronic laziness?

b. Vince Lombardi's now-famous view of winning is as follows: "Winning isn't everything—it's the *only* thing." Is this a healthy view to bring to athletic competition? To other forms of competition?

c. Should parents be held legally and financially responsible for children over the age of sixteen who live at home?

9. *Group discussion exercise:* Select one of the cases you analyzed in application 8 and discuss it with two or three of your classmates. Try to reach a consensus on the issue. Be prepared to present your idea(s) to the class.

CHAPTER EIGHTEEN

CLARIFYING ISSUES

Many people make the scope of their analysis larger than they can manage. Uncertain as to whether they can find enough about one aspect of a topic, they address the whole topic. Unfortunately, by grouping all aspects together rather than separating them, such people tend to ignore important distinctions, miss subtleties, and distort the relationships among ideas. Any inquiry and judgment that follow such a beginning are likely to be shallow and oversimplified.

Skilled analysts, on the other hand, understand that if they conduct their inquiry carefully, they will usually find more than enough to say about even a small aspect of an issue. They know that a quality analysis, particularly of a controversial matter, usually demands that their focus be severely limited. They realize that unless they are writing a long *book*, they must sacrifice breadth of treatment to achieve depth. In other words, they have learned the wisdom of the saying "Less is more."

◇ How to Clarify an Issue

To get the most out of our thinking we must, like the skilled analysts, limit our topics appropriately. That is, we must determine at the outset what aspect or aspects of the broad general issue we are concerned with.

We should select the particular aspect we wish to focus on, and in doing so settle not for a rough, vague notion but only for a precise one. The following steps provide a quick yet effective way to select and clarify an issue.

1. *List as many specific subheadings as you can that are included under the broad general issue you have chosen.* In the case of an important controversial issue, your list may include more than a dozen subheadings, each of which is a minor issue in itself and therefore a challenge to your critical thinking.

2. *Decide exactly which specific issue (subheading) you are concerned with.* Seldom will you be able to treat all specific issues adequately. The one or ones you choose should not only meet your interest but also fit the occasion and purpose of your analysis and the amount of time and space you have available.

3. *Express the specific issue (subheading) you are concerned with in one or more clear, carefully focused questions.* Doing this helps keep the subsequent inquiry focused and prevents your drifting from the issue. If the questions are written out, when your thoughts move in a certain direction, you can quickly glance at the questions and decide whether that direction is likely to be productive.

Let's see how these three steps apply to some actual issues.

◇ SAMPLE ISSUE: ABORTION

In January 1973 the U.S. Supreme Court decided in *Roe* v. *Wade* that abortion was legal. Yet, in this final decade of this century, the American people are sharply divided on the matter. Like most controversial matters, the issue of abortion is not merely a single issue but *a cluster of smaller issues.* No contribution to the discussion of abortion is likely to be worthwhile unless it begins with an awareness of that fact. Here is how our three-step approach can help you separate the individual parts of that cluster and deal with them meaningfully. (For the sake of brevity, the left column presents the subheading in the form it might first occur to you, and the right column shows how, after deciding that you were concerned with it, you might refine the subheading into a question.)

The Subheading	*The Question*
A woman's right over her body	Does a woman have the right to decide how her body will be used? If so, should the fetus be considered a part of her body?

The Subheading	*The Question*
The doctor's role	Does the doctor have an obligation only to the patient (the woman) or to the fetus as well?
The status of the fetus	At what point, if any, during a pregnancy does the fetus become a human being?
The role of the law	If the fetus at some point during the pregnancy becomes a human being, do the enforcers of the law (the police and the courts) have any obligation to protect its rights?
The stage of the pregnancy	At what times during a pregnancy, if any, should an abortion be permitted? (First three months? First six months? Any time before birth?)
The age of the woman	Should the woman's age be a factor in the decision whether to permit an abortion? Should a child of thirteen be treated the same as a woman of forty?
Cases of rape and incest	Should cases of rape and incest be treated differently from other cases? That is, does the fact that the woman was raped or impregnated by a close relative create a special warrant for abortion?
Parental consent for minors	Should parental consent be required before abortions are performed on minors?
Government assistance for poor	Should the government, through Medicaid, pay for the abortions of women who

	lack the financial means to pay for them themselves?
The rights of the father	Does the husband or lover of a woman who seeks an abortion have any rights? If he opposes the abortion, should the woman be permitted to have it anyway?
A constitutional amendment to ban abortion	Should the U.S. Constitution be amended to ban abortion (or to extend the guarantees of law to the unborn from the moment of conception)?

◇ SAMPLE ISSUE: BOXING

The Ring Record Book lists 337 professional boxers who have died from injuries sustained in prizefights since World War II. In the United States alone, 120 boxers have died from such injuries.[1] With the death of a Korean fighter, Duk Doo Kim, following a barrage of punches by Ray "Boom Boom" Mancini, an issue that had received the public's attention many times previously raged once again: *Should boxing be outlawed?* Like the abortion issue, this one is really a cluster of smaller issues. Here is how the three-step approach to clarifying issues would apply to it:

The Subheading	*The Question*
The boxer's right to earn a living	Would the outlawing of boxing be an unfair denial of the boxer's right to earn a living?
Boxing and mental health	Is the expression of violence that takes place in a boxing match an emotionally healthy experience for the fighters themselves? For the spectators?
The popularity of boxing	How valid is the argument that boxing should be allowed to continue because it has historically been, and continues to be, very popular?

The Subheading	*The Question*
The classification of boxing as a sport	Is boxing properly classified as a sport? That is, does the fact that the contestants aim to strike potentially harmful blows disqualify it from that classification?
Overcoming the dangers	Is it possible, perhaps by modifying the rules or the equipment, to eliminate or at least reduce the physical danger to fighters?
The effects of being punched	Exactly what effect does a punch have on the human body, particularly the brain? What is the cumulative effect of the punches received during ten or fifteen rounds of boxing? During a career?

◇ SAMPLE ISSUE: JUVENILE CRIME

For much of this century juvenile criminals have been accorded special treatment in the courts. Because the emphasis was on rehabilitating rather than on punishing them, the charges were different—"juvenile delinquency" rather than assault or murder—as were the proceedings and disposition of the case—"hearings" rather than trials, sealed records rather than publicity, and lectures rather than imprisonment. In recent years, however, the public has become dissatisfied with that system. Many people are demanding that juveniles who have committed criminal acts be treated as criminals, regardless of their age. The broad issue is usually expressed as "Should juvenile criminals be treated the same as adult criminals?" However, like the other issues we have examined in this chapter, this broad issue represents a cluster of smaller issues, which you might clarify as follows:

The Subheading	*The Question*
Causes of juvenile crime	Are juvenile delinquents alone responsible for their criminality? Are parents

and others in society (makers of violent films, for example) also responsible? If others are responsible, should the law "get tough" with them? How?

The age of responsibility

Is it reasonable or fair to hold people responsible for their actions before they are old enough to understand their moral and legal quality? At what age does a person reach such understanding?

Similarities or differences between juveniles and adults

Is it reasonable to hold a fourteen-year-old (or a sixteen- or eighteen-year-old) as accountable as a twenty-one- or thirty-year-old?

Effect of publicity on juvenile crime

Will publicizing young people's crimes deter juvenile crime? Will it assist in the process of rehabilitation?

Effects of imprisonment on juveniles

What effects will imprisonment have on teenagers? On preteens?

Differences in crimes

Should all juvenile crimes be handled alike? That is, should the criminal's age be considered in certain crimes (vandalism and shoplifting, for example), but not considered in others (rape and murder, for example)?

Recidivism

Should chronic juvenile offenders be treated differently from first-time offenders? If so, in what way?

Prisons

If juvenile offenders are sent to prison (say, for crimes of violence), should they be housed in the same institutions as adult criminals?

By identifying precisely the issue we wish to examine, we not only ensure a clearer focus and increase the chance that we will not exceed our competency, but we also make the job of analysis easier. The fewer aspects competing for our attention, the less distracted and confused we are likely to be. Even on those rare occasions when we will be addressing the entire issue in all its aspects, careful identification of those aspects can make our inquiry more orderly and purposeful. Finally, precise identification of the issue lessens the chance of oversimplifying complex matters.

▨ APPLICATIONS

1. This chapter explains three steps that are helpful in selecting and clarifying an issue for analysis. Apply those steps to *two* of the following topics. Be sure to select topics that interest you because applications in subsequent chapters will build on this one.

    a. Should the federal income tax system in the United States be reformed?

    b. Is sex education desirable in elementary and secondary schools?

    c. Should the divorce laws be tightened so that obtaining a divorce is more difficult?

    d. Is it possible for a sane person to commit suicide?

    e. Does a government ever have the right to impose the death penalty for a criminal offense?

    f. Should prostitution be legalized?

    g. Should lobbying by special interest groups be outlawed?

    h. Should advertising be banned from children's TV (for example, from Saturday morning cartoon shows)?

    i. Are people who practice devil worship insane?

    j. Is it reasonable to believe in UFOs?

    k. Are male athletes naturally superior to female athletes?

2. The following topics were included in the applications for Chapter 1. Choose one of the topics and apply the three steps presented in this chapter for clarifying an issue. (Disregard your earlier analysis of the issue.)

a. Should freshman composition be a required course for all students?

b. Should athletes be tested for anabolic steroid use?

c. Should creationism be taught in high school biology classes?

d. Should polygamy be legalized?

e. Should the voting age be lowered to sixteen?

f. Should extremist groups like the Ku Klux Klan be allowed to hold rallies on public property?

g. Should the prison system give greater emphasis to the punishment or to the rehabilitation of inmates?

h. When they prescribe birth control devices for minors, should doctors and clinics be required to notify the parents of those minors?

CHAPTER NINETEEN

CONDUCTING INQUIRY

Inquiry is seeking answers to questions, investigating, gathering evidence to help us draw conclusions. It enables us to get beyond our first impressions, feelings, preconceived notions, and personal preferences.

There are two basic kinds of inquiry—inquiry into facts and inquiry into opinions. Opinions, remember, can be informed or uninformed. Except in cases where the purpose of our inquiry demands that both varieties of opinion be gathered, we should be more interested in *informed* opinion.

Often we will need to inquire into both facts and opinions. How much inquiry into each is needed will, of course, vary from situation to situation. If the specific issue were "Which U.S. income group is most inequitably treated by the present federal tax laws?" we would have to examine the tax laws to determine what they specify (*fact*) and consult the tax experts for their interpretations of the more complicated aspects of the laws (*informed opinion*). But to determine the degree of inequity we would have to know the amount of income necessary to provide living essentials (food, shelter, and clothing). So we would also have to examine cost-of-living statistics (*fact*), and consult economists about more subtle factors affecting the various income groups (*informed opinion*).

◇ Some Inquiry Results Inconclusive

Because the state of human knowledge is imperfect, not every question is answerable when it is asked. Some issues remain unsolved for years, even centuries. Before we traveled into outer space, no one knew exactly what the effects of weightlessness on the human body would be. Many respected doctors argued that the rapid acceleration at blast-off would increase an astronaut's heartbeat to a fatal level. (There was strong medical evidence to support this view.) Others believed that weightlessness would cause vital organs to malfunction and atrophy.[1] Both dire predictions proved mistaken, but any inquiry into the issue undertaken before the first successful launch would necessarily have been incomplete.

Which mountain in the Sinai desert did Moses really climb? The Bible gives it a name (actually *two* names), but scholars differ on where it is located. Strong claims are advanced for three different mountains in three countries. No conclusive answer has been reached despite over 3,000 years of inquiry.[2]

Some questions are even more resistant to inquiry—for example, the question "Are there intelligent life forms in our solar system or other systems?" Our sun is one of billions of stars. The farthest ones we have discovered are believed to be nine billion light-years away. (In miles, that's 54 followed by 21 zeroes.)[3] It's conceivable that any inquiry into this question made in the next million years will be inconclusive. Perhaps the answer will *never* be known.

However resistant to solution a question may be, though, inquiry is still useful. Even if it yields no more than the *untestable* opinions of experts, those opinions are more valuable than the casual speculations of the uninformed. So we shouldn't be intimidated by difficult issues. We should merely be realistic about how complete and final our answers are likely to be.

◇ Where to Look for Information

Whenever possible, we should consult our own experience and observation. Even if what has happened to us or we have seen happen to others pertains only indirectly to the issue or touches just one aspect of it, it should not be overlooked. Our observation of how people use stereotypes or face-saving maneuvers in everyday situations may help us evaluate a political candidate's speech or a party's platform. Our experience with conformity in ourselves and our friends can provide us with an insight into the effects of TV programming on the public. Being alert to the relevance of our experience to the issue we are investigating not only can give us valuable ideas; it can also suggest important questions. Thus, it can provide our inquiry with better direction.

Of course, our own experience and observation will seldom be adequate by itself, especially on complex and controversial matters. We will need to consult other sources. What follows is a brief guide to what to look for and where to find it.

BACKGROUND ON THE ISSUE

Think of several general headings under which the issue might be classified. For example, if the issue concerned criminal investigation, the headings might be "crime," "criminology," "police," and one or more specific kinds of crime, such as "burglary." Then look up those headings in the *index volume* of a good general encyclopedia, such as *Encyclopedia Americana* or *Encyclopaedia Britannica*. (*Americana* has a separate index volume. *Britannica* is divided into two sets of books: the macropaedia set, which contains detailed articles on a limited number of subjects, and the micropaedia set, which contains brief articles and cross-references on a large number of subjects.) The articles you find there are written by authorities in the various fields. At the end of each article is a list of books and other articles you can consult for a fuller or more specialized treatment of the issue.

In addition to the general encyclopedias, there are numerous special ones: encyclopedias of art, business, history, literature, philosophy, music, science, education, social science, and many more. Most of these contain not only discussions of the history of the field but also titles of other books and articles you may find helpful.*

FACTS AND STATISTICS

Almanacs are treasuries of information, published yearly, on myriad subjects. *World Almanac* is available from 1868. *Information Please Almanac, The New York Times Encyclopedic Almanac,* and *Reader's Digest Almanac* are more recent publications. Because any almanac is arranged

---

*Remember that background reading, though a helpful start toward analyzing an issue, is never an acceptable substitute for analysis. Your instructor will expect more from you than just background information.

very compactly for efficient use, it is important to study the index before using it.

INFORMATION ABOUT PEOPLE

A number of biographical dictionaries and encyclopedias are available. Two of the most helpful ones are *Current Biography: Who's News and Why* and *Webster's Biographical Dictionary.*

INFORMATION ABOUT THE ENGLISH LANGUAGE

Many reference books are available, including the *Oxford English Dictionary (OED), Webster's New Dictionary of Synonyms,* and Eric Partridge's *Dictionary of Slang and Unconventional English.*

ARTICLES IN NEWSPAPERS, MAGAZINES, AND JOURNALS

The most basic index to articles is the *Reader's Guide to Periodical Literature.* This guide lists articles from over one hundred magazines by subject and by author. As with an encyclopedia, you should begin by thinking of the various headings under which the issue might be classified. Then select the volumes for the appropriate years (more current years are listed in unbound pamphlet form), and look up those headings. The entries will list the title and author of the article and the name and issue of the magazine it appeared in.

Many other indexes are available, even in moderate-sized libraries. The following is a partial list. (For a complete list, consult Eugene O. Sheehy's *Guide to Reference Books.*)

*Social Science Index

*Humanities Index

New York Times Index

Essay and General Literature Index

General Science Index

Education Index

United States Government Publications: Monthly Catalog

Applied Science and Technology Index

Art Index

Biography Index

Business Periodicals Index

Biological and Agricultural Index

Book Review Index

Business Periodicals Index

Engineering Index

*Before 1965, these indexes were combined under the title *International Index.*

Index to Legal Periodicals	*Music Index*
MLA International Bibliography	*Philosopher's Index*
Magazine Index	*Religion Index One: Periodicals*

After you locate the article and read it, be sure to check the reader response in the letters-to-the-editor section of subsequent issues. Most newspapers and magazines have a "letters" section, and it will often provide reaction by informed readers supporting or challenging the ideas in the article. In weekly magazines, responses usually appear two issues after the article; in fortnightlies and monthlies, one issue later.

BOOKS

In addition to the lists of books provided in encyclopedias and those you find mentioned in the articles you read, you can consult your library's card or computer catalog, the key to the books available on its shelves.* Occasionally, if your library is small or if the issue you are investigating is obscure, the library holdings may be limited. In such cases, as in any situation where you are having difficulty finding information or using the reference books, ask your librarian for help. (Remember that librarians are professionals trained to solve the kinds of research problems you may experience.)

COMPUTER DATABASES AND ABSTRACTING SERVICES

Modern information retrieval technology has made it easier than ever to conduct a data search. Ask your librarian about the computer databases available to you. Ask, too, about the abstracting services; among the best known are *Psychological Abstracts, Sociological Abstracts, America: History and Life,* and *Dissertation Abstracts International.*

All of this may suggest long, monotonous, time-and-energy-consuming research like that required for a doctoral dissertation. But that is a misconception. With a little practice, it is possible to use quickly and efficiently all the reference sources mentioned. Even books needn't be waded through page by page to find something useful. In a few seconds you can turn to the index (usually at the end) and look for the several headings your issue might be found under, then turn to the appropriate

*One valuable source of information is college textbooks in fields related to the issue you are investigating.

pages and read *just those pages.* If the book has no index, you can turn to the table of contents, read the chapter titles and decide which chapters seem most relevant, and then scan them.

◇ HOW MUCH INQUIRY IS ENOUGH?

It would seem that deciding when an inquiry is complete should be easy. More often than not, however, it is not easy at all. One insight can make a great difference. A single fact can upset a mountain of evidence. For example, in the late 1960s and early 1970s most social psychologists would probably have agreed that crowded living conditions are harmful to human beings. Numerous experiments seemed to have settled the matter. Then anthropologist Patricia Draper studied a southwest African tribe of hunter-gatherers, the !Kung bushmen. Though their land offers ample space to spread out their settlements and huts, they crowd their dwellings together and often sit in tight groups, literally brushing against one another. Yet they have none of the medical conditions (such as high blood pressure) usually associated with crowding.[4] This one fact has caused reexamination of a scientific truism.

The aim of inquiry is to produce evidence. Chapter 2, you will recall, stated that evidence is sufficient in either of two circumstances:

1. **When it permits a judgment to be made with** *certainty.* Wishing, assuming, or pretending that a judgment is correct does not constitute certainty. Certainty exists when there is no good reason for doubt, no basis for dispute. It is rarely attained, especially in controversial issues.

2. **When certainty is unattainable yet one view of the issue has been shown to have the force of** *probability.* This means, in other words, that the view in question is demonstrably more reasonable than any competing view. Demonstrating reasonableness is, of course, very different from merely asserting it, and all possible views must be identified and evaluated before any one view can be established as most reasonable.

How much inquiry is enough? There is no easy answer. It depends entirely on the issue. In some cases, a brief inquiry will be more than adequate. In others, an exhaustive inquiry will be incomplete. However, though no absolute statement may be made about the amount of inquiry required, you can be reasonably sure your inquiries are complete when you have made a thorough and careful effort to learn the relevant facts and to consult informed opinion in all fields of study that have a direct bearing on the specific issue you are analyzing. The number of fields to be researched will, of course, vary with the nature of the issue. Here, for example, is a list of the fields that have a direct bearing on three specific issues we identified in Chapter 18:

Specific Issue	Fields with Direct Bearing
At what point, if any, during a pregnancy does the fetus become a human being?	Biology Law Ethics Metaphysics Psychology
Exactly what effect does a punch have on the human body, particularly the brain? What is the cumulative effect of the punches received during ten or fifteen rounds of boxing? During a career?	Anatomy and physiology Medicine Psychology
Is it reasonable or fair to hold people responsible for their actions before they are old enough to understand their moral and legal quality? At what age does a person reach such understanding?	Education Psychology Medicine Ethics Law

A special problem frequently arises with an inquiry into opinion. When we have found one or two respected thinkers who agree with what we believe or want to believe, we are inclined to feel satisfied. "Case closed," we're tempted to say. "This is the answer." Precisely at that moment we need to be especially cautious. To understand why, consider the following situation. In early 1992, then-President George Bush forced John E. Frohnmayer, the chairman of the National Endowment for the Arts, to resign his position. If you lived in Louisville, you might have read the following editorial on the subject.

WHEN HE CANNED the head of the National Endowment for the Arts last week, President Bush reminded us of the middle management executive who, after being chewed out by the boss, goes home to yell at his spouse, punish the kids and kick the dog.

On Tuesday, voters in New Hampshire gave Mr. Bush a stern warning by casting a lot of protest votes for columnist Patrick Buchanan. And what did our "kinder and gentler" hero of

Operation Desert Storm do? Did he face his opponent to discuss the issues head on or defend his administration against the xenophobic and racist slurs of the Buchanan campaign?

Dream on. Instead, he picked the easiest target available—arts endowment chief John E. Frohnmayer, and offered him up as a sacrifice on Friday. It was Mr. Bush's cheap play for the right-wing claque that loves Jesse Helms and has its doubts about most art more modern than Grant Wood.

This campaign has just begun, and, quite frankly, it's not encouraging to see the nation's chief executive behaving like a petty tyrant. Until Nov. 3, "kinder and gentler" are out.[5]

By not mentioning any possible reason other than the purely political one, the editorial implies there was no good reason. Thus, if this were the only view you read, you might well have concluded that the president acted arbitrarily for purely political motives. But if the scope of your inquiry was a little wider and you sought other views, you might have encountered the following editorial.*

WE CANNOT HELP but wonder if Pat Buchanan's strong showing in New Hampshire had some connection to John Frohnmayer's resignation Friday as chairman of the National Endowment for the Arts. The NEA's funding of filth, indecency and blasphemy could have become a major political liability for George Bush as he heads into the southern primaries.

Mr. Frohnmayer never seemed to understand why the NEA's funding of gross and offensive alleged art upset many Americans. He recently described as "emotional, intense and serious" a sexually graphic poem describing Jesus Christ sodomizing a 6-year-old boy who says he could kill his mother, which appeared in an NEA-funded collection called "Queer city." And despite public and congressional protests, Mr. Frohnmayer this year approved still another grant to the infamous Annie Sprinkle, for her latest pornographic video, "The Sluts and Goddesses of Transformation Salon."

Mr. Frohnmayer always viewed the battle over the arts agency as one over censorship. That never has been the real issue. What made his management of the NEA so objectionable was not the content of the so-called art itself but that taxpayers were being forced to pay for it. There is hardly a city in the country that does not tolerate, to some degree, the existence of strip joints and porn palaces specializing in entertainment that many people find dis-

---

*The source of these editorials was *Editorials on File*, a collection of editorials from around the nation and, on occasion, foreign countries on timely issues. Available in many college and public libraries, it is a good preliminary source. Because editorials are by nature very abbreviated, your inquiry should go beyond editorials to sources that analyze issues in depth.

tasteful or offensive. But the difference between those and the NEA is that the former involve private transactions, so no one is forced to pay. If Annie Sprinkle and her ilk want to put on their shows, display vile and disgusting photographs or publish blasphemous poetry, that's their business—so long as it is not at taxpayers' expense.

Unfortunately, throughout the NEA controversy Mr. Bush bought the "censorship" line and vigorously defended his appointee, Mr. Frohnmayer. America is engaged in a battle for its culture, a war in which George Bush claims to be on the side of right and good. But the NEA under Messrs. Bush and Frohnmayer often has been on the other side. Perhaps that is about to change.

The NEA's funding of pornography is not a matter of a few isolated grants slipping through the bureaucratic cracks. Thus, Mr. Bush should be careful to choose as a replacement for Mr. Frohnmayer someone who would aggressively work to enforce traditional American values in grantmaking.

In a statement to NEA staff, Mr. Frohnmayer said he expects "to work in the private foundation or legal world for the growth and enrichment of our society—for quality art, for less hate and for a generosity of spirit that allows us to live with our differences in a real community." Even in leaving, Mr. Frohnmayer does not understand the issues involved, but we shall wave a fond farewell as he flies off into the sunset to his Oregon home.[6]

This editorial almost seems to be talking about a different issue entirely. It goes beyond speculation about the president's political motives and discusses Mr. Frohnmayer's actions. Whatever position you might eventually reach on the president's action, you would be considerably more informed for not having cut your inquiry short. A controversial issue, by definition, is one on which informed, careful thinkers may disagree, on which there is something to say for both sides. The more generous your examination of that disagreement, the wiser your judgment is likely to be.

◇ MANAGING EXTENDED ARGUMENTS

When you conduct more extensive inquiry, you encounter extended arguments. These are more difficult to appraise than brief ones because the core argument is seldom presented neatly, compactly, in a form that permits ready analysis. This is not because the authors intend to make analysis difficult—it is simply the nature of the writing process. Authors of journal articles and books do not merely present lists of bald assertions; they support their views with evidence. They also add sufficient explanation to satisfy the demands of clarity and make clear the path their reasoning has taken. Sometimes the path has numerous turns, so secondary assertions must be added to complement and refine primary ones. As anecdotes multiply, as experimental and statistical data are reported and annotated, and testimony is detailed, the essential argument can become almost as concealed as the hidden premises it sometimes contains—one premise may appear on page 2, another on page 5, and the conclusion on page 12. Before you can evaluate arguments in these cases, you need to consolidate the argument. Here is a strategy for doing so:

1. *After reading the article or book, go back and identify the key assertions.* Most paragraphs contain one or more assertions (topic sentences). Scan these and determine which are central to the argument. Subheadings usually signal important assertions, as do capitalizing and italicizing. Look, too, for intensifying words such as *moreover, indeed, more (most) important, more (most) significant.*

2. *Identify the argument's conclusion.* The conclusion may appear anywhere, but commonly it appears as follows: in an article—right after the introduction, in the conclusion, or in both places; in a book—in the first or second chapter, in the last chapter, or in both places. Expressions like *for these reasons, thus, consequently, so,* and *therefore* signal conclusions.

3. *Notice any qualifying words used in the key assertions or the conclusion.* Is the writer speaking of *all* people, places, or things? Or is she speaking of *most, many, some, several, a few,* or *certain specified ones?* Is she saying *always, usually, sometimes, occasionally, seldom, never,* or *at certain specified times?* Often writers will make an assertion and then balance it in the next sentence. They often lead into the second sentence with words like *but, however, nevertheless, on the other hand, still,* or *yet.*

4. *Note the amount, kinds, and sources of evidence used to support the assertions.* As explained in Chapter 2, the broad classifications of evidence are anecdotal, experimental, statistical, and testimonial.

5. *Notice the conditions the author includes.* Saying, for example, "Drug pushers should be given long jail terms if they are not themselves drug users and have been previously convicted of drug pushing" is very different from saying, "Drug pushers should be given long jail terms." The "if" clause adds a special set of conditions. Similarly, "The United States should never fire a nuclear missile at another country unless first subjected to nuclear attack by that country" is quite different from saying, "The United States should never fire a nuclear missile at another country." Expressions like *if, unless, as long as, until,* and *before* can significantly alter the meaning of an assertion.

6. *Compose an accurate summary of the article or book from your analysis in steps 1–5.* This enables you to focus your attention and analyze the argument. The summary needn't be long; a paragraph or two is adequate in most cases. The summary should be a capsule version of the original work. (There is no room for carelessness in quoting or paraphrasing the original: If it says something *may be* a certain way, it is not saying that it *is* that way; similarly, *is* does not necessarily mean *should be*.) Here is a sample summary of an article recommending the abolition of grades. Although it extended to more than ten printed pages in the original, it is here condensed into a single paragraph without sacrificing accuracy.

> One of the biggest obstacles to learning—in grade school, high school, and college—is grades. The fear of bad grades hangs over the heads of young people from the time they are six to the time they are twenty or twenty-two. Their anxiety to do well, to succeed, to please their parents so fills their minds that all the natural joy in learning evaporates. As a result, conscientious students are driven to view their schoolwork as oppressive drudgery, and marginal students are tempted to cheat and bluff their way to a degree. For these reasons I say grades should be abolished at all levels of education.

⊞ APPLICATIONS

1. Extend your inquiry into the firing of the NEA chairman following the approach explained in the chapter.

2. Summarize each of the following editorials. Be as concise as you can without sacrificing accuracy. Then extend your inquiry on the issue using the approach explained in the chapter.

SHOOT THE MESSENGER. That seems to be the impulse behind the boycott-Time Warner movement, aimed at punishing the company for issuing an album by rap star Ice-T that contains a song called "Cop Killer."

In the song, Ice-T takes on the voice of an angry young ghetto resident who says, among other things, "I'm going to bust some shots off. I'm going to dust some cops off." It does not, contrary to actor Charlton Heston's suggestion, "celebrate the killing of police officers." Nor does it contain lyrics that tell young people to go out and kill police. It's an expression of ghetto anger, and it scares people, as well it should. But trying to stifle such a statement would be even scarier.

Imagine, for a moment, that such language were contained

not in a rap song but came from a character in a novel. Would the author be denied the right to write the dialogue? Would serious citizens' groups ask people to boycott the publisher? Almost certainly not.

Last year, some feminist groups urged a boycott of Alfred E. Knopf, the parent company of the publisher of "American Psycho," a book that depicted grisly and sadistic scenes of violence against women and other people. This newspaper defended the company's right to publish such a book, and the author's right to use such shock tactics. It wasn't a pleasant book and it wasn't great literature, but that was no reason to deny it publication.

Stung by the accusation that he is just using hate to make money, Ice-T has asked time Warner to reissue his album without the offending song, to prove that he's not just out for profit. He'll distribute the single free at concerts, he says.

This should have been unnecessary, however. Rap is the literature of the ghetto. It's true that such songs may confirm antisocial attitudes in angry young people. But they arise out of a culture that already has these attitudes; they don't create them. In the '60s, similar debates took place when the psychedelic rock scene produced songs that were about drug experiences. The songs both reflected and legitimized a culture that was antiestablishment and celebrated illegal practices. Trying to control the phenomenon was fruitless.

Police groups that have called for a boycott of Time Warner, especially those that operate in big cities, should try to understand what produces the kind of anger and alienation expressed in rap songs.

In fact, this controversy could be used as a way to communicate with the followers of Ice-T, to let them know that even for the residents of South Central Los Angeles there are some advantages to being American. The First Amendment comes to mind.[7]

In 1990, RECORD company mogul David Geffen was asked to distribute a rap album that included descriptions of graphic violence and necrophilia. His answer: A definite "No."

"It's not a matter of censorship," Geffen told the Associated Press. "It's a matter of responsibility. You can make money selling cocaine. I choose not to." Record companies, he said, should set limits on the kinds of materials they distribute.

Time Warner executives would do well to consider Geffen's words. The company was let off the hook this week by rap performer Ice-T, who said he would voluntarily pull the song "Cop Killer" from his album and give away copies of the song as a single.

Police officers and their families exercised their freedom of expression when they angrily called for the company to pull the song. Ice-T and some—but not most—other rap artists exercised their own freedom of expression in songs that describe such acts as killing policeman, raping women and sodomizing young girls.

But just because a singer wants to express something doesn't mean a record company has to distribute it.

Time Warner executives were wrong when they said pulling "Cop Killer" from distribution would be censorship. Censorship would be the passage of laws banning the sale of certain record albums. What Time Warner was called on to do—and what the company should have done— was exercise some responsibility to the public by declining to distribute "Cop Killer." Instead, Ice-T took the heat and Time Warner avoided making a tough decision it should have made a long time ago.[8]

3. Choose one of the specific issues you clarified in application 1 or 2 of Chapter 18. Conduct your inquiry into this issue in the manner explained in this chapter. Take careful notes.

4. Choose one of the specific issues presented in Chapter 18 in the discussion of abortion, boxing, or juvenile crime. Conduct your inquiry into this issue in the manner explained in this chapter. Take careful notes.

CHAPTER TWENTY

FORMING A JUDGMENT

Judgments are conclusions arrived at through examination of evidence and careful reasoning. They are the products of thinking. Unlike feelings, judgments are not spontaneous and unconscious. They may, of course, contain elements of the spontaneous—such as intuition—but, like other data, these have first been weighed and evaluated.

The fact that judgments are products of evaluation and reasoning does not guarantee their worth. There are foolish as well as wise judgments, superficial as well as penetrating ones. A judgment can easily reflect misconceptions about truth, knowing, and opinion. Or it can involve one or more of the errors in thinking detailed in Chapters 6 through 15.

The strategy we have discussed for thinking critically about issues is designed to promote thoughtful judgments. By knowing ourselves and being observant, we improve our perception and guard against error. By systematically clarifying issues and conducting inquiry, we rescue our thinking from preconceived notions and first impressions. Next we must evaluate the evidence we have obtained, deciding what it means and how significant it is. One of the most common questions concerns the resolution of apparent conflicts in evidence. As we have seen in previous chapters, experts do not always agree. Because people often view the same event quite differently, even the eyewitness reports of honest people can conflict.

It is a popular view that the more scientific the procedure, the less need exists for evaluation. But that view is mistaken. Scientific procedures generate or discover factual information which must be classified and interpreted to be meaningful. Consider, for example, this unusual case. An ancient tomb was unearthed in Central China containing the body of a woman who died about 2,100 years ago. Great care had been taken in burying her. She was placed in an airtight coffin filled with a special fluid. The coffin was encased in five larger boxes lined with five tons of charcoal. That larger unit was buried in a sixty-foot hole and surrounded by white clay.

Because of this extraordinary burial, when the woman's body was found, the flesh was still moist, the hair still rooted in the scalp, the joints still flexible, most of the internal organs intact. Specialists conducted a careful autopsy. They performed chemical analyses of the woman's hair, stomach, muscles, bones, lungs, gallbladder, intestines. They X-rayed her bones. To be useful, however, the mass of facts they obtained had to be *interpreted*. Only by studying the data, raising questions about it, and deciding what judgments were most reasonable did they conclude, for example, that she had borne children, had eaten a melon shortly before her death, and had probably died suddenly as the result of an obstructed coronary artery.[1]

Evaluation plays an important role not only in science but also in other fields. In fact, because in other areas the information may be less clear or more fragmentary and opinions may be more sharply in conflict, the quality of a judgment may depend even more heavily on evaluation.

◇ EVALUATING EVIDENCE

The focus of our evaluation depends on the kind of evidence we have obtained. Evidence from our own direct experience or observation poses different questions from evidence given us by others and evidence obtained through research. The following questions are arranged by category.

If the evidence is from your own experience or direct observation, ask:

1. How accurately did I observe? What kinds of inaccuracies in perceiving could have been caused by the circumstances of the event or issue? (Did it occur quickly? Were there any physical imped-

iments such as my distance from what happened, the time of day, or weather conditions?) What kinds of inaccuracies could have been caused by my state of mind? (Was I tired? Afraid? Distraught? Angry?) What kinds of inaccuracies could have been caused by my mood or my attitude toward the issue, the people, or the place? Was I predisposed to view the matter one way?

2. Is what I experienced or observed typical of all such cases? Is it possible that it is more the exception than the rule? Were the circumstances unusual enough that it was different from what it would usually be?

If the evidence is from the experience and observation of other people, ask (in addition to *the questions you'd ask of your own experience and observation):*

1. Did the person who reported the matter to me experience or observe the matter herself? Or was she reporting someone else's experiences?

2. Does the reporter's reputation warrant my accepting the report at face value? (Is she regarded as a careful observer? Are her statements generally accurate and precise?)

3. If more than one person experienced or observed the matter, do their reports agree?

If the evidence is from your research (that is, from an article or book or television program), ask:

1. If the evidence is found in a magazine article, how reputable is the magazine? Is it given to the sensational? Is it considered a responsible publication?

2. How careful does the writer seem to be about avoiding unsupported assertions, oversimplifications, sweeping generalizations? How impartial is the writer? (It's only reasonable to be a bit skeptical about a writer with an obvious bias, such as the chairwoman of a political party explaining the virtues of her candidate. She may be speaking impartially, but she will be more prone to unconscious one-sidedness.)

3. If the article, book, or TV program refers to the results of research, does it provide important details? For example, if the research involved interviews, how many people were involved? What was the range of geographical areas, occupations, and ages of those interviewed? What questions were asked? (Not every research project is sufficiently comprehensive to answer the questions it proposes to answer. In the nineteenth century Cesare Lombroso, chairman of the criminal anthropology department at

the University of Turin, Italy, theorized that all criminals had certain peculiarities in common. One special distinguishing characteristic he believed all criminals possessed was a skull deformity. The criminal skull shape, he believed, resembled that of primitive man. His research in prisons seemed to verify the theory, and it was very influential until a British researcher, C. Goring, found as many college students and professors with that head shape as convicts!)

It's important to remember that writers may, consciously or unconsciously, include the evidence that supports their view and omit any evidence that challenges it. So an article or book that seems to present an overwhelming case may actually be a "loaded" argument.

◇ Evaluating Your Sources' Arguments

In addition to evaluating the evidence we have obtained, we must examine the arguments others have advanced. (When we deal with testimonial evidence, the argument—the author's professional judgment—is itself a form of evidence.) The summaries of books and articles we examined in our inquiry facilitate this examination. Here, for example, is the article summary presented in Chapter 19, followed by the questions we would raise in evaluating it. For ease of reference, each sentence in the paragraph is numbered, and the questions that apply to it are numbered correspondingly.

THE SUMMARY

1. One of the biggest obstacles to learning—in grade school, high school, and college—is grades.

2. The fear of bad grades hangs over the heads of young people from the time they are six to the time they are twenty or twenty-two.

3. Their anxiety to do well, to succeed, to please their parents so fills their minds that all the natural joy in learning evaporates.

4. As a result, conscientious students are driven to view their schoolwork as oppressive drudgery, and marginal students are tempted to cheat and bluff their way to a degree.

5. For these reasons I say grades should be abolished at all levels of education.

THE QUESTIONS

1. Are grades an obstacle to learning? If so, are they at all three levels?

2. Do any young people between these ages fear bad grades? Do all of them? Is the fear a serious one (as "hangs over the head" implies)?

3. Is there any natural joy to begin with? For all subjects? Do grades cause anxiety? If so, does the anxiety eliminate the joy? For all students?

4. Do any conscientious students view schoolwork as oppressive drudgery? Do all of them? Do many view it that way in certain circumstances but not in others? If they do view it as oppressive drudgery, is it grades that cause them to? Are any marginal students tempted to cheat and bluff? All of them? If some are, is it grades that tempt them to do so?

5. Would abolishing grades solve all these problems? Some of them? Would it create any additional problems? If so, would the resulting situation be more or less desirable? Would the effects differ at different levels of education?

Here is another example, the response of popular psychologist and author Joyce Brothers to a reader's question.[2] (Because the response is brief, no summary is necessary.) As in the previous example, numbers have been assigned to our paraphrase of Dr. Brothers's response and to our analysis.

THE LETTER AND RESPONSE

The reader explained that she works with a homosexual man and has formed a close platonic relationship with him. Her husband, however, disapproves of the man, calling him "sick," and becomes angry when she and the man converse on the telephone. (No other details of the situation were included in the published letter.)

Dr. Brothers said in her response:

1. That in her view the woman's husband is afraid of homosexuality.

2. That, as is characteristic of all people who suffer from homophobia, the basis of the husband's fear is not concern that the man might proposition him, but a perceived threat to his ego and apprehension about discovering that at some level he, too, has some "feminine" characteristics.

3. That homophobia can have harmful effects, including—in this woman's case—a possible weakening of her marriage.

4. That the woman should discuss the situation fully with her husband and encourage him to examine his feelings rationally.

5. That such an approach could help the husband gain greater insight into the problem.

6. That if for some reason this approach does not produce the effect the wife desires, she should consider seeking joint counseling, giving the husband an opportunity to change his viewpoint.

7. That regardless of the outcome of the counseling, whether the husband comes around to the wife's way of thinking or not, the wife should continue her relationship with her homosexual friend.

THE QUESTIONS

1. Could his reaction be based on anger or revulsion or a firmly held belief or simple jealously that she shares much of her time with another man? Is it possible that his derogatory comments about her friend are masking jealousy (rather than expressing any deeply felt antagonism toward gays)? Nothing in the letter *requires* the conclusion that he is afraid.

2. The reference to homophobics in general moves the discussion beyond the individual case. It suggests that no homophobic is ever afraid that a homosexual will make advances toward him or her. But what of people who were molested by homosexuals as children? Wouldn't it be normal for them to fear reliving that experience, just as people heterosexually molested would fear reliving their experience? It is possible that the husband's ego is threatened and that he is apprehensive about his own feminine qualities, but given the lack of details in the letter, it is far from certain that this is the case.

3. No reasonable person would dispute this idea.

4. What does it mean for the wife to discuss the matter with her husband: to have her mind made up in advance about his feelings and thoughts or to ask him to explain them and listen to his answer with the expectation of learning something?

5. Should the wife not be willing to explore her behavior as honestly as she expects her husband to explore his feelings? Shouldn't she, too, be attempting to achieve a new and deeper understanding of the situation than she presently has?

6. Is counseling likely to be more successful if one partner begins with the conviction that he or she is entirely right and the other person wrong?

7. Is maintaining a friendship necessarily more important than saving a marriage? Is more information than is provided in the reader's letter needed before concluding that the friendship in this case is worth more than the marriage? Wouldn't it be helpful to know how long the couple has been married; whether they have children and, if so, what ages; and whether their relationship was harmonious before this situation arose? (If the husband cherished her companionship, is it not possible that he is more motivated by feelings of neglect and loss than by homophobia?) Is it reasonable for Dr. Brothers to *assume* the woman is being fair to her husband and he is being unreasonable without knowing how often, at what times of the day, and for how long the woman talks on the phone to her gay friend? What if both husband and wife work and share responsibility for housework and parenting, but she now spends hours on the telephone every evening? Would not the best advice in that case be for *her* to get counseling and find out what's wrong with *her*?

As the examples demonstrate, taking the time to ask appropriate questions has several benefits. First, it gets us beyond judging on the basis of appearances. That is good because ideas that might seem appealing to us at first glance may not remain so when we examine them more closely. Second, it protects us from our own visceral reactions and permits us to get beyond a blanket, overall yes or no and consider the position in its various parts. Even the best thinkers, after all, are human and therefore fallible. So on a complex issue, any statement longer than a sentence or two could easily be neither perfectly reasonable nor perfectly unreasonable but partly each. And the longer the passage, the greater the likelihood that it is flawed and that we can therefore find both things to agree with and things to disagree with, strengths and weaknesses. Finally, it suggests to us a structure around which to arrange our thoughts.

The answers we develop for the questions we raise comprise our response to the viewpoint. If we write out our response, we may either follow the organization suggested by the order of the questions or use a different organization. The decision depends on what order of presentation makes our ideas most coherent and provides the emphasis we intend.

◇ MAKING IMPORTANT DISTINCTIONS

Still another important consideration in evaluating evidence is making careful distinctions. The exact distinction needed, of course, depends on the situation. However, here are six kinds of distinctions that are frequently necessary to avoid faulty evaluations:

1. *Between the person and the idea.* It's easy to confuse the person with the idea. Just as we tend to overlook the faults of our friends and exaggerate those of our enemies, so we tend to look favorably on the ideas of people we like or admire and unfavorably on those we dislike or do not admire. Similarly, we tend to disregard the ideas of people who we feel *ought not to have* ideas on certain subjects—for example, white scholars on black history or men on "women's issues." Such reactions are irrational because ideas are not synonymous with the people who hold them: Admirable people can be wrong, despicable people can be right. Further, a person's gender, color, nationality, or religion is not a proper basis for accepting or rejecting his or her ideas. It is possible for a man to be an authority on feminism (or for that matter to *be a feminist*), a white scholar to have insights about African-American

history, a Chinese Buddhist to make a valuable contribution to the subject of American Protestantism. Therefore, we should make a conscious effort to keep our analysis of ideas separate from our feelings for the people who hold them.

2. *Between what is said and the way it is said.* Style and substance are quite different matters. Unfortunately, the person with the clearest and most graceful expression does not always have the soundest idea. So though it is natural for us to be impressed by effective writers or speakers, it's unwise to assume that their ideas are necessarily sound. As Augustine once said, "Our concern with a man is not with what eloquence he teaches, but with what evidence."

3. *Between why people think as they do and whether what they think is correct.* It's common to judge people's *motives* for thinking and acting as they do. Though such judging is sometimes rash, at other times it is very helpful. Finding out that a senator has connections with the handgun manufacturing industry, for example, raises interesting questions about the senator's opposition to gun control laws. But it is important for us to remember that unworthy motivations do not necessarily contaminate the position. The soundness of an idea doesn't depend on the motivations of those who support it. It depends on how well the idea fits the realities of the situation.

4. *Between the individual and the group or class.* The individual person or thing may differ from the group or class in one or more significant respects. Therefore, the characteristics of the individual should not be carelessly attributed to the group, and vice versa.

5. *Between matters of preference and matters of judgment.* Matters of preference concern taste, which it is pointless to debate. However, matters of judgment concern interpretations of fact and theory, which are debatable. It is therefore appropriate to question the evidence supporting judgments and fallacious to claim that matters of judgment are preferences.

6. *Between familiarity and correctness.* It is natural to respond less guardedly to the familiar than to the unfamiliar. Yet familiar ideas are not necessarily correct. Accordingly, when judging correctness, we should disregard the familiarity or unfamiliarity of the idea. Then we will be open to insights from both sides of issues, not just from the side we favor.

Being open to unfamiliar arguments often has an additional benefit: By preparing us for the unpredictable, it enables us to appreciate situations in which an author challenges vogue thinking. Noted columnist William Safire, for example, once committed no fewer than three acts of heresy in a single brief column, and produced three interesting arguments worthy of serious consideration. First, he asserted that the second trial of the police officers responsible for the infamous Rodney King beating was an "affront to the Constitution" because it amounted to double jeopardy (being tried twice for the same crime). Second, he claimed that the organizers of the St. Patrick's Day Parade in New York City were on solid legal ground when they barred gay rights groups from marching because governmental licensing should "never be twisted into a power to enforce conformity to one opinion." Third, he argued that Oregon Senator Bob Packwood, when pressured to leave office because of allegations of sexual harassment, was being made into a scapegoat by senators still embarrassed over their handling of the Anita Hill case. Safire did not condone Packwood's crude, offensive behavior, but he advised the Senate to turn their attention to "real sexual harassment," discriminatory hiring and promotion policies.[3]

◇ EXPRESSING JUDGMENTS

The act of expressing a judgment can alter it. Therefore, no matter how clear your judgment of an issue might be, it is best to consider it formless until you have expressed it accurately in words. The following guidelines will help you express all your judgments effectively:

Strive for a balanced view.

Deal with probability.

Make your subject appropriately specific.

Make your predicate exact.

Include all appropriate qualifications.

Avoid exaggeration.

Let's look more closely at each of these guidelines.

STRIVE FOR A BALANCED VIEW

A balanced view of an issue is one that reflects all the subtlety and complexity of an issue. The prevailing view exerts considerable force on most people's thinking, particularly when the issue is controversial and emotion is running high. Without realizing it, people typically adopt identical perspectives and use identical arguments, and even identical words. This happens even with people who are normally critical thinkers.

At such times, hordes of liberal thinkers sound alike, as do hordes of conservative thinkers. When someone finally exercises the mental discipline to break the pattern and take a balanced look at the issue, the result is a refreshingly original, and often insightful, view.

Consider the case of Salman Rushdie's book *The Satanic Verses.* Many Moslems, convinced that the book ridiculed their religion and the prophet Mohammed, reacted angrily. The Ayatollah Khomeini went so far as to put out a contract on the author's life and to threaten any individuals involved in publishing or distributing the book. The literary, journalistic, and intellectual communities' response to this extreme reaction was to hold rallies and publicly support Rushdie and his publisher. The theme of these rallies and statements was that freedom of expression is an absolute right.

There is no question that freedom of expression is a worthy principle and that the extreme reaction of Khomeini and his followers to Rushdie's novel was totally unjustifiable. And that is precisely why it was so tempting for sensitive people to support Rushdie and condemn Khomeini without qualification. (Adding to that temptation was the fact that Khomeini had previously earned the enmity of Westerners.) Yet intellectual balance means making a conscious effort to moderate our reactions even in the face of strong temptation to overstatement.

At least a few writers displayed intellectual balance on this issue by reminding us that other principles are also important—notably, the principle of respect for the religious beliefs of others. Columnist John Leo spoke of "the fact that our [principle of tolerance] calls for a certain amount of deference and self-restraint in discussing other people's religious beliefs."[4] And Professor John Esposito of Holy Cross College observed that "the First Amendment right doesn't mean you should automatically say everything you want to."[5] *What made these views balanced is that they were made without denying the importance of freedom of speech and the unacceptability of Khomeini's threat.*

Consider another issue—the question of building self-esteem in people. For more than twenty years writers of self-improvement books have emphasized the importance of self-esteem, particularly in young children. So great has been this emphasis that many people assume that success or failure in school and later life is largely a reflection of this factor. Almost any effort to make people feel good about themselves is applauded.

But Barbara Lerner, psychologist and attorney, was able to resist the powerful lure of the prevailing view and examine self-esteem critically. Her reward was the insight that self-esteem is not always good. In some cases it can be an *obstacle* to achievement. There is a difference, she notes, between "earned" self-esteem and "feel good now" self-esteem. The former can lead to achievement and even excellence, whereas the latter promotes complacency and, ultimately, incompetency.[6]

To achieve a balanced view of the issues you address, you must be willing to look for the neglected side of the issue and, when there is good reason to do so, challenge the prevailing view.

DEAL WITH PROBABILITY

Despite our best efforts to investigate issues, there are times when we cannot accumulate sufficient evidence to arrive at a judgment with certainty. This is especially true with controversial issues. At such times, the irresponsible often raise their voices, choose more forceful words, and *pretend* certainty. That is a grave mistake, first because the pretense seldom fools good thinkers, but more important because it is intellectually dishonest.

As long as we have made a sincere effort to gain the evidence necessary to achieve certainty and are not deliberately choosing to ride the fence, there is no shame in admitting, "I cannot say for certain what the correct judgment is in this situation." On the contrary, there is virtue in doing so. Yet in such situations there is one further obligation we must, as responsible thinkers, meet. It is to explain, if possible, what judgment is supported by probability—that is, what judgment the evidence *suggests*, as opposed to *proves*, is correct.

The evidence, for example, may be insufficient to say with certainty that cigarette smoking *causes* lung cancer or that viewing television violence *definitely harms* people. Nevertheless, there is sufficient evidence on both issues to warrant your judgment about *probable* cause–effect relationships.

Whenever you cannot achieve certainty, focus on probability.

MAKE YOUR SUBJECT APPROPRIATELY SPECIFIC

The subject in a careful judgment is appropriately specific. Consider these sentences:

> *Today's college students* are less proficient in grammar and usage than their counterparts were ten years ago.

> *Today's U.S. college students* are less proficient in grammar and usage than their counterparts were ten years ago.

> *Today's U.S. two-year college students* are less proficient in grammar and usage than their counterparts were ten years ago.

> *Today's students at this college* are less proficient in grammar and usage than their counterparts were ten years ago.

If the evidence covers only students at a particular college, only the last judgment can be sound. The other three are too generalized. To avoid this kind of error in your writing and speaking, choose the subjects of your judgments with care.

MAKE YOUR PREDICATE EXACT

The predicate in a careful judgment asserts exactly what you want to assert. Compare these sentences:

Peace *has been* achieved.

Peace *can be* achieved.

Peace *must be* achieved.

Peace *should be* achieved.

Peace *could be* achieved.

Peace *will be* achieved.

Though these sentences are very similar in construction, their meanings are very different. Unless we deliberately choose ambiguity (in which case we should expect to cause confusion), we should choose our predicates judiciously. A good example of the kind of confusion that can result is shown in the sentence that triggered theological debate in the 1960s: "God is dead." It made a nice slogan, but exactly what did it mean? Taking it by itself, a person would have great difficulty answering. In addition to the obvious possibility, "There is no supreme being," there are at least seven others:

People no longer *want* to believe God exists.

People are no longer *able* to believe God exists.

People are no longer *certain* God exists.

People no longer *act* as if God exists.

People no longer *care* whether God exists.

People no longer *accept* some particular conception of God.

People are no longer *satisfied* with the limitation of traditional human expressions of belief in God's existence.

Anyone who wished the message to be understood would have been better off using whichever of the above (or some other) sentences expressed the judgment clearly rather than saying, "God is dead."

INCLUDE ALL APPROPRIATE QUALIFICATIONS

Saying that something usually happens is different from saying that it frequently happens or that it happens every other Tuesday. The more care you take to make the qualifications necessary to say what you wish, no more and no less, the more defensible your judgment is likely to be. And that includes not only qualifications of time but those of place and condition as well. In the judgment "American men over forty who never attended college tend to be opposed to the idea of women's liberation advocated by the National Organization for Women" (which may or may not be true), almost every word is a qualification. It says: (a) not all men but *American* men; (b) not members of all age groups and educational levels but those *over forty who never attended college*; and (c) not the idea of women's liberation in general but the idea *advocated by the National Organization for Women.*

AVOID EXAGGERATION

Most of us know one or more people for whom every occasion is "memorable," every problem is a "crisis," every enjoyable film is "worthy of an Academy Award nomination," every attractive new car or fashion "incomparable." To such people nothing is merely good or bad—it is the best or worst. Their vocabulary is filled with superlatives. When someone is late for an appointment with them, they wait an "eternity." When they go to the dentist, the pain is "unbearable." Their debts are "titanic."

When such people report something to us, we have to translate it, scale it down to realistic proportions. If they say, "He was the biggest man I've ever seen, at least seven feet ten," we conclude he was about six feet six. If they say, "You've got to hear Sidney Screech's new record—it's the most fantastic performance he's ever given," we conclude it was a bit better than usual.

We make such translations willingly if the people exaggerating are close friends. But we may still grow weary of the superlatives. If the people exaggerating are only acquaintances or if we know them only through their writing or speaking, then we tend to be less patient. We cannot help losing a certain amount of confidence in them. We cannot help seeing them as people who misjudge the world around them. Moreover, they seem to lack a balance, a necessary sense of proportion in their seeing.

If you want your judgments to stand the test of scrutiny by others, you will do well to avoid any such exaggerations. Where you cannot be certain your judgment is accurate, you should tend to err on the side of understatement rather than overstatement. In other words, you should take the more modest interpretation, the less extreme conclusion. That way, if you are wrong—as every human must sometimes be—you will at least have the saving grace of having demonstrated a sense of control and restraint.

If your evaluation and judgment meet the standards explained in this chapter, you have a right to be proud, for judgment carefully arrived at is the hallmark of humanity. It is the capstone to your capacity for thinking. As such, it separates you most dramatically from other creatures, enabling you to grow in knowledge and, considerably more important, in *wisdom*, and to improve your own life and the lives of others.

⧉ APPLICATIONS

1. Analyze *two* of the following summaries in the manner demonstrated in the chapter. Be sure to get beyond your first impressions and to avoid the errors in thinking discussed in Chapters 6 through 15. Answer all the questions you raise, deciding exactly in what ways you agree with the idea and in what ways you disagree.

a. Feeling and intuition are better guides to behavior than reasoning. We need immediate answers to many of our problems today, and feeling and intuition are almost instantaneous, while reasoning is painfully slow. Moreover, feeling and intuition are natural, uncorrupted by artificial values and codes imposed on us by society. Reasoning is a set of programmed responses—tight, mechanical, and unnatural. Thus, if we wish to achieve individuality, to express our real inner selves, the part of us that is unconditioned by others, we should follow our feelings and intuitions instead of our thoughts.

b. It is commonly accepted that the best way to improve the world and relations among its people is for everyone to curb his or her own self-interest and think of others. This concern with others is the basic idea in the golden rule and in most religions. It is, of course, questionable whether that goal is realizable. But more important, it is mistaken. It is not selfishness but the pretense of altruism that sets person against person. If everyone looked out for himself or herself, pursued his or her own interests, there would not only be less hypocrisy in the world, there would be more understanding. Each person would be aware of where everyone else stood in relation to him or her. And no one would be dependent on others.

c. The institution of marriage has outlived its usefulness. More and more people today, particularly young people, are realizing that it makes more sense to have informal relationships. A couple should live together only as long as both want to. Whenever one wants to end the relationship, he or she should be able to do so, neatly, without legal complications. This could be done if marriage were abolished. Everyone would benefit. Individuals would retain their individual freedom and be able to fulfill their own need to develop as a person, responding to their own changing values and interests.

d. College instructors should not be permitted to set restrictive attendance policies; they should be made to treat students as responsible adults, leaving each student free to decide his or her attendance behavior. By the time students are eighteen years old, they know their own strengths and weaknesses better than anyone else does and are mature enough to decide which classes they need to attend. Some courses will be new and challenging to them. Others will merely duplicate what they had in high school. Some instructors will add to the students' store of information and challenge their intellect. Others will read the textbook to students, adding nothing more than they can get by reading it themselves. Left to exercise their own judgment, students can use their time wisely, attending the classes of the good, interesting, dedicated teachers and avoiding those of the dullards and deadbeats.

e. Every time parents tell their children how to look at an issue, they close the children's minds to other views. Every time parents present their political views or their philosophy of life (the principles they live by), they narrow their children's perspective. Every time parents take their children to church or make them sit in Sunday school, they shackle the children to one spiritual outlook. In each of these cases parents rob the children of their freedom and independence and individuality. For these reasons, wise and loving parents, who wish their children to become free beings and not slaves to the thinking of others, will not teach them their principles and values but will leave them free to develop their own.

f. One of the reasons crime is so rampant in our society is that we put too much emphasis on determining why the criminal committed the crime and whether the police treated the criminal fairly. Those are important matters, but other, equally important ones seem to be neglected lately—like protecting law-abiding people from dangerous, irresponsible people and making punishments severe enough to deter crime. We cringe at primitive societies' handling of crime—for example, cutting off a thief's hands or a perjurer's tongue. But at least such punishments reflect a recognition that crime is an outrage against society that should not be tolerated. I am not suggesting that we return to such a standard of justice, only that we get tough with criminals. Two steps that would provide a good start would be setting determinate sentences for crimes instead of giving judges the wide latitude they now enjoy and refusing to let legal technicalities set aside a conviction when a person is clearly guilty.

g. Every year there is at least one major scandal involving a college athlete illegally accepting money from the coaching staff, alumni, or other supporters of the team. In recent years the number of scandals seems to be increasing. The best way to eliminate this problem is to discard the National Collegiate Athletic Association (NCAA) prohibition against playing for pay. Athletes get paid for their efforts at the professional level. There is no good reason to make them wait until graduation to be rewarded for their talents. The coaches are paid a salary and the colleges often receive substantial sums of money from television rights to games. Only the athletes, the ones mainly responsible for generating the income, are deprived of financial gain. By continuing its archaic rule, the NCAA is being both unfair and hypocritical.

2. Apply what you learned in this chapter to the inquiry you completed for either application 3 or 4 in Chapter 19.

IV

SOME
CONTEMPORARY
ISSUES

The following applications cover not merely Chapter 20 but all the chapters in this book. In other words, they are designed to provide exercise not only in forming careful judgments but also in the various steps leading to such judgments. Each issue is or has been the subject of public debate. Each is controversial. Though some are relatively recent issues, many have a long, complex history. For most, a sizable amount of written interpretation and argument is on record.

Before addressing these applications, review the chapters briefly. Doing so will make it easier for you to remain aware of the broad intellectual context in which the issues must be discussed, to recognize and avoid the problems that impede clear thinking, and to pursue effectively the strategy you have learned.

Keep in mind that these applications identify the issues in a very general way. It is up to you not only to find and study the available information but also to select the particular aspects you will focus on. As you have seen, it is better to treat one or two aspects in depth than a larger number superficially.

⊞ APPLICATIONS

1. In the season before his retirement from the National Basketball Association, Michael Jordan's gambling activities received national attention. League rules forbid players only from wagering on their own sport, but gambling on *any* sport is frowned upon. Is the latter position reasonable? In other words, should professional athletes be held to a higher standard than others concerning gambling? If so, should this standard be adopted by professional leagues?

2. Several television information programs have sent undercover reporters to apply for jobs or purchase automobiles and other products to determine whether women applicants/consumers are treated differently from men. The general conclusion has been that many employers and salespeople harbor negative stereotypes of women—for example, that they are less intelligent than men, less able to understand complex matters, less interested in matters of substance, and less qualified to perform work assignments that are more demanding than answering a telephone or carrying out simple tasks. Is the behavior depicted in such reports typical of society's treatment of women, or is it a dramatic *exception* to the rule?

3. The rise in the number and the violence of crimes in this country is causing increasing concern among many Americans. As a result, more and more citizens are arming themselves. What effect is this having on crime? On the average person's safety? What effect is it likely to have if the trend continues?

4. In recent years debate has continued, sometimes heatedly, over "family values." The principal issues have been whether America has lost them, who has been responsible for the loss (if, indeed, there has been one), and who can best restore them. Many debaters seem to have taken for granted that the term itself has one meaning that everyone understands. Your challenge is to find out if their assumption is warranted. Investigate and determine the meaning (meanings?) of "family values." If you find significant differences in people's definitions, build a reasonable composite, explain it thoroughly, and answer the objections critics might raise about it.

5. Popular talk shows seem to proliferate endlessly. In the beginning there was Donahue, who begat Oprah, who begat Geraldo, Sally Jessie, Vicky (Lawrence), Montel (Williams). And the list goes on. Critics say that ratings competition has driven such shows to increasingly sensational and bizarre topics and guests. The result has been, claim the critics, that the socially disruptive and dysfunctional behavior the shows loudly deplore is, by being publicized, actually glamorized and encouraged. Investigate this issue and determine whether there is any validity to these charges.

6. "What people view on television or in films can't affect their thinking and actions," argue many in the artistic community. Those who disagree point out that the same artistic community creates public service messages aimed at changing people's minds about drinking and driving, sex without condoms, and abusing the environment. These critics reason that if a medium has the power to help, it also has the power to harm, and they urge artists and programmers to take an honest look at the messages they put on the screen. Investigate this issue and decide which point of view is more insightful.

7. In recent years the contract negotiations of professional athletes have been given considerable attention by the news media. Better known players frequently demand and receive salaries that were unheard of ten or fifteen years ago. Numerous questions have been raised about players' salaries. Among them are the following: How much higher than the average are the superstars' salaries? Is there anything wrong with players earning more than senators and presidents? What effect is the present trend of asking more and more likely to have on sports? On the economy?

8. In education the term *tenure* means "permanent position." The teacher who is given tenure cannot be fired, except for very grave reasons (such as a serious moral offense or the school's decision to eliminate the program in which he or she teaches). Some argue that tenure is essential to guarantee academic freedom and good teaching. Others believe that it destroys initiative and undermines good teaching. Should the tenure system be retained in its present form, modified, or eliminated?

9. In Asian cultures, marriages have traditionally been arranged for young people. In our culture young people are free to choose their own spouses. Might it be a good idea, with our divorce rate soaring and so many families in disarray, for our culture to follow the Asian custom?

10. Since television became a major entertainment medium in the late 1940s and early 1950s, the TV commercial has become as familiar as the newspaper. Yet few people know very much about commercials. How much do they cost? Who really pays for them? What effects do they have on our lives? Would pay TV be more desirable?

11. Animal intelligence has been a matter of scientific interest since at least the time of Darwin. Can animals "think" in any meaningful sense of the term? Can they form categories (friend, master, my species, and so on)? Are they aware of themselves and their activities? Do they have a sense of past and future, or do they perceive only the present moment?[1]

12. Interscholastic and intercollegiate sports competition is as American as apple pie. To many people the mere suggestion that these programs should be abolished is the ultimate heresy. But should they be so sacred? Where did the idea of varsity sports originate? Is it older than intramural competition? What are its good and bad points?

13. The philosophy of "spare the rod and spoil the child" has a long tradition in parenting. But the modern attitude is that physical punishment comes close to being, and may indeed *be,* child abuse. What kinds of punishment, if any, are appropriate for parents to use?

14. Proponents of a guaranteed annual wage argue that by giving every adult person an assured amount of money, we would not only eliminate poverty and its terrible effects, but we would also eliminate an entire bureaucracy—the giant welfare system—and perhaps even save money. Opponents see more harmful effects. What are some of those effects? Might they outweigh the benefits?

15. Laugh tracks and applause tracks are so much a part of television comedy shows that most people undoubtedly give them little thought. But some people object strongly to them, regarding them as manipulative and insulting. They propose banning them. Would you support such a proposal?

16. In this country, gambling was traditionally prohibited by law. Yet today laws have been rewritten to permit states to sponsor lotteries and off-track betting. Is the movement to legalize gambling a healthy one for our society?

17. Historically in this country, high school and college athletic budgets have been divided unevenly, with men's teams getting a larger share than women's. Many object to this unequal treatment; others believe it is justified because men's teams have traditionally demonstrated a higher level of skill. Which view is more reasonable? What changes, if any, should be made in the distribution of funds?

18. Compulsory education is so common today that we tend to forget it is a fairly recent historical development. However, some social critics are not only aware of its recency—they are convinced it is no longer a sound idea. In their view children, even as young as six or eight, should be permitted a free choice of whether they will study or not and, if they decide to do so, of what and where they will study. Among the important questions to be considered are these: Why was compulsory education begun? Was it a good idea then? Have the social conditions changed significantly since that time?

19. In some states the testimony of a woman who has been raped is not considered sufficient to bring charges against her assailant. There must be corroborating testimony. Many women and men feel that the reasoning that underlies such a law is specious. In their view any such law is discriminatory and should be abolished. Others maintain that without such laws innocent men could be easily victimized. Which view appears to be the more reasoned? Are there other alternatives?

20. Yale University's Dr. José Delgado dramatized the effectiveness of electrical stimulation of the brain (ESB) as a means of controlling behavior. He demonstrated that by "wiring" the brain of a fighting bull and merely pushing a button that transmits an electrical charge to the animal's brain, he can stop it in the middle of an enraged charge. He also established that repeated electrical stimulation diminishes a bull's natural aggressiveness. Similar experiments have shown that chemical stimulation of the brain (CSB) by the strategic placement of tiny tubes of time-released substances is similarly effective. Some people believe it would be desirable to use these techniques on criminals or mental patients or students with certain impediments to learning. Others see any such use as an Orwellian nightmare. What might be the dangers of the use of such techniques on humans? Might their use be regulated to minimize abuses?

21. Should the parents of students who attend private and parochial schools be allowed to deduct tuition expenses from their federal income tax returns? For several decades, advocates of the idea have argued that fairness demands it because such parents already support the public schools through taxes and must at present bear an additional financial burden for exercising free choice over their children's education. Opponents argue that the proposal violates the principle of separation of church and state (at least in the case of parochial schools) and would harm the public school system.

22. The 1990s have witnessed the beginning of a new phenomenon—children *divorcing* their parents. What possible effects could this phenomenon have on the relationships between children and parents, government and families? Which of these effects are most *likely* to occur? Decide whether they are desirable or undesirable.

23. Top executives of large corporations often earn millions of dollars a year in salaries, bonuses, and benefits, whereas the vast majority of people who work for them earn modest wages, sometimes no more than the minimum hourly amount the government requires they receive. Some people believe that an economic system that permits such disparity to exist is wrong and should be changed. Others argue that no change is possible without stifling human initiative. How might the economic system be changed? Should it be changed?

24. In 1982, in a 5–4 decision, the U.S. Supreme Court ruled that current and former presidents enjoy "absolute immunity" from lawsuits seeking monetary damages for misconduct in office. Justice Byron White, one of the four justices who opposed the decision, wrote this dissenting opinion: "[As a result of this decision] a president acting within the outer boundaries of what presidents normally do may, without liability, deliberately cause injury to any number of citizens even though he knows his conduct violates a statute or tramples on the constitutional rights of those who are injured."[2] Do you share Justice White's opposition to the decision?

25. Because journalists serve the important function of collecting information for public dissemination, they have traditionally claimed the right to keep their sources of information confidential, even from the courts. That claim has been challenged many times in the courts, and reporters have on occasion been held in contempt of court and sent to jail for refusing to divulge their sources. In taking such action, judges have not denied the basic principle of confidentiality; they have merely asserted that it has definite limits. Do you agree with them?

26. Are video games harmful to young minds? C. Everett Koop, former surgeon general of the United States, believes they are. Because of the emphasis in most games on "eliminate, kill, destroy," he says, the games produce "aberrations in childhood behavior." Needles to say, not everyone shares Koop's view. Some psychologists and educators believe that, far from being harmful to children, video games are in some ways helpful.[3]

27. One of the causes of the antisocial behavior that is so prevalent today, according to some analysts, is the fact that the old-fashioned hero has been largely replaced by the anti-hero. If the media offered more wholesome, virtuous individuals for young people to model their lives after, these analysts reason, crimes of violence would decrease. Do you agree?

28. On at least two occasions the city council of Evanston, Illinois, considered a proposal to tax the students of Northwestern University to offset the cost of unpaid services provided by the city. The Association of American Universities opposed the proposal, which they believed would serve as a lamentable model for other college communities.[4] But some people disagree, asserting that such a tax represents the fairest way of having everyone share the costs of the services they use, and suggesting that municipalities across the country adopt the idea. What is your view?

29. In two separate cases, the U.S. Supreme Court ruled that the use of trained dogs to detect drugs is legitimate under certain circumstances. In the first case, it ruled that citizens' rights are not violated when dogs are used to sniff airport luggage if police have reason to suspect that drugs are present. In the second case, it approved the use of dogs to sniff students' lockers, cars parked on school property, and students themselves when they are suspected of drug possession. (However, it outlawed the use of dogs for mass searches of students.)[5] Do you believe the Court judged wisely?

30. Should adults be held financially responsible for their elderly parents when the parents are too poor or ill to care for themselves?

31. In the past couple of decades, student evaluations of teachers have become one common measure of teacher effectiveness. Typically, students are given an opportunity, toward the end of the term, to fill out a questionnaire and rate their teachers. The overall ratings are then compiled and become one criterion for salary raises, promotion, and tenure. Not all teachers approve of students' evaluating them, however. Some argue that students are not trained evaluators and can too easily confuse popularity with effective teaching and punish the very teachers who are serving them best. What is your view?

32. In early 1989 Whittle Communications Corporation tested a new approach to the use of television in the classroom. They offered pilot schools free installation of television equipment and a twelve-minute news program, with the provision that they be allowed to include two minutes of advertising in the program. Some educators hailed the idea as the beginning of a new partnership between big business and education. Others adamantly opposed it. What is your view?

33. Suppose that a single woman becomes pregnant, has the baby, and then decides to give it up for adoption. Suppose, too, that the biological father learns of her adoption decision. Under what circumstances, if any, should he be able to block the adoption and claim the baby as his own?

34. Do wealthy people have any obligation to share their riches with poor people? Does your answer depend on whether their wealth was honestly or dishonestly obtained (by themselves or their ancestors)? If they do have such an obligation, how should it be enforced if they choose not to honor it? Do rich countries have a similar obligation to poor countries?

35. Most computer software carries a warning against copying, yet many people feel the warning is unreasonable. They believe that if they buy a program, it is theirs to do with as they wish, and that includes giving or selling a copy to someone else. Are they right?

36. When television dish antennas first became available, owners were able to receive HBO and other pay-channel signals directly from the satellites, without paying for them. Then the pay-channel companies began to scramble their signals to prevent the owners of dish antennas from receiving pay channels without paying. Do you think the companies were within their rights to do so?

37. Should a lawyer defend a client that he knows is guilty of the charge against him? Does your answer depend on the seriousness of the offense? For example, would your answer be the same for driving while intoxicated as it would be for murder?

38. Since the onset of the AIDS epidemic, many people have experienced the pain of seeing their loved ones die a slow death. When the victims have begged to be assisted in committing suicide, some people have been moved by pity to grant their request. Such actions are against the law. Should the law be changed? If not, should people who aid others in committing suicide be charged with a crime?

39. Fear of contracting AIDS has caused people to behave in untypical ways. For example, many refuse to have any social contact with a friend who has contracted the disease. Dentists and doctors have refused to work on patients with the disease. Undertakers have refused to embalm victims. Is such behavior justifiable?

40. Is the Asian practice of acupuncture pure superstition, or does it produce a real anesthetic or curative effect?

41. For many years it was believed that children who receive early formal education have an advantage over those who start school at age five or six. Today, some educators challenge that view. They speculate that intellectual and emotional *harm* can result from putting very young children into structured learning situations. Which view is the more reasonable one for parents to accept?

42. The increase in violence in this country (and a number of other Western countries) in recent years has given new currency to an old issue. Are human beings naturally, instinctively aggressive, or is aggression *learned* behavior?

NOTES

CHAPTER ONE: WHO ARE YOU?

1. Maxwell Maltz, *Psycho-Cybernetics* (New York: Pocket Books, 1969), pp. 49–53.

2. Viktor Frankl, *The Unheard Cry for Meaning* (New York: Simon and Schuster, 1978), pp. 35, 67, 83.

3. Viktor Frankl, *Man's Search for Meaning* (New York: Washington Square Press, 1963), pp. 122–123.

4. Frankl, *Unheard Cry*, pp. 39, 90, 95.

CHAPTER TWO: WHAT IS CRITICAL THINKING?

1. Maya Pines, "We Are Left-Brained or Right-Brained," *New York Times Magazine*, September 9, 1973, pp. 32ff.

2. Thomas R. Blakeslee, *The Right Brain* (Garden City, N.Y.: Anchor Press/Doubleday, 1980).

3. John Dewey, *How We Think* (Lexington, Mass.: D.C. Heath, 1933), p. 4.

4. Ibid., pp. 88–90.

5. R. W. Gerard, "The Biological Basis of Imagination," *The Scientific Monthly*, June 1946, p. 477.

6. Ibid., p. 478.

7. "Teacher Uses Prayer," *Binghamton* (New York) *Press*, November 16, 1982, p. 4B.

8. "Religious Group Aims TV Boycott at NBC," *The* (Oneonta, New York) *Star*, March 5, 1982, p. 1.

9. *Binghamton* (New York) *Press,* March 27, 1989, p. 1A.

10. "When 'News' Is Almost a Crime," *Time,* March 21, 1983, p. 84.

CHAPTER THREE: WHAT IS TRUTH?

1. Quoted in Francis L. Wellman, *The Art of Cross-Examination* (New York: Collier Books, 1962), p. 175.

2. *Time,* August 14, 1972, p. 52.

3. "Chaplin Film Is Discovered," *Binghamton* (New York) *Press,* September 8, 1982, p. 7A.

4. "Town's Terror Frozen in Time," *New York Times,* November 21, 1982, Sec. 4, p. 7.

5. "A Tenth Planet?" *Time,* May 8, 1972, p. 46.

6. Herrman L. Blumgart, "The Medical Framework for Viewing the Problem of Human Experimentation," *Daedalus,* Spring 1969, p. 254.

7. "Back to School," *New York Times,* March 11, 1973, Sec. 4, p. 4.

8. "The Murky Time," *Time,* January 1, 1973, pp. 57ff.

CHAPTER FOUR: WHAT DOES IT MEAN TO KNOW?

1. Karl-Erick Fichtelius and Sverre Sjolander, *Smarter Than Man? Intelligence in Whales, Dolphins and Humans,* translated by Thomas Teal (New York: Random House, 1972), p. 147.

2. Karl Menninger, *Whatever Became of Sin?* (New York: Hawthorne Books, 1973).

3. Thomas Fleming, "Who Really Discovered America?" *Reader's Digest,* March 1973, pp. 145ff.

4. "Scientists Say Chinese 'Discovered' America," *The* (Oneonta, New York) *Star,* October 31, 1981, p. 2

5. "Shibboleth Bites Dust," *Intellectual Digest,* July 1973, p. 68.

6. "Empty Nests," *Intellectual Digest,* July 1973, p. 68.

7. "Psychic Senility," *Intellectual Digest,* May 1973, p. 68.

8. *Time,* August 20, 1973, p. 67.

9. "*Nova,*" PBS-TV, September 21, 1993.

10. Herbert Kupferberg, "Why Scientists Prowl the Sea Floor," *Parade,* July 29, 1973, pp. 12ff.

11. Louis Lasagna, "Special Subjects in Human Experimentation," *Daedalus,* Spring 1969, p. 459.

12. "Beer Test," *Parade,* May 13, 1973, p. 4.

13. David Egner, "Sioux Fight to Keep Black Hills Holy Land," *Binghamton* (New York) *Press,* December 7, 1982, p. 5A.

CHAPTER FIVE: HOW GOOD ARE YOUR OPINIONS?

1. "Couple Awaits Resurrection of Their Son," *Binghamton* (New York) *Press,* August 27, 1973, p. 11A. Also, "Two Arrested in Son's 'Faith Heal' Death," *Binghamton* (New York) *Press,* August 30, 1973, p. 8A.

2. "20/20," ABC News, July 22, 1982.

3. "Aid for Aching Heads," *Time,* June 5, 1972, p. 51.

4. Francis D. Moore, "Therapeutic Innovation: Ethical Boundaries . . . ," *Daedalus,* Spring 1969, pp. 504–05.

5. *Adolescence: Its Psychology and Its Relations to Physiology, Anthropology, Sociology, Sex, Crime, Religion, and Education,* Volumes 1 and 2 (New York: Appleton, 1904).

6. "Egyptian Artifacts Termed Fakes," *The* (Oneonta, New York) *Star*, June 16, 1982, p. 2.

7. "Venus Is Pockmarked," *Binghamton* (New York) *Press*, August 5, 1973, 2A.

8. "Which Psychiatrist Can a Jury Believe?" *New York Times*, January 21, 1973, Sec. 4, p. 7.

9. John Locke, *The Conduct of the Understanding*, part 3.

10. "Hashaholics," *Time*, July 24, 1972, p. 53.

11. Walter Sullivan, "New Object Seen on Universe Edge," *New York Times*, June 10, 1973, p. 76.

12. Karl-Erick Fichtelius and Sverre Sjolander, *Smarter Than Man? Intelligence in Whales, Dolphins and Humans*, translated by Thomas Teal (New York: Random House, 1972), pp. 135–36.

13. Ray Marshall and Marc Tucker, *Thinking for a Living: Education and the Wealth of Nations* (New York: Basic Books, 1992), pp. 17–20.

14. Bill Katz and Linda Sternberg Katz, *Magazines for Libraries* (New York: R. R. Bowker, 1992).

15. "A Current Affair," Fox TV, April 28, 1989.

16. "Bars' Ladies' Nights Called Reverse Sexism," *Binghamton* (New York) *Press*, January 12, 1983, p. 5B.

CHAPTER SIX: THE BASIC PROBLEM: "MINE IS BETTER"

1. Ambrose Bierce, *Devil's Dictionary* (New York: Dover Publications, 1958), p. 66.

2. Edmond G. Addeo and Robert E. Burger, *Ego Speak: Why No One Listens to You* (Radnor, Pa.: Chilton, 1973).

3. The descriptions of ethnocentrism in this paragraph and the preceding two paragraphs reflect the findings of a number of studies. Principal among them are T. W. Adorno, *The Authoritarian Personality* (New York: Harper & Brothers, 1950) and James G. Martin, *The Tolerant Personality* (Detroit: Wayne State University Press, 1964).

4. Gordon Allport, *The Nature of Prejudice* (Reading, Mass.: Addison-Wesley, 1954), pp. 355–56.

5. G. K. Chesterton, *Charles Dickens* (New York: The Press of the Readers Club, 1942), p. 15.

6. "Theologian: U.S. Too Tolerant," *The* (Oneonta, New York) *Star*, May 30, 1981, p. 15.

7. Letter to the Editor, *New York Times*, May 9, 1982, Sec. 4, p. 20.

8. "Jailed Rabbi Seeks Kosher Diet," *Binghamton* (New York) *Press*, May 23, 1982, p. 5A.

9. Reported on "Good Morning, America," ABC News, November 4, 1982.

10. "Pregnant Teacher Stirs Town," *Binghamton* (New York) *Press*, December 22, 1982, p. 1A.

CHAPTER SEVEN: RESISTANCE TO CHANGE

1. Ellen J. Langer, *Mindfulness* (Reading, Mass.: Addison-Wesley, 1989), pp. 43–44.

2. "Darwin Doubted in Scopes's Town," *New York Times*, October 1, 1972, p. 24.

3. Robert K. Merton, "The Self-Fulfilling Prophecy," *The Antioch Review*, 1948, pp. 193–210.

4. Thomas A. Harris, *I'm OK—You're OK: A Practical Guide to Transactional Analysis* (New York: Harper & Row, 1969), pp. 22–23.

5. "Anna Freud, Psychoanalyst, Dies at 86," *New York Times*, October 10, 1982, p. 46.

6. Rona and Laurence Cherry, "The Horney Heresy," *New York Times Magazine*, August 26, 1973, pp. 12ff.

7. This approach was used in the 1982 California primary and reported in "Game Show Prizes Entice CA Voters," *The* (Oneonta, New York) *Star*, June 4, 1982, p. 1.

8. This idea was tested by an education researcher, Eileen Bayer. It proved successful. (Fred M. Hechinger, "Grandpa Goes to Kindergarten," *New York Times,* October 29, 1972, Sec. 4, p. 11.)

9. The Reagan Administration discussed this plan and indicated it was not opposed to it. "U.S. Considering National ID Cards," *The* (Oneonta, New York) *Star,* May 21, 1982, p. 1.

10. Karla Valance, "This Time, the Rebel's on the Right," *Christian Science Monitor,* January 27, 1983, p. B1. Also: George Basler, "Student Paper Urges Theft and Graffiti," *Binghamton* (New York) *Press,* January 25, 1983, p. 1F.

11. Harry Atkins, "Football, Hockey Are X-Rated," *Binghamton* (New York) *Press,* December 19, 1982, p. 60.

CHAPTER EIGHT: CONFORMITY

1. "Groupthink," *National Catholic Observer,* January 27, 1973, p. 24.

2. See, for example, "Methodists Battle About Gay Cleric," *The* (Oneonta, New York) *Star,* May 15, 1982, p. 8.

3. "Witch's Church Tax Free," *The* (Oneonta, New York) *Star,* April 8, 1982, p. 17.

CHAPTER NINE: FACE-SAVING

1. "T.A.: Doing OK," *Time,* August 20, 1973, p. 44.

2. Harold Kolansky, M.D., and William T. Moore, M.D., "Toxic Effects of Chronic Marijuana Use," *Journal of the American Medical Association,* October 2, 1972, pp. 35–41.

3. "Abortion Sought for Retarded Woman," *Binghamton* (New York) *Press,* September 23, 1982, p. 8B.

4. "Bar License Church Veto Struck Down," *Binghamton* (New York) *Press,* December 14, 1982, p. 4A.

CHAPTER TEN: STEREOTYPING

1. Quoted in William E. Vinacke, *The Psychology of Thinking* (New York: McGraw-Hill, 1952), p. 338.

2. Gordon Allport, *The Nature of Prejudice* (Reading, Mass.: Addison-Wesley, 1954), pp. 189–90.

3. Bruno Bettleheim and Morris Janowitz, *Social Change and Prejudice* (London: Collier-Macmillan, 1950), p. 137.

4. "A Policeman Complains . . . ," *New York Times Magazine,* June 13, 1971, pp. 28ff.

5. Robert K. Merton, "The Self-Fulfilling Prophecy," *The Antioch Review,* 1948, pp. 201–02.

6. James G. Martin, *The Tolerant Personality* (Detroit: Wayne State University Press, 1964), p. 19.

7. Ibid.

8. Ibid., p. 129.

9. Allport, *Nature of Prejudice,* p. 173.

10. Michael J. McManus, "Jerry Falwell Moves into Social Action," *The* (Oneonta, New York) *Star,* January 26, 1982, p. 4.

11. "Unwed Father Barred from Delivery Room," *The* (Oneonta, New York) *Star,* May 14, 1982, p. 2.

12. "Donahue," WIXT-TV, Syracuse, N.Y., November 18, 1982.

13. "Ex-Policeman Says Sex Shift Cost His Job," (Schenectady, New York) *Gazette*, August 28, 1982, p. 14

CHAPTER ELEVEN: OVERSIMPLIFICATION

1. "FAA's Regulations Ruffle Feathers of Hang Gliders," *Binghamton* (New York) *Press*, September 3, 1982, p. 1A.
2. "The 'New Intolerance,'" an excerpt from Justice Clarence Thomas's speech at Mercer University School of Law, *St. Petersburg Times*, May 30, 1993, p. 5D.
3. "States Must Educate Illegal Alien Children," *The* (Oneonta, New York) *Star*, June 16, 1982, p. 1.
4. "Paternity Battle," *New York Times*, December 12, 1982, p. 57.
5. "Minister Proposes Public Executions," *The* (Oneonta, New York) *Star*, June 16, 1982, p. 1.

CHAPTER TWELVE: HASTY CONCLUSION

1. Ruth Ellen Thompson, "Lawsuits Link Human Catastrophes, Drug," *Binghamton* (New York) *Press*, March 13, 1973, p. 9A.
2. "60 Minutes," CBS-TV, October 3, 1993.
3. "Long Sentences Sought for Repeat Offenders," *New York Times*, April 25, 1982, p. 63.
4. "Possessed Teen Gets Long Prison Term," *The* (Oneonta, New York) *Star*, December 19, 1981, p. 2.
5. "Woman Convicted of Making Ethnic Slur," *The* (Oneonta, New York) *Star*, May 14, 1982, p. 2.
6. "High School Class Uses Human Cadavers in Lab," *Binghamton* (New York) *Press*, December 15, 1982, p. 2C.

CHAPTER THIRTEEN: UNWARRANTED ASSUMPTION

1. Seth S. Oldschlager, "There Was a Real Count Dracula and He Was Not a Good Old Boy," *New York Times*, August 27, 1972, Sec. 10, p. 9.
2. "Visitors Say China Delivers Better Health Care Than U.S.," *Binghamton* (New York) *Press*, July 16, 1972, p. 5D.
3. "Navajo Psychotherapy," *Time*, June 12, 1972, p. 68.
4. "'Love Addicts,'" *Parade*, April 1, 1973, p. 9.
5. J. H. Plumb, "The Great Change in Children," *Horizon*, Winter 1971, pp. 4–12.
6. "Reagan Proposes Prayer Amendment," *The* (Oneonta, New York) *Star*, May 18, 1982, p. 2.
7. "Liberation Lawn," *New York Times*, May 23, 1982, Sec. 4, p. 11.

CHAPTER FOURTEEN: LOGICAL FALLACIES

1. "State Rules Let Gays and Crooks Adopt Children," *Binghamton* (New York) *Press*, August 8, 1982, p. 1A.

CHAPTER FIFTEEN: THE PROBLEMS IN COMBINATION

1. "An Exercise in Educational Flimflam," *Parade*, May 12, 1974, p. 17.
2. "Court Order Blocks Big Inmate Release," *The* (Oneonta, New York) *Star*, December 22, 1981, p. 12.

3. "Ruling Strikes Down Tax Exempt Status," *The* (Oneonta, New York) *Star*, March 27, 1982, p. 1.

4. Romans 13.

5. "Tough—But Flawed—Alcohol Tests," *Christian Science Monitor*, March 3, 1983, p. 24.

CHAPTER SIXTEEN: KNOWING YOURSELF

1. *New York Times*, November 28, 1982, p. 31; December 12, 1982, Sec. 4, p. 6.

2. "Questioning Campus Discipline," *Time*, May 31, 1982, p. 68.

3. "Holiday Songs Haunt Schoolmen," *Binghamton* (New York) *Press*, December 16, 1982, p. 3A.

4. "Elizabeth Taylor vs. Tailored Truth," *Time*, November 8, 1982, p. 71.

5. Interview with Shirley MacLaine, *USA Today*, June 16, 1983, p. 11A.

CHAPTER SEVENTEEN: BEING OBSERVANT

1. Lawrence K. Altman, "Discovery 60 Years Ago Changed Doctors' Minds on Heart Attack Survival," *New York Times*, December 10, 1972, pp. 56–57.

2. Earl Ubell, "Lysozyme: One of the Body's Miracle Workers," *New York Times*, November 12, 1972, Sec. 4, p. 6.

3. "Attacking Disease," a dialogue between Jacques Monod and Jean Hamburger, *Intellectual Digest*, May 1974, pp. 12–14.

4. *Binghamton* (New York) *Press*, March 22, 1989, p. 1A.

CHAPTER EIGHTEEN: CLARIFYING ISSUES

1. "Tragedy May Haunt Mancini," *Binghamton* (New York) *Press*, November 16, 1982, p. 4D.

CHAPTER NINETEEN: CONDUCTING INQUIRY

1. Lee Edson, "Will Man Ever Live in Space?" *New York Times Magazine*, December 31, 1972, pp. 10ff.

2. Gordon Gaskill, "Which Mountain Did Moses Really Climb?" *Reader's Digest*, June 1973, pp. 209–16.

3. James R. Miller, "The Speeded-Up Search for Life in Space," *Reader's Digest*, May 1973, pp. 255–64.

4. Lucy Burchard, "The Snug Way," *Intellectual Digest*, February 1974, p. 67.

5. Editorial, *The Courier-Journal* (Louisville, Kentucky), February 26, 1992. Reprinted with permission.

6. Editorial, *Richmond* (Virginia) *Times-Dispatch*, February 22, 1992. Reprinted with permission.

7. Editorial, *The Hartford* (Connecticut) *Courant*, July 30, 1992. Reprinted with permission.

8. Editorial, *Albuquerque* (New Mexico) *Journal*, July 31, 1992. Reprinted with permission.

CHAPTER TWENTY: FORMING A JUDGMENT

1. "The 2000-Year-Old Woman," *Time*, September 17, 1973, pp. 55–56.

2. Joyce Brothers, "Answers to Your Questions," *Good Housekeeping*, November 1993, p. 100.

3. William Safire, *St. Petersburg Times,* March 2, 1993, p. 21A.

4. John Leo, "In Search of the Middle Ground," *U.S. News & World Report,* March 6, 1989, p. 30.

5. Ibid.

6. Barbara Lerner, "Self-Esteem and Excellence: The Choice and the Paradox," *American Educator,* Winter 1985.

PART IV: SOME CONTEMPORARY ISSUES

1. See, for example, Carolyn A. Ristau, "Do Animals Think?" in R. Hoage and L. Goldman, editors, *Animal Intelligence* (Washington, D.C.: Smithsonian Institution Press, 1983).

2. "Court Exempts Presidents from Damage Suits," *The* (Oneonta, New York) *Star,* June 25, 1982, p. 1.

3. "Pacman Ilk Nips Surgeon General," *Binghamton* (New York) *Press,* November 10, 1982, p. 1A.

4. "Evanston, Illinois, May Tax University Students," *Time,* November 7, 1982, p. 33.

5. "School's Out for Drug-Sniffing Dogs," *USA Today,* June 28, 1983, p. 7A.

INDEX